Leopold Pospíšil

Adventures in the 'Stone Age'

A New Guinea Diary

Edited by
Jaroslav Jiřík and Martin Soukup

Charles University
Karolinum Press 2021

KAROLINUM PRESS
Karolinum Press is a publishing department of Charles University
Ovocný trh 560/5, 116 36 Prague 1, Czech Republic
www.karolinum.cz

Language supervision and translation of afterword by Robert Russell
Set and printed in the Czech Republic by Karolinum Press
First edition

A catalogue record for this book is available
from the National Library of the Czech Republic.

ISBN 978-80-246-4751-7
ISBN 978-80-246-4807-1 (pdf)

Contents

Note on the Title

We understand that readers may be taken aback by the title of this book.

Anthropologists have been concerned for good reason and for quite some time about the power dynamics between anthropologists and their subjects, who traditionally were viewed as 'the other.' Already in 1983, in his seminal work *Time and the Other*, Johannes Fabian challenged the allochronistic approach of anthropology that presented anthropologists and their subjects as being from different ages or times. However, the potentially politically incorrect title of this book, which at the time of the author's arrival situates the Kapauku in the Stone Age, has been kept for three reasons.

The first is that Leopold Pospíšil's research took place almost seventy years ago. Anthropology's ethnocentric emphasis on an evolutionary development from the Stone Age through the Bronze Age to the Iron Age was prevalent in scholarship and higher education at the time. Anthropology has come a long way since then, but the diary entries which form the basis for this book come from a time before such a shift in anthropology occurred.

The next reason is that when the author lived among the Kapauku, stone was indeed an essential piece of raw material — utilized for axe-blades, arrow-heads, and in cooking, just to mention a few of its uses. The importance of stone to the culture Pospíšil describes should not be discounted or underestimated.

Finally, we trust that readers of the book will quickly understand the author's respect for the Kapauku and see that his comments about the Stone Age are usually tongue-in-cheek as he insists that the culture of the Kapauku was very often more sophisticated and advanced than those of the Western anthropologists' observing them.

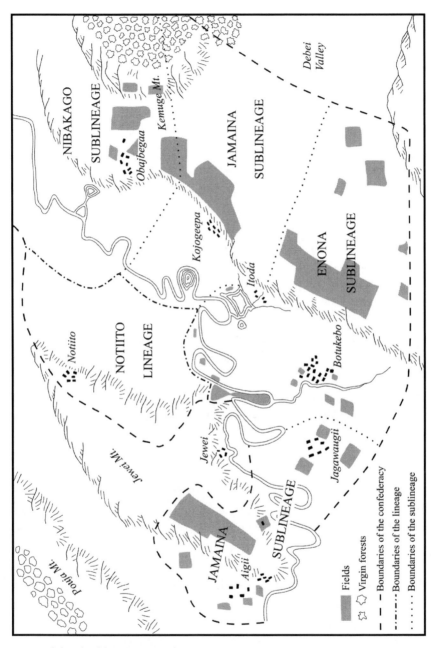

Map with local sublineages. (Scale: 1 : 50,000)

How I Became
an Anthropologist

Since boyhood, I have been interested in nature: in animals, plants, stones, lightning — simply in the phenomena of the natural world that surrounded me. Later on I focused my attention on human biology, especially after having read Paul Kruif's The Microbe Hunters. I planned to be a physician and fantasized about becoming another Semmelweis or Robert Koch. My life and intentions radically changed with the occupation of my country, Czechoslovakia, by the Nazis in 1939. All Czech universities were closed, my father was taken away to the German concentration camps — Dachau and later Buchenwald — and thus another interest came to occupy my mind. I wanted to know how it was possible that my German friends, who came from good, usually Christian families, could become SS men, young men who before had played and skied with me and taught me their language. Now they would not hesitate a minute to kill me for the glory of Hitler and his Reich. Thus my other interest arose — in the social sciences and the study of social control. This interest was fortified by the involvement of non-Nazi intellectuals in Marxism-Leninism, a system as murderous and vicious (if not more so) than Nazism itself. My basic question was: How can decent and often well-educated people, indeed even scholars, be brainwashed into believing outdated and demonstrably false theories from the nineteenth century? I have studied these theories, always checking them against empirical facts, and regardless of who said what and how important and popular they were. I have always been interested in what actually and objectively existed out there, so that for me the only authority has been objective reality rather than the dogmatic -isms and proclamations and prophesies of commonly regarded "wise" men and women. In fact many of them have not appeared to me to be really wise.

In 1945, after the "liberation" of my country from Nazism, the safe return of my father from the German concentration camps (only to be imprisoned a few years later by the communists), and the opening of the universities, my interest in biology re-emerged and prompted me to enrol in the medical school of my city of birth, and to study anatomy, biophysics, and biochemistry. However, with the ever-increasing influence of communism, with the Soviet Union and Stalin in the background, and the imprisonment of my father, this time by the illustrious followers of Marxist doctrine, my interest in social control and socio-psychological phenomena were again aroused. I quit the study of medicine and, of necessity, enrolled in the law school of Charles University of Prague — in the absence of any proper social science programs, this was the pursuit of knowledge closest to my interest. In 1948 I completed all the obligatory law courses; unfortunately, law was unable to answer all my burning questions and so I turned to philosophy, which I continued to study in Germany after my escape from Czechoslovakia following the communist takeover in 1948. I finally received my doctoral degree in law from my Czech alma mater, but not until the collapse of communism, in 1991.

Although philosophy showed me some interesting avenues of thought and taught me logic, it failed to provide me with unambiguous answers based on solid empirical evidence. So when I arrived in the United States I studied first economics and then sociology, receiving a bachelor's degree in the latter discipline. Again, however, I became dissatisfied, and this time I meandered into anthropology. Here, for the first time, I received answers to some of my inquiries, based upon cross-cultural empirical evidence. At last I had found a discipline that was neither arbitrarily limited to a single segment of culture (as are economics, sociology, political science, and psychology) nor ethnocentrically restricted to the study of Western Civilization. And so I became a student of anthropology in general, and comparative law in particular.

My professor H. G. Barnett at the University of Oregon first suggested that I should combine my past study of law with anthropology and write my master's thesis in that subject. This I did, accomplishing the task in 1952 by studying literature pertinent to the theory of law and legal and social control in fifty-five societies. In the summer of that year I accepted an offer from Professor Edward Dozier to try my first field research among the Hopi-Tewa Indians of the Hano village of the First Mesa in Arizona. This research was brief, lasting about two months. I lived in the house of Faye Ayach, sharing my room in the pueblo with three other students and my wife. Although I had collected a heap of material on socio-political structure and social control, I did not dare to publish because of my ignorance of the language and the Tewa culture as a whole. Without these prerequisites, I knew I could not write anything definitive on the Hopi-Tewa culture. I did not want to join those anthropologists who published on people of whose language and whole culture they were ignorant. Rather, my examples were Bronislaw Malinowski and Clyde Kluckhohn. In his thorough study of the whole culture and language of the Trobriand Islanders, Malinowski introduced the participant-observer method. And Kluckhohn's long-term study of the Navajo Indians provided the very important dimension of time.

My first opportunity to carry out such a definitive study came at Yale University, where I had to decide on a culture and topic for my Ph.D. dissertation. By then I realized the shortcomings of the various theories of law, which were mostly speculative rather than based on solid cross-cultural evidence. So I wanted to design a cross-culturally valid theory of law based on solid fieldwork in several societies, complemented only by the necessary library research of the pertinent anthropological literature. These societies had to be at different evolutionary stages (hunters and gatherers, tribesmen, chieftainships, and civilized societies) and, as far as possible, unaffected by the influence of colonization. It had become clear to me that as their first task colonial governments destroy, of necessity, native legal systems by imposing their own law and "justice," and that my colleagues writing on such societies typically studied remnants of the aboriginal legal systems — some sort of "decomposed legal cadavers" — rather than viable systems of social control.

Thus my first choice was to go to the southern part of the Guianas or to the northern part of the Amazon Basin to study an isolated Indian tribe. However, my professor George Peter Murdock talked me out of this scheme by pointing out that I would have to study another Western language (Portuguese) and travel many miles into the interior, while there were still unexposed societies in the eastern part of New Guinea, not far from the coast, where the official language of the colony was English. So I settled on New Guinea. I corresponded with Siegfried Nadel at the Australian National University, asking for advice and possible support. His answer was not satisfactory to me: there would be support, but I would have to get my Ph.D. at his university. Then I had a stroke of luck. During the spring semester of 1954 at Yale there was in our department a visiting professor from Utrecht University, Theodore Fischer. He and Professor Murdock recommended I do my research in the western part of New Guinea (then a Dutch colony) that had the anthropology professor Jan Van Baal as its governor. In subsequent correspondence he expressed interest in my project and promised support and permission to conduct my research in "an uncontrolled territory," a place where most of the people had never seen a white man. This was a very exciting offer, and I accepted the invitation immediately.

In September 1954 I left New Haven by train to Oregon, where I stopped to visit my parents. From Portland I flew to Hawaii and, after having spent several days there visiting friends, flew via Canton Island and Fiji to Sydney, Australia. There I stayed for six days with my old Czechoslovak friend Jaroslav Latal and, while visiting Sydney University, made the acquaintance of professors Adolphus Peter Elkin and Arthur Capell. From Sydney I flew to the international airport on the island of Biak, part of Dutch New Guinea. From a propeller plane, the sight of the island where I planned to spend about one and a half years of my life impressed me. Flying from the south at an elevation of about fifteen thousand feet we flew over the central mountain chain of New Guinea, which rose from sea level in one heave to a peak of over sixteen thousand feet (Carstenz Toppen) towering above us on the east. This gigantic rocky "frozen wave," covered with an uninterrupted green carpet of tropical rain and mountain moss forests, would be my new home for the duration of my research. After crossing the highlands we descended over the immense forested plains of the northern part of New Guinea, bisected by silvery ribbons of rivers, half covered by the overhanging canopy of the endless tropical rain forest. From above, these plains showed no evidence of human habitation.

We landed on the raised coral island of Biak. I took a room in a simple but clean and comfortable KLM hotel located next to the airport. During my brief stay on Biak I had an exciting encounter with a waterspout, a sort of a small tornado rotating over the sea. It approached while I was lying in a sling chair on the beach near the hotel. Its rotating funnel was picking up water, lifting it into an overhanging black cloud from which it was raining back onto the sea. I wondered whether I, too, was about to be lifted, but my sling chair neighbour assured me that there was no danger, that the waterspout would disintegrate as soon as it hit the nearby coral reef. I took several pictures of the waterspout as I prepared to run for my life. And then, over the outlying coral reef, the spout disintegrated and collapsed in a spectacular cascade of colourful, glittering water drops magically illuminated by the late afternoon tropical sun.

After several days of exploring the local beaches, an old U.S. World War II airport overgrown by jungle, and rusting, crippled vehicles and landing crafts along with a downed airplane in a lagoon, I flew in an old Dakota plane to Hollandia, then the capital of the Dutch colony. There I moved to the government hotel, located next to the governor's residence in Hollandia Binnen. The accommodation was excellent. I had a room, a shower, and a terrace facing the adjoining jungle, and at six o'clock each morning hot tea was served. I shared the terrace with an Australian businessman. This arrangement was fortunate for me for several reasons. The Australian gentleman acquainted me with the life and bureaucratic procedures of the Dutch administration, along with all the local gossip. On one occasion he proved very helpful. When we were having our six o'clock tea a large venomous snake slithered out from the jungle and studied our appearance with great interest. Somehow I was more appealing than my acquaintance, and so it slid menacingly within striking distance from me. "Don't move," ordered the Australian, then screamed some words in Malay and assured me that help would be coming. Meanwhile the snake and I watched each other. I recalled John Wayne spitting into the eyes of a coiled rattlesnake and readied myself to employ the same trick. The only trouble was that I had no experience of spitting at snakes or, for that matter, at anybody or anything. So instead of using Wayne's remedy I just stared and sweated. Finally a Kanaka, a local coastal Papuan, appeared with a machete and slowly moved behind the snake. Then with a swish of steel the snake collapsed and my ordeal was over. Without the Australian's help and the Kanaka's skill, my acquaintance would have probably had to share his tea with the snake.

After two days of waiting for an appointment with the governor I decided to try to see him without the normal protocol. I walked to the governor's mansion, the former residence of General MacArthur, passed the sentry with little difficulty, and climbed up the veranda steps. Suddenly the door to the interior of the house opened and two gentlemen stepped outside, followed by a man in a dressing gown. Here was Governor Van Baal. After saying good-bye to his visitors he turned to me and asked: "And who might you be?" I introduced myself as a student of Professors Murdock and Fischer, who supposedly had written to the governor about my arrival. The governor admitted that he was surprised I had not been shot by the sentry and remarked that probably all successful political assassins in history got close to their noble victims. After this observation he kindly told me to come to his house at the same time tomorrow, and that now he would like to finish shaving. Thus I succeeded in making a swift appointment without being shot.

The next day the governor seemed transformed. Properly dressed and very cordial, he not only granted me permission to study a group of unpacified Papuans who had never seen a white man, but introduced me to a young anthropologist, Van den Leeden, whose job it was to acquaint me with local conditions, help me with purchasing equipment, and introduce me to important members of the administration and other individuals who might help me with my fieldwork. He himself, having just finished work among the coastal Papuans of the Sarmi region, proved to be an invaluable adviser in my research. Thus I met the legendary Victor de Bruijn, an experienced Dutch administrator known for his brave fight against the Japanese during World War II. At that time he was "kontroleur" in charge of the administration of the Wissell Lakes area, a region occupied by the Kapauku around the three lakes Paniai, Tigi, and Tage. The lakes were discovered by a pilot named Wissell who flew over them in 1937. The outbreak of war surprised de Bruijn there, so he decided to fight behind the Japanese lines with a bunch of Kapauku warriors. These exploits earned him the title "Jungle Pimpernel," and a book of the same title was published about his experiences.

For my research area de Bruijn suggested two central mountain areas which would suit my purposes: the Grand Baliem Valley, recently "opened" by some missionaries, and the unmapped and unpacified Kamu Valley, a part of the Kapauku territory to the southwest of the three lakes that had not yet been brought under governmental control. My advisors were in favor of the Dani tribe because, they claimed, they were more formally organized and had an established headmanship, while the Kapauku were believed to be so egalitarian that they lacked any kind of leadership, and therefore also law. Since I did not believe in any truly egalitarian and leaderless society, the Kapauku would be a challenge and I made my decision. This choice had one great advantage: in Enarotali on the Paniai Lake, the only Dutch administrative outpost in the interior of western Dutch New Guinea in 1954, Marion Doble was stationed. Doble was an American missionary who, having had training in the Summer School of Linguistics, had succeeded in analyzing the Kapauku-Paniai dialect and written a dictionary of about two thousand words and a grammar of the language (1953). In previous correspondence she had assured me of her help with learning the complicated Kapauku language. Although the people in Hollandia advised me to learn Malay, an easy language, and take with me a Paniai Kapauku as an interpreter, claiming that I would never learn the Kapauku language, I decided otherwise. If a three-year-old could learn the language, I reasoned, so could I.

My fourteen-day stay in Hollandia was made very pleasant for me by Governor Van Baal. Not only did he provide me with advisors and access to supplies from the government store, he also loaned his chauffeur and car to help me with these purchases and my visits to various administration officials. This generous loan, in one instance, resulted in a memorable a comedy of errors. One afternoon when I was swimming in Sentani Lake the governor's chauffeur appeared with his black limousine flying the governor's flag, informing me that I had been invited to a dance and reception for the captain and crew of a Dutch warship, at a restaurant on the pier in Hollandia harbour. I was to go to my hotel, change into formal dark dress attire loaned by the governor, and be driven to the pier for the festivities. There, to my surprise, the crew and the captain of the ship were lined up with the inevitable brass band, awaiting the arrival of the governor. As my car, flying the governor's flag, moved past the row of military personnel, the brass band started to play. Everybody saluted me, obviously mistaking me for the governor. Out of courtesy I responded with a salute. The car stopped in front of the captain, who was startled to see a new young governor unknown to him step out of the official car. The bandleader, also shocked, hesitantly stopped swinging his baton, while the puzzled musicians, one by one, slowly muted their instruments. Some of the guests broke into laughter; while the captain and I, trying to maintain propriety and decorum, shook hands. It was then that I introduced myself as a Yale student. I think the greatest "kick" (as he said) of the incident was had by the governor, who later even toasted me on my "promotion."

Purchases made, official and unofficial visits completed, and full of advice, I finally departed by plane to the island of Biak. Two days later I boarded a World War II amphibious plane, a Catalina, and started my journey to the highland country of my research. After a brief stop on Japen Island to deliver some people and goods, we flew into the interior of New Guinea. The flight was fascinating. To look down upon the "sea" of the tropical rain forest with its meandering silver ribbons of glittering rivers, the green vastness broken occasionally by a red blooming tree or a white heron gliding over the canopy, was certainly the experience of my life. It was extraordinary to think that all this country was still unexplored, with people living in it who had not yet experienced the blessings as well as the ecological devastation that Western civilization brings with it. In fact, my elation at nature's beauty was punctured periodically by the mental image of the future devastation civilization would exact on this virgin paradise. Humanity's greed and short-sightedness would certainly cut down those forests, destroy the habitat of exotic fauna with its marsupials and birds of paradise, expose the natives to the ravages of introduced diseases and exploitation, and destroy their culture, especially their political and legal structures and religion.

I was jolted from my daydreams by the fast approach of the foothills and mountain chains of the Central Highlands, with their towering peaks and razor-sharp tree-clad ridges. On the horizon to the east were the blue walls of the massif, which rises to the glacier-covered Carstenz Toppen, the highest mountain in the Pacific (nearly 16,500 feet). The weather was splendid, and small cumulus clouds floated beneath and around us. As we passed one mountain crest there appeared below us three huge lakes glittering like diamonds and sapphires set between the green cliffs and forest-covered mountains. We started to descend upon the northernmost and largest lake, Paniai. In the early anthropological accounts the lake's name was falsely attributed to the then mysterious inhabitants of this highland region. The mistake originated with some explorers of the southern coast of New Guinea who, being ignorant of the local language, pointed to the mountains and asked who lived there. The coastal Papuans, not understanding the question, indicated the most spectacular feature of the mountain: the huge lake. In this way, the mysterious inland dwellers became the "Paniai mountain pygmies." As it turned out Paniai was neither the name of the people nor the mountain, but a lake; and the people, who were over five-foot tall, were not pygmies.

After landing smoothly on the lake we cruised to the pier of the village of Enarotali and anchored the plane about 200 feet offshore. A motorboat with two uniformed officials set out from the pier to meet us and took us ashore. One of them was Raphael Den Haan, the district officer of the Paniai region. He addressed me in French, and so I, assuming he spoke no English, replied in the same language as best as I could. We talked about the flight and my research. Finally Den Haan asked me, "But you are not French?" This was the biggest compliment I have ever received concerning my proficiency in French. When I apprised him of the fact that I am an American citizen of Czech origin he switched to perfect English.

At the pier, another surprise awaited me. A row of people awaited our arrival. Most were local natives, some were Dutch officials, and among them was Marion Doble. From our correspondence I had pictured her as an elderly unmarried woman. To my amazement there stood instead a most attractive smiling young blonde dressed in white and pink as though she were about to attend a Sunday church service. This was not the only surprise. I received a real shock as I looked more closely at the rest of the group. Next to this beautiful, smartly dressed young woman stood a row of natives in their local costumes, the women bare-breasted with a garment consisting of a strip of bark that passed between their thighs and tucked behind and under a belt. Their buttocks were fully exposed. The males were completely naked except for a belt holding an orange bottle gourd, a penis sheath, surmounted by a kangaroo fur stopper and held in an upright position by an orange belt. They gave the impression of all having a magnificent erection. The contrast between Marion Doble and these Kapauku, the first I had ever seen, was so stark that I lowered my eyes and did not dare look up again. As the amused Miss Doble explained to me later, "It was quite a sight to see an adult man blush." My entrance into Kapauku society was certainly not heroic.

Not everything went wrong on my arrival. I made such a good impression on the district officer that he invited me to stay in his house as his guest. His residence stood on a hill overlooking the large lake, swamps, forest-covered mountains, and a Dutch village with a picturesque Catholic church. The interior of the house was very well designed, comfortable and well furnished. The drawing room was equipped with an excellent and well-stocked bar. There were constant visitors to the place, so I could certainly not complain of boredom. Den Haan made it his business to introduce me to the local residents, especially the physician and his nurse who ran a small hospital, the parish Catholic priest of the Franciscan order, the manager of the government shop, and Mr. Post, the head of the Protestant missionaries of the American Mission Alliance. Mr. Post and Marion Doble invited me to several dinners, so that during my short stay I became acquainted with most of the mission personnel.

While waiting to trek into the unchartered territory of the Tage Lake region and beyond, I had an interesting opportunity to witness the trial by the Dutch government of an elderly Kapauku woman accused of murdering a child. The charge was serious indeed. The woman had allegedly killed a four-year-old boy, and subsequently eaten the body. So it seemed that I was going to study cannibals. This was another surprise for me. A young government official translated the court proceedings for me so I could follow the arguments. The accusers and witnesses were very specific in their statements and extended testimonies. The accused woman sat still, her head lowered. She did not speak at all and did not object to the charges. After the hearings were concluded the district officer decided that the evidence, although quite solid, was still inconclusive. He explained to me that in similar cases the testimonies, although well-delivered and convincing as to their accuracy, were subsequently proven to be biased and based at least partially on personal prejudice. No matter what the actual outcome, however, the charge of cannibalism was certainly a serious matter.

So, it looked like I would be studying cannibals for about one and a half years, which I did not find to be an encouraging prospect. I surveyed my physique in the mirror and concluded that since I was rather skinny, I would not be considered appetizing. I recalled that even sharks preferred fat seals and sea lions to skinny sailors and swimmers. Also, it was likely that the cannibals focused on their traditional enemies. However, this knowledge of cannibalism did not invoke any fear with me. As strange as it may appear to the reader, I was not afraid or worried of what would happen to me if I were killed. Indeed, I was not even afraid of death.

This lack of fear dated back to my childhood when, at the age of five, I was afflicted with appendicitis which ultimately burst causing peritonitis. It was 1928 when there was no penicillin or other antibiotics to help me recover. The hospital believed I was doomed and advised my parents that my case was hopeless. My father refused to accept this verdict, boarded his private plane and flew to a summer resort where he unceremoniously picked up my vacationing uncle Robert Pospíšil, M.D. who was a well-known surgeon. Together they flew to my native town, where my uncle operated on me in his sanatorium at eight o'clock in the evening. He had to flush out of my abdomen the mess my treacherous intestine had produced. During the operation, he discovered that the cause of my appendicitis was tuberculosis of my abdominal glands, which he removed. During these operations my heart stopped and I had a strange dream that haunted me afterwards but later fortified me for the rest of my life. I dreamed I was running on a parquet floor with cracks big enough for me to fall though into a fiery glow beneath. In front of me was a brilliant golden light which I was trying to reach. Suddenly, my feet left the floor and I floated into the embrace of the golden light. What a marvellous experience! Though I survived the operation, my abdomen remained open for several months. During the first five weeks, it had to be opened and cleaned every afternoon around four o'clock. What I dreaded most was the closing of the wound with spiked clamps due to the intense pain it produced.

The aftermath of this childhood experience was a relative tolerance of pain, no fear of death, and a deep scar in my abdomen which proved to be most helpful in my New Guinea research, as I will explain later. My lack of fear of death was most helpful during my resistance to Nazism and its brutality, which sent my father to the concentration camps of Dachau and Buchenwald and three of my uncles to the various "accommodations" of the Gestapo. Beside such experiences, of course, made my initial stay in the strange "Stone Age" of the Kapauku Papuanas was not only bearable, but actually very pleasant and exciting.

After ten days at Enarotali, my leisure period ended. The district officer introduced me to some natives and helped me organize my party. He also suggested the southern and southwestern parts of the uncontrolled Kamu Valley as the most promising areas for my study.

My communication with the natives was most rudimentary. During my brief stay at the lake I was able to stutter a few of the most common words and sentences in the Kapauku language. There were, of course, no interpreters and no Pidgin English as lingua franca. Thus the sentence of most importance for my immediate future and survival was "Kapauku maa mana?"— "How do you say it in Kapauku?" With such stellar linguistic skills, and with supplies, porters, and a police patrol composed of native constabulary provided by the district officer, I left Enarotali by motor boat. Unfortunately the pleasant voyage did not last long. After going down the Jawei River in a southerly direction for a few miles, we had to leave the boat at a place called Udateida and start our long trip overland.

At the end of the first day we reached Waghete village on Tigi Lake, the seat of one Mr. Lawrence, the Dutch police commander of the newly "opened" area. I stayed in his house for one day. The next day, Lawrence led our expedition across the huge lake in boats. We arrived at the entrance to the mountainous Debei Valley, a region traditionally hostile to intruders. As I had been told, Dutch expeditions had been attacked and turned back, and even a Japanese platoon that succeeded in penetrating it during the Second World War had been massacred.

As we proceeded through the valley the local natives learned about a very strange white man who was coming to live with them and who, oddly enough, was neither a missionary nor a policeman. He was not coming to teach them any new religion or customs, nor was he going to force any of the white man's laws upon them. On the contrary, he claimed that he intended to learn their language and study their way of life. Although many of the natives were suspicious of these strange assertions (communicated to them by a native who spoke Malay and had learned about my research from the Dutch administration), they became interested in my project. The first confrontation with the Debei people occurred not far from the entrance to the valley. Suddenly we were surrounded by about two hundred warriors. In front of us, on a hill, stood the headman of the local political unit. With one interpreter (Kapauku-Malay), Mr. Lawrence started to climb the slope.

I took his picture. At the time I feared it would be my last one. When we reached the top of the hill the headman — still sporting Japanese epaulettes that testifed to his war exploits — received us. Mr. Lawrence engaged him in conversation for half a day and was quite successful. He convinced our "host" that I posed no threat to them and their political freedom. I showed the headman a book I was carrying with me into the field (the British "Notes and Queries" Committee of RAI, 1951) to demonstrate what my future work on Kapauku culture would look like. The headman agreed to our free passage through his territory but warned us that their neighbours to the west, another Kapauku political confederacy of lineages, were really dangerous. To protect us, he persuaded about fifty of his followers, armed with bows and arrows, to join our procession.

During our passage through the Debei Valley such discussions and arrangements were repeated each time we entered another political territory. At the outset our party numbered about forty individuals (including carriers and native constabulary). As we continued more and more natives joined us for our "protection," so that by the time we entered the low-lying Kamu Valley (about 4,300 feet above the sea level) from the lofty threshold of the Debei Valley (about 6,000 feet above the sea level) my native following numbered well over three hundred people.

In this way, the trip through the traditionally hostile Debei Valley proved to be quite peaceful. Walking through the jungle on a narrow winding path was another matter, however. The ground was soft, usually with ankle-deep mud, traversed periodically by slippery tree roots that made me slide sideways. How I appreciated my heavy Australian army boots with their copper studs, which kept me from losing my footing and rolling in the mud! Indeed, my journey well befitted the title of Pierre-Dominique Gaisseau's film *The Sky Above — the Mud Below*. Above me were tall trees and the canopy of the tropical forest. Making our trip less monotonous were native "bridges" over streams in deep ravines, which we crossed by balancing often on a single pole, without the luxury of a railing. These crossings resembled more of a circus tightrope act than a forest trek. We also waded through swamps, often knee deep in mud and water, steadying ourselves on poles. Sometimes I preferred to simply swim.

Finally, on the third day, we stood at the end of the Debei Valley, about 1,500 feet above the low-lying Kamu, a huge dried-out (naturally drained) lake bed with the Jewei Mountain rising in the middle. It was a magnificent sight, enhanced by my three days of claustrophobia in the jungle. The vastness of the valley floor below me, the magnificent mountains reaching into the clouds, the savanna and reed-covered valley flats, and the verdure of the surrounding tropical rain forests around me was simply overwhelming. That such beauty could exist in our "developed world" was beyond my comprehension.

After a few minutes of silence as I took in the beauty, I began to think about what the "civilized" world would eventually bring to this paradise: mountain slopes denuded of forests by Japanese lumber companies and turned into a tropical desert; the swampy lake bed and the savanna carved into rice paddies and traversed by paved roads; smoke and toxic fumes emitted from industrial enterprises and tractors; the crystal-clear streams polluted by human and industrial waste; and the introduction of malaria and an additional assortment of white man's and Asiatic bacteria. I finally managed to shake off these mental images and concentrate on the glorious present. It was 23 November 1954.

As I gazed from my lofty perch over the expanse of the Kamu Valley my first intuition was to cross it and settle in the villages I could see faintly in the south-west. My escorts informed me that these were the villages of Bibigi, Degeipige and Ginopigi. However, as we descended to the valley floor the natives of the first village we entered, Botukebo, persuaded me to change my plan and stay in their territory. They staged a great welcoming party during which they presented me with a pig. On the advice of Mr. Lawrence I immediately reciprocated with a gift of several steel axes. The people, led by the young headman of the village of Aigii, Jokagaibo, offered me a nice piece of land called Itoda (Kapauku meaning: place of sand), through which ran a creek with clear, ice cold water that was safe to drink without any purification. The creek originated from a mountain cliff some distance back in the jungle at the foot of the Kemuge Mountain, which towered over the place. What better place could I have wished to settle in? I accepted the headman's generous offer, and with the help of the police I pitched my tent and unloaded my supplies.

Slowly a crowd of several hundred of people gathered around the place, all watching my every move. To them, each tiny item of my supplies was a treasure, especially my used Gillette razor blades. On the morning of the second day the police and the natives started to clear the ground in preparation for my future house. With the help of machetes provided by the police, they tore at the groundcover, exposing a beautiful alluvial layer of yellow sand. While this was going on, many native men and children approached me in order to subject me to closer scrutiny. A couple of courageous fellows even touched my cheeks to find out whether I was painted or not. Once they were convinced I was not, they concluded that I was immortal. Why? To them this conclusion was empirical and logical. The only pinkish white animals they knew in their environment were crayfish that had recently shed their dark, hard skin. This rejuvenation cycle was thought to go on indefinitely — proof that the animal was immortal. Because the crayfish were intensively fished, the Kapauku never had the opportunity to see any of them die naturally. So, by analogy, these notions were applied to me. When I objected, they refused to believe that the white man was mortal. They maintained that in the past I had gone through cycles similar to the crayfish. Later on this idea was "empirically" confirmed when my body, exposed to the tropical sun, slowly acquired a deeper and deeper tan. "You see", they exclaimed, "you lied to us! You are now getting dark like us (I did indeed tan a deep bronze) and then you will shed your dark skin like the crayfish and start the process over again." This contention and my "lying" was proven a couple weeks later, when my skin started to peel. The people assured me, however, that they did not think of me as a bad man because of my "lying." I was simply being modest, not wanting to flaunt my superiority. At that time I wished my wife were there to hear this evaluation. She has always been aware of my status as a flawed mortal.

What slowly started to unnerve me was that I was constantly the center of everybody's attention. Every move I made was carefully watched, and if I wanted to open a can and bent over it, I soon had at least ten natives bending over it with me. The initial native shyness diminished remarkably after I appeared in shorts and without a shirt. Although my clothes scared them at first, the people could see that the body underneath was built like theirs, with a proper belly button in the right place. One thing, however, aroused excitement and brought me immediate prestige: the deep scar on my abdomen, a relic of my uncle-surgeon's operation to remove my appendix. Because there were no antibiotics in the twenties, my abdomen had to be kept open for antiseptic purposes for about half a year, causing a large, deep, depressed scar. Not knowing anything about surgery, the people attributed my scar to combat and I became immediately not only *jape uu*, a war hero, but also some sort of superman. No Kapauku could survive such a stab in the belly. Not conversant in the language, and thus ignorant of their interpretation of the reason for my scar, for several months I enjoyed the highest reputation as a macho man. Appearing to them to be very rich and physically tough and brave, I was given their highest honorary title of *ibo* (big) and *ibome* (big man or "big shot"). After they learned that I was American, I became known far and wide as *Americ-aibo* — something like a big shot from America. For practical reasons I did not object to such a distinction.

On my first day, however, the people's reaction to me had one undesired effect: the terrific hollering and screaming of hundreds of culturally extroverted Kapauku. This noise and the omnipresent multitude rendered me completely exhausted that first day, and in the evening I collapsed into a deep sleep in my tent. The next morning at about six o'clock I woke up and with apprehension listened for the presence of the multitude. Absolute quiet and the chirping of birds in the forest enveloped the tent. Finally alone, with the people dispersed to their close and distant villages, I could relax and wash and shave myself in the brook in much appreciated solitude. I picked up my toilet supplies, opened the tent, and stepped out into what I expected to be a glorious day. But there, in front of my tent in a large semicircle, five hundred people sat in complete silence, their eyes glued to the entrance. The minute I stepped outside, noise and screaming and yelling erupted like a salvo. While I washed and shaved, hundreds of pairs of eyes stared at me from every quarter. It seemed that the entire jungle around me was alive.

As the days passed, the people continued to follow me about, constantly surrounding me. At least ten of them tried to teach me Kapauku words for different objects — all, of course, at the same time. The direst moment came when I had to use the toilet. I tried to disappear in the bush, but a procession followed me. Finally, in desperation and acute discomfort, I screamed and swung my arms at them, trying to make it clear that they should leave me in peace. In order not to antagonize them, I tried to laugh at the same time. They laughed back at me — but they did retreat! From then on I used this technique any time I needed compliance with an order or suggestion that the natives were reluctant to follow. As a matter of fact, this also worked marvelously with my students at Yale: castigate and smile at the same time.

The people's reactions to the various items I had brought along with me were varied and often surprising. They placed great value not on clothes but on blankets. The smell of my aftershave frightened them at first, but later some said *enaa* (good, nice), while others maintained their aversion. My little toy teddy bear elicited amazement and, after some tentative touching, lots of laughter. Similarly my magazine pictures were a great success. Above all, they admired pictures of animals that were familiar to them (especially birds); they could not comprehend my picture of a horse. No one commented on the beauty of the cover girls on these magazines, though they did show interest in their clothes. To my surprise, my harmonica failed to impress them, whereas when I played on my comb covered with paper, I was quite a success, especially when I produced high-pitched tones.

During my initial contact I tried to be cool toward people who overeagerly offered advice and help, remembering Professor Barnett's warning that most likely such people were misfits in their own culture, trying to compensate by attaching themselves to a foreigner. Indeed, one of two such Kapauku proved to be a generally disliked man, while the other, Ijaaj Bunaibomuuma, was a recidivist criminal who later in my stay was tried for his life. I filmed the trial.

The real adventure for me started with the departure of Mr. Lawrence and his police escort on 27 November, leaving me with one policeman named Darobo. We had just begun the daunting task of building a solid house as headquarters for my research. It was to stand on the place given to me and called Itoda, between the villages of Botukebo and Kojogeepa. Its location outside of a village and on a main trade route proved most advantageous. It permitted me to live close to Kapauku communities while minimizing the disturbing influence my arrival and presence might have had upon the village life of the natives. It also prevented my identification with any one single village, thus allowing informants from other villages and, thanks to the trade route, even those from other political confederacies or lineages — as well as free access to my house. At the same time the proximity of the village of Botukebo permitted close and continuous observation of the life of its inhabitants.

We started to build my house on 25 November. I drew up a plan of a square house with a three-foot elevated floor for sanitary reasons and as protection from crawling insects and reptiles. I drew two windows, a door, and a partial partition that created the effect of two rooms. Behind the partition I constructed a bed. Since this was made of thin, crude poles, offering what only a most imaginative individual would call comfort, I called it "the bed of Procrustes."

The floor was made of large poles with gaps between them so that sweeping it was an easy task indeed; all the dirt simply fell underneath the house, where it was scraped away once a month. A gabled roof topped the four walls. The roof was made of hewn planks, provided by the villagers. They labored fantastically on the construction. Adolescent boys brought freshly cut poles from the jungle, stripped nicely of their bark, and a Papuan even donated the entirety of his old house, whose planks were freshly shaved by natives with their stone maumi axes and the steel axes supplied by us. Of course I reciprocated the gift with counter-offerings of axes, machetes, and knives.

The work proceeded satisfactorily. Although I had to wait until 5 December for nails to arrive from Enarotali by special courier, we proceeded with construction. The natives lashed poles and planks together with steel-like rattan vines. As it turned out, this lashing was the bond that held my house together for seven months, by which point the nails had rusted away. On 5 December we finished the frame and the walls, on the next day the door, one window, and the internal partition. On 8 December the floor and the second window were completed. And on 9 December the roof was installed, although later it had to be covered with a layer of oak bark weighted down by a mesh of poles lashed together in order to make it watertight and to prevent *toto*, "dripping holes," which appeared later anyway and had to be sealed periodically.

While working on the building, we had to climb up onto the ridge pole, rafters, and horizontal beams. The boys climbed the perpendicular poles while I, with my training at the Czechoslovak Sokol gymnastic organization, jumped up, grasped a horizontal beam, and swung my legs up over it in a couple of seconds. The boys screamed in surprise and enthusiastically tried to imitate my gymnastics. The result was almost a catastrophe. With five or more of the boys swinging on a pole simultaneously, the whole structure bent dangerously, threatening to collapse. I had to stop this performance. The natives, however, were so taken by the elegance of the swings and turnovers on the beams that the very next day they erected a horizontal bar next to my house, on which the Papuans began diligently practicing. Periodic outbursts of laughter came from onlooking girls when an unfortunate boy broke his koteka gourd penis sheath on the bar. The embarrassed athlete jumped down and swiftly disappeared in the reeds, wherefrom he shouted for help. His friends supplied him with a new genital cover in his hideout. In a couple of days an enterprising Kapauku entrepreneur appeared with a large supply of gourds, selling these to the gymnasts in need. I eventually ruined his business by supplying the boys with shorts. I showed them other tricks, so that in about fourteen days there was something like a Papuan gymnastics team surrounding my house, exercising on bars, throwing spears (there were no spears prior to my arrival), playing team games, and pulling on poles. I was even able to film the first headstand, handstand, and somersault ever made in the interior of New Guinea, possibly even on the entire island.

To complete my habitat I added four structures to my house: a chicken coop, fireplace, toilet, and garden. Since I had received two chickens from the district officer, bought another from the local people, and then added a handsome rooster, the natives built a chicken house for me. This was on 16 December. Although the coop was quite attractive, some of the birds preferred to roost in a shrub nearby. Even worse, they laid their eggs in the jungle and the boys had to look for their nests. Sometimes there were more than fifteen eggs in the same place. Many boys and adults reproached me for eating eggs, claiming that it was a bad business not to give the birds in the eggs a chance to hatch and enjoy life. They themselves used the adult birds only for meat and feathers. The latter use became a problem. In order to keep my chickens and rooster, I had to feed them sweet potatoes every morning and evening. At sunset I would stand in front of my house and produce, with my pursed lips, a shrill purring sound and the fowl would come flying out of the jungle to get their food. The rooster would usually emerge from the forest, descending from the steep mountain slopes, spiralling down to me, his magnificent metallic-coloured plumage glittering in the rays of the setting sun. One evening, however, his arrival was not as spectacular as usual. To my horror I found that his beautiful tail feathers had been plucked. The culprit was a boy whom I later named Robertus (the natives pronounced it as Gubeeni); he had used the feathers to make a headdress for himself. I castigated him severely and put a halt to the plucking practice as far as my birds were concerned.

Since we had to search constantly for the egg nests in the jungle, I decided to use an old trick from my native country to induce the chickens to lay eggs in the same place. In my house I blew out six eggs, consumed the contents and filled the empty eggshells with sand, sealing the two apertures with wax. Then I lined up the final products on a shelf above my desk. When I had time, I would place them in the nests and remove the real eggs. The chickens would not know the difference and would come to lay eggs in the same place.

While I was contemplating all this, in came one of my boys, named Ogiibiijokaimopaj, and admired my products, not knowing they were not real eggs. He asked me whether he could have one. Having lived in this place for three months, I was able to speak some Kapauku, and was familiar with the natives' penchant for playing practical jokes. I generously replied, "Take all of them, if you wish." "*Nagajaawege*," he thanked profusely, and took the eggs and went home. The next day many young boys and other villagers came to my house, laughing and telling me that I was quite a clever trickster. They told me that Ogiibiijokaimopaj had invited some of them for an egg feast (by that time the people were already imitating me and enjoyed eating eggs), where he planned to roast the eggs in red-hot ashes. Once they broke the shells and discovered the sand, they realized the joke. They went from house to house, laughing and telling about their unfortunate host and this new kind of trick. Ogiibijokaimopaj was not offended or even annoyed, as we Westerners would have been. As a good Kapauku he laughed along with his guests and upon seeing me, slapped my back, declaring, "It was a good trick. You got me this time, I'll get you next."

In order to heat my house at night, when the temperature routinely dropped into single digits on the Centigrade scale, and as a means of cooking, I decided to build a fireplace. Of course I had neither bricks nor mortar. I decided to use large flat stones instead of bricks, and clay mixed with sand, dried moss, and straw as mortar. A crew of boys and young men rolled large stones and even boulders down the mountainside. This activity provided lots of excitement as the rocks rolled down through the jungle and shrubs, tearing down smaller trees and branches and leaving trails in the greenery on the slope. I proceeded to build the fireplace chamber onto the outside of the house, using huge rocks covered by large flat stones. At the end of this megalithic structure, away from the house wall, I built a more or less square chimney of smaller stones. The clay mortar worked fine and held the structure together. Amazingly, even the heavy rains did not dissolve my achievement, which the Kapauku called *mogo owa* (the stone house). The whole construction was finished by 29 December, in twelve days. It proved magnificent, keeping me warm in the evenings, providing a place to cook my meals, and giving my new home a coziness and distinction.

To provide me with regular fresh food the boys made a garden nearby my house and fenced it in. I cultivated vegetables that were rarely grown by the natives or quite unknown to them: onions, cucumbers, melons, two kinds of tomatoes, American multicolored corn, string beans, chili peppers, and Irish potatoes. I also tried cabbage, cauliflower, broccoli, and kale, but these plants were rapidly devoured by ochre-colored beetles, in spite of our efforts to eradicate them. In addition to these introduced crops (seeds I received from my parents in Oregon), the natives planted some types of marrow, bottle gourds, and ginger. Later I used ginger roots for trade with the Paniai Lake residents in exchange for imported goods. Of course the people were keen on tasting my strange vegetables. All except one were received with enthusiasm. Corn had the greatest success, spreading from my seeds across the Kamu Valley and beyond. One year later I found fields of it in the Pona Valley, which to my knowledge I was the first white man to enter.

The only failure proved to be the tomato. People had no use for them until an incident gave the plant a new function. Once while I was weeding my garden, my "adopted" native boys were playing a war game nearby, hitting each other with balls of mud. One of the missiles missed its target and hit me in the back. Being the retaliatory type, I grabbed the first projectile I could find, a ripe red tomato hanging next to my face, and with beautiful accuracy hit one of the boys in the middle of his forehead. The tomato splashed magnificently, covering the warrior with red juice and yellow seeds. Seeing this fabulous effect the boys screamed with delight. They instantly invaded my tomato patch and engaged me and the other group in an all-out tomato fight. At first I was apprehensive about the prospect of losing my entire crop, but after receiving several spectacular hits I succumbed to the boys' enthusiasm and helped them finish off my tomato inventory. Objectively speaking, tomatoes were far superior to mud balls in this war game. There could be no stones hidden inside, and they splashed so extraordinarily over the warriors' naked bodies, an effect no mud ball could produce. One lucky and unexpected outcome of our battle was that the splashed tomato seeds eventually sprouted and grew in the reeds and the adjoining jungle, wherever the stray or inaccurate missiles had landed. In two months, tomato fighting around my house became a favourite pastime of the younger generation. This was my first contribution to the native culture.

Other additions to my food supply grew outside my house. One was a bush with fruits that resembled giant lemons, larger than grapefruits. The juice, however, was disappointing, tasting like something between a lemon and grapefruit. The fruit had lots of white pulp, which the people ate together with the juicy flesh. Another citrus fruit cultivated by the natives was called *mukwa*. It was the shape and size of a large lime, but its skin had a rich yellow colour when ripe. The juice was excellent, superior to our limes and lemons. I used to squeeze one daily, sweetened with sugar. What a treat it was to have plenty of ice-cold fruit juice in this tropical jungle! Another natural food source was a banana grove that the people planted for me on the southern side of my house. My grove had five varieties of bananas: two kinds of non-ripening green plantains and three ripening varieties: one medium-sized white, the other medium-sized yellow (a most common variety), and one smaller orange variety, the most delicious of all.

To complete my building project I had to construct an outhouse toilet. The natives took care of it by building one over a small inlet into the swamps that stretched in front of my house, insisting that the crayfish would prosper on my products. The toilet was most adequate, located a short distance from the house and with one unique quality: it was alive and grew. The poles the natives used for construction came from freshly cut trees and were not stripped of their bark. About a year later, a Dutch officer came to stay in my house for three days. In the morning, he watched me as I prepared to visit the outhouse, a machete in my hand. "Where are you going?" asked the officer. "To prune my toilet," I replied. The toilet was interesting from another point of view. On each visit I was entertained by all these insects, spiders, and lizards crawling on the living walls. The greatest improvement to toilets in the Kamu Valley was of course made by the people themselves. When I returned to New Guinea in 1959 and 1962 I observed with amazement the Kapauku version of my toilet in the "modernized" villages of Idabagata and Obadoba. The natives not only had living outhouses like my own, but they made use of their walls as support for my introduced string beans, which they planted all around the structures. Thus, a visit to the privy was also a time to observe and scrutinize the growing crop.

My house did not stand alone under the mountain wall. The boys who helped build my quarters also erected flimsy shacks of branches about twenty yards away from my house. There they slept and cooked while working on my residence. Later, on 12 January 1955, they built themselves an extraordinary Kapauku house of planks with an elevated floor. For political reasons two headmen decided to build themselves houses near mine, so that when they stayed long into the night in my house, discussing various issues, instructing me systematically in Kapauku culture, and enjoying my food and the warmth of my fireplace, they did not have to take the long walk back to their home villages. These were only small buildings; their main residences were, of course, their family homes with their wives and children. Thus Ijaaj Auwejokaamoje of Jagawaugii had a house built just beyond my brook on 26 December 1954, followed by Ijaaj Jokagaibo of Aigii, a man who became my *noogei* (Kapauku formal best friend). He built his shelter on the same bank about twenty yards toward the foot of the steep walls of the Kemuge Mountain, on 6 January 1955. In this way, I enjoyed the company of two of the most important local politicians.

Language

In my research among the Kapauku I was faced with an initial problem: there was no lingua franca and no interpreter was available. That meant I had to learn the native tongue right from the start if I wanted to communicate with a living soul. Luckily, Marion Doble had offered me her analysis of the Kapauku dialect spoken at Lake Paniai, and supplied me with that dialect's vocabulary and a brief grammar and text booklet written for the use of other missionaries staying at the lake. Thus I was able to start learning the language as soon as I arrived in the Kamu Valley. Several people in the valley knew the Paniai dialect well, so I could read the Paniai words from Doble's vocabulary and add *"Kamu maa mana?"* which means "How do you say it in Kamu?" In this way I had a working vocabulary of about two thousand words in fourteen days. In that dialect many words were the same as in Kamu, some had only a phonetic shift (e.g. "my mother" in Paniai is *noukwai* and in the Kamu, *niikai*), and only few were unrelated (in Paniai fire is *bodija* and in Kamu, *utu*. In Kamu the word *bodija* was used for the largest cowry shells of the cowry currency).

The Kapaukan language is an unbelievably complicated affair, especially the verb forms. Paul Taylor — a Yale student who in the seventies did research among the Papuan speakers of the island of Halmahera in the Moluccas — and I calculated an astonishing quarter of a million or in some cases half a million forms per verb.[1] I am sure

---

1] The Kapauku verb changes with subject and number (four forms for singular, three for dual, and three for plural) which results in ten forms. It also changes with direct object and indirect object (e.g., "I hit you because of her"), thus producing one thousand forms. Then there are twenty-four tense aspects, some of which may be combined in one verb (e.g. past tense and durative, past tense and iterative, past tense and repetitive, etc.) so that the twenty-four thousand forms have to be again multiplied by twelve. Also, the verb expresses positive or negative aspects (the

that in the history of the Kapauku people, not a single Kapauku has ever pronounced all the forms of a single verb. So how does one learn such a language? Certainly not by memorizing idioms, as in English or French. One has to learn it the way we learn Latin (I had six years of it in a Czech *gymnasium*) — one memorizes the rules and the sequence of prefixes, suffixes, and infixes of the verb (the verb structure) so that one can produce or understand a verb instantaneously without previous experience of each and every specific form. In Latin you do not learn all the forms of a verb but only the necessary suffixes — so not necessarily *amo, amas, amat*, etc., but only the infinitive *amare* (to love), and then the suffixes for the various persons: *-o, -as, -at, -amus, -atis, -ant.*[2]

My complete isolation from non-Kapauku speakers forced me to learn the native tongue intensively. The people proved to be patient and enthusiastic teachers. At the beginning of my stay they were so insistent that I learn their tongue swiftly that in order to get any quiet moments, I had to pretend I was sleeping in the morning, when I was actually plodding through my grammar and vocabulary. My daily target was to learn at least ten new words. After three months I could converse fairly fluently on topics of daily life. This success was due to two factors. First, I had a good training in linguistics from Floyd Lounsbury at Yale, and prior to that from T. Stern at the University of Oregon and from Prague University. This linguistic knowledge allowed me to analyse systematically the Kamu-Kapauku dialect structure, phonetics, phonemics, and semantics and to relate them to Marion Doble's analysis of the Paniai dialect (1966) Second, I had had to learn several languages in my early life. By the age of eleven I was bilingual (in Czech and German); and in the Czechoslovak *gymnasium* I learned

---

288,000 forms times two produce 576,000 forms). A few verbs combine three tense aspects, making them most formidable. Fortunatelly not all verbs are so complicated. What does such a verb look like? Like this, for example: *tekaawagimakaipiga*: "I shall not finish him off by hitting him because of you in the immediate future."

2] In this verb the first syllable, *te*, means "no" (negative); *kaa* means because of you; *wa* means him; *gi* carries the meaning of to hit; *makai* is a infinitive form, to finish; *pig* is the infix of the immediate future tense aspect; and *a* means I.

Latin (six years), French (four years), and German eight years. These studies required not only reading, writing, and speaking of all these languages, but also a knowledge of their literature. Indeed, I had to learn by heart many poems, which I can recite to this day. Later on, when I was in a German camp waiting to emigrate to the United States, I learned Spanish and English from textbooks.

At Yale a great majority of our students had no foreign language training prior to entering college, and the language examinations there, administered in "reading" the language (certainly not in writing or in speaking), could at best be called decipherment tests. How anthropologists with such a gap in their education, having no speaking knowledge of even a single foreign European language, are able to learn a non-Indo-European language is hard to comprehend and, of course, they often don't. In the past they used interpreters, and in the present many avoid foreign languages and cultures by studying their own, thus necessarily falling into the trap of ethnocentricity. To learn a foreign language means not only to acquire the skills specific to that language but also, and more importantly, to learn how to learn another language. With each additional language, learning comes easier. Kapauku was my seventh.

After my first six months among the Kapauku, I had made such progress that I was able to curtail my intensive study of the Kapauku language. I did not reveal my knowledge immediately, though. I pretended not to understand when they spoke rapidly amongst themselves. My teachers, of course, were not much pleased with my progress. They were especially embarrassed to tell visitors from other villages, *"Aki tuanima kojaa mana wegai to. Okai mekaa mana mijo epi to"* ("You have to speak with the master only very slowly. He knows the human language only a little"). This pretense of mine, however, proved very rewarding when individuals had to talk in my presence about something I was not meant to hear; they simply chatted with each other and I pretended not to understand. At such times the speakers were grateful to my teachers for my ignorance, while I was able to learn things that otherwise would have been hidden from me.

To gain knowledge and understanding of a foreign culture, one has to understand fully and speak fluently the language of the people one is studying. There is no substitute for this basic requirement, made plain by Malinowski's work early in the twentieth century. So it is sad to find anthropologists not speaking the language of their objects of study and using interpreters or lingua franca instead. Indeed, ignorance of the native language has even been defended by such well-known anthropologists as Sally Moor and Laura Nader (Starr and Collier 1989, p. 20). Since when is ignorance justifiable in a scholarly work?

Even the use of lingua franca is not acceptable. To talk to a Kapauku in Malay or Indonesian is like a Chinese scholar talking to an American in Esperanto! Most work based on ignorance of the native language I consider not only incomplete but generally unreliable. I have therefore always insisted on my students learning the language of the people they studied. Similarly, if one wants to understand any single segment of a foreign culture one has to know the culture as a whole, and only then concentrate on the field of one's special interest. In order to demonstrate the indispensability of knowing the native language as well as the overall culture, I present here the problem of deciding upon and deciphering the Kapauku concept of ego and its consequences in understanding seemingly unrelated parts of these people's culture heritage.

During the initial five months I spent studying the Kapauku language and culture, several phenomena emerged that defied simple explanation. First, Kapauku never took prisoners of war. Either they killed their enemies or they let them go. Also there were no servants, slaves, or subjects of any kind. In the Paniai region the people hated and condemned as inhuman ("not even pigs or dogs behave like that") the institution of *wanee owa* — the house of the white man's prison. They preferred death to imprisonment. In jail they would fall sick, and many did not survive. Second was their behaviour toward their children. Youngsters were never ordered or forced to do anything, and punishment was aimed at addressing past mischief rather than inducing an individual to behave in a specific way. Third, while the people believed in the soul, they expected no afterlife. Death was simply their ultimate end. Also, their soul was not them (their ego) — they prayed to their souls as in the West one might address one's guardian angel. Neither was the body the essence of ego, since if one lost a body part, the ego was not diminished. The central question underlying these mysteries was "What am I?" If ego is neither the body nor the soul, what is it? No one could tell me. Obviously the concept of ego belongs to the covert culture of the Kapauku, the part that people possess but are not aware of. It resides in their subconscious.

For answers, I first turned to the Kapauku religion. There, a child's soul is said to enter the mother's body when she becomes pregnant. However, the soul is not synonymous with the self, because the soul is called *ani ipuwe enija*, which means "the spirit that owns me." Indeed it cannot be, because I pray to my soul and treat it as an entity different from myself. The Kapauku concept of death tells us that while the body slowly decays and, apart from the skeleton, disappears, the soul, being a true spirit, is unaffected by death. It leaves the body and departs to the virgin forests and mountains, where it stays during the day. The Kapauku have no clear conception of the soul. It is simply immaterial, and and thus beyond human comprehension. It is thought to embody the good qualities of the deceased. During the night the soul of a deceased person may return to the village and linger around the houses it once frequented. Its relationship to the living depends on the character of the person prior to his or her death, and upon the way the body was disposed of during the funeral. If it has been given a decent burial, the soul is pleased and becomes a guardian to the inhabitants of the house. It is believed to shield them especially from the attacks of evil spirits (manifested as disease).

While the good qualities of the deceased are preserved in the soul, death separates the bad qualities and malevolent potentialities of the dead person and associates them with *tene*, the departed shadow — an ethereal, dark outline of the dead (an actual shadow is called an *aija*). While the *tene* occasionally helps his "protégé," it is believed to be motivated either by its own interest and profit, or by the harm it can do to other people. For this reason it is much feared. Although the

Kapauku may request help from the departed souls of their relatives during the performance of white magic, in the areas of black magic and sorcery, when the objective is killing other people, they usually turn to the *tene*. The ego does not survive death — it is not part of the decomposing body, nor of the departing soul. Except for the reflection of its bad qualities it has little to do with *tene*. Death, then, is not only a destructive force, destroying the body and eliminating the ego — it also creates a new, malevolent spirit. Thus Kapauku have an additional reason to fear death.

When I started to discuss religion with the Kapauku, I was shocked by their initial response. To my question *"Ugatame topi?"* ("Is there God?") the answer was "No." I asked the question several times until, exasperated, I argued: "You claim there is no God, but you have a word for him — *Ugatame*." "Yes, we do have the word, but God does not exist." I continued: "But you pray, for example, *Ugatame nadouje, ani kamutaine* (Creator of mankind, look at me, I want to perform white [curative] magic). So there is a God!" "No, there is no God but we believe (in him)!" I began to suspect that the Kapauku had a radically different conception of existential reality than I. But the reality was much simpler: it all came down to the meaning of certain words. Their word *tou* or *topi* — to stay, to be — means to stay in space. When I say *tou*, I imply that the being or thing "is" because I can see it, hear it, smell it, taste it, or touch it. The Kapauku verb "to be" applies to phenomena, to entities that are empirically verifiable. Spiritual perception is referred to as *umii* (to sleep) or *bagume dou* (to see dreams). Another reality is *umijogoo gai* (thinking while dreaming or sleeping). This dimension I call spiritual conceptualization. *Umii* and *umijoggo gai* are are considered to be a function of the soul. To complete the logical construct there should be a verb for conceptualizing physical phenomena while awake. There is indeed the word *gai* (to think), but according to several of my philosophically minded informants, to think and make decisions is an activity involving both the soul and the body — the only human cognitive process that entails the combined activity of both, and an anomaly in the logical scheme I had conceived. This anomaly, of course, bothered me and pricked my interest. So the thinking process *gai* is unlike the other three realities, a combination of endeavours of body and soul, a murky concept.

With this well-defined conceptualization of the fourfold realities, I turned to the language again and realized a surprising truth: while my body (*tou*) remains in physical space and my soul (*umii*) dreams, my ego (*umii-tou* — the Kapauku word for living) lives. Thus "to live" means the combination of bodily and spiritual activity. And what is this combination of the activities of body and soul in the Kapauku epistemology as discussed above? *Gai*, to think. And here finally was the answer to all the mysteries. "Ego" in the Kapauku covert (subconscious) culture means nothing other than the process of thinking — the free cooperation of the body and the soul. Consequently for the Kapauku, as for some European philosophers, to think means to be, to live — *Cogito ergo sum*. Thus, strictly speaking, "I" exists only when I am awake and think. During sleep and dreaming or in a vision, ego ceases temporarily to function. The dream is the experience of the soul and not of ego. So my body stays in space (*tou*), my soul dreams in my sleep (*umii*) and I live (*umii-tou*). When presented with my discovery, my friends exclaimed, "Of course, that's it," but in reality they had not been aware of it before. I could not have discovered or understood any of these connections without knowledge of the native language.

The consequences of this subconscious conception of ego's nature in the Kapauku culture and behaviour are profound. Whenever the free cooperation of the body and soul are impeded, ego either ceases to function temporarily (during a dream, disease, or vision) or may be annihilated forever if the cessation of the cooperation is permanent (in death). The free cooperation of body and soul and thus free thinking itself is certainly impeded (according to the Kapauku) when the soul cannot determine the actions of the body — we would call this a lack of freedom. Such an obstruction to free cooperation is tantamount to an obstruction to life itself and is consequently regarded as dangerous and often as fatal. It occurs when an individual is in a coma and cannot move. It is also present when a person is forced to conform with the behaviour of others, or to perform certain tasks (forced labour), or if physically prevented from moving freely by being tied up or locked in a jail administered by white people. Because of these beliefs, the Kapauku people abhor the concept of the white man's prison, and in their own cultural inventory they have no place for slavery, serfdom, war prisoners, imprisonment, or any kind of compulsory behaviour.

To them, personal freedom is essential to living. In bringing up their children, the Kapauku never force their offspring to behave in a certain way. Punishment is always a reprimand for wrong behaviour, or a settling of scores between the accuser and the accused, but never a demand to behave. In 1962, during my third research trip to New Guinea, a Dutch doctor became aware of this when, with my assistance, he inoculated the Kamu Valley Kapauku against one of their dreadful diseases, yaws (framboesia). The people were well aware then of the necessity and advantage of the injections and came in large numbers to my house in Itoda to receive treatment. Because of the highly infectious nature of the disease, the doctor insisted on injecting all the members of each family. Among the people was a man with his six year-old son. So after the father had received his injection the doctor turned to his son. The boy became frightened of the needle and refused treatment. When the doctor tried to proceed despite the boy's objections, the father stopped him abruptly: "You heard the boy. He said no." And no it was. To the father, his son's freedom to decide was more important than protecting him from disease. In despair, the doctor tried to explain (through my interpretation) to the father the necessity of the injection. The father agreed with the doctor that it was unwise not to get the injection, but he said that nothing could be done as long as the boy objected. The doctor turned to me: "Can anything be done?" What was I to do? I bribed the little boy with cowry shells, a glittering mirror, and a small knife. Holding the bribe in his other hand he cried from the pain, but almost at the same time he smiled into the mirror. There is usually a way to accomplish some social or political task without the necessity to use force.

In light of the Kapauku concept of ego one can also understand their system of social control and law. One does not use torture or other physical threats to force an individual to conform to a prescribed behavior — the law. A dangerous criminal or a captured enemy may be killed but never tortured or deprived or his or her liberty. A culprit may be punished with a beating, or by shooting an arrow into his or her thigh, but during the administration of these penalties the individual always has a chance to fight back or run away. If the culprit fails to do so, this often indicates that he prefers to accept his punishment and then resume a normal life. Inducement rather than compulsion is the main agent of social control here. Legal sanctions work either to even the balance between the two sides of the dispute — called *uta-uta* (half-half, or more colloquially, fifty-fifty) — or as an inducement to behave in the future rather than as an immediate enforcement. Similarly, a Kapauku leader's decision is most frequently issued not in the form of an order that is enforced physically; rather, it is made in the form of an opinion or suggestion and the headman's followers are persuaded to accept it. Because wealth is one of the highest goals of an individual, inducement may often take the form of economic advantage. By the same token, economic disadvantage can also be used, such as fines, withdrawing credit, or the threat of these.

The subconscious concept of ego and the consequent emphasis on individual freedom and independent action dramatically influences the Kapauku economy and cultural personality. For example, their extreme individualism makes common property unthinkable. Communal economic enterprise (such as the now almost defunct Marxist anthropologists would have us believe exist in every "primitive society") would be regarded as a bad joke. Even work in the family's gardens is done individually. Young boys already possess their own fields, and every wife has her own plot to weed and harvest.

Knowledge of the language and the culture as a whole is essential to understanding the basic principles of the covert culture. Many cultural features escape the detection of anthropologists unless they know the language thoroughly and participate in native life as much as the situation allows. For example, I would not have understood important features of the Kapauku legal system had I used interpreters and neglected the non-legal aspect of the culture. One night I slept in the house of my best friend, Jokagaibo, the headman of the Ijaaj-Jamaina sub-lineage. All men of a household sleep in the *ema*, the common men's dormitory of a Kapauku house. Their feet are next to the fireplace located in the center of the floor, while their heads are near the walls. Thus the pattern of the sleeping men resembles a star. The floor is well insulated, being elevated about three feet above the ground and covered with *tiba*, the linoleum-like bark of a species of pandanus tree. We ate our evening meal of roasted sweet potatoes, steamed spinach-like amaranth greens with a little pork, and water from an elongated bottle gourd container. I slept next to my friend. Next to him lay his grandfather. The fire ebbed, the young men and boys sang softly a *tuupe* resembling a lullaby, and one by one we fell asleep.

When the last voice had died down, silence fell on the house, save for the occasional movement of someone elsewhere in the dormitory or behind the thin partition wall of the adjacent women's quarters. I was nodding off when I heard my friend whispering with his grandfather. As a good anthropologist, with a more dubious moral sense, I stretched my ears to eavesdrop on the conversation. The contents of this dialogue held one of the great surprises of my life. My friend, who was supposed to adjudicate a legal case the next day, was consulting his grandfather about the forthcoming proceedings. First the grandfather wanted to know the charge, the claims, and all the available evidence. Then he gave his grandson his opinion and advice. If this or that fact came out during the trial, the case should be settled this or that way, based on well-known Kapauku statutes (*leges*); abstract rules (*daa mana*), remembered often verbatim especially by the eldest and most knowledgeable, and precedents. He outlined all the possible settlements according to any aggravating or alleviating circumstances that might come up during the trial. Thus clearly, the old legal sage combined the precepts of formal justice — the statutes — with consideration of special features of the factual evidence presented, that is, the justice of each individual case. In Kapauku society, formal and case justice combined to form an admirable legal edifice of which Western legal scholars as well as old Roman jurisconsults, such as Ulpian, Papinian, or Gaius, would be proud. Thus I learned of the existence of a Kapauku jurisconsult and of the intricacies involved in legal decision making and thinking of the ancient *tonowi*, the old Kapauku headmen-judges. Could legal anthropologists, using only informants and often communicating through interpreters or in a lingua franca (be it Swahili or broken Spanish) and specializing in law (their excuse for ignorance of the rest of the culture) ever get information like this? In fact, they tend to substitute speculations, called "interpretive anthropology," for facts.

But I was more interested in understanding what the Kapauku were really like than inventing a brilliant interpretive theory.

Ignorance of language may often lead to grotesquely distorted "analyses" and incidents. The Kapauku have a keen sense of humor, and they especially enjoy practical jokes. A poor command of the language by incoming white men provided them with ample entertainment of this sort. I witnessed one such occasion when visiting the pastor of Ugapuga, Father Steltenpool, in 1959. The priest was an accomplished scholar of Chinese culture and language (having spent many years in China as a missionary), and later of the Kapauku language, having published an excellent Kapauku (Ekari) vocabulary (1969). But in 1959 his Kapauku was still wanting. While traveling from my place in the Kamu Valley to Enarotali on the Paniai Lake, I stayed with the father overnight, as I had done on several previous occasions. It was afternoon and the priest was in the picturesque church that he and his parishioners had built. He was delivering a sermon. I silently entered and sat down next to an elderly Kapauku on the last bench in the rear of the church. With interest I listened to the sermon delivered in rather good Kapauku. However, one thing was incomprehensible and, to me, bewildering in his address. Father Steltenpool spoke very frequently of *kedi*, which means fingernails. Never before had I realized that human fingernails were of such importance in Christianity. Fingernails were burned in eternal fire, they floated in the sky, they entered heaven or hell, and in general exhibited extraordinary properties and feats. I was completely perplexed, so I asked my neighbor if he understood the sermon and especially the parts about the fingernails. He turned to me rather indignantly and whispered: "Of course I do not. But you be still, listen, and pretend to understand and enjoy. *Patoge* (the pastor) is an old, dignified, and good man and so do not make him unnecessarily mad with your questioning. When you are good, he gives you tobacco after the service." After this castigation I sat quietly, following the escapades of fingernails to the end of the lecture. Then I greeted the father and complimented him on his knowledge of the Kapauku language. "Only one thing puzzled me quite a bit, though," I admitted. "This constant reference to fingernails." "Fingernails?" he asked. "I did not speak about fingernails!" "Well, you did. Fingernails, which are *kedi*, burn, fly, are punished, etcetera." He gave me a surprised look and exclaimed, "But *kedi* is the soul, not fingernails." "No," I said, "*Kedi* means fingernails, whereas the human soul is called *ani ipuwe enija.*" At this point I noticed that the father's Papuan assistant, a boy of about fifteen years of age, quietly giggled and backed away from us toward the sanctuary door. Father Steltenpool turned to him and asked him what *kedi* meant. "Fingernails, of course," he replied, and then fled. "What in the world, that boy lied to me and made a fool of me by pulling this undignified joke. And I trusted him!" "You shouldn't be so trusting, Father," I proclaimed. "I don't trust any of my informants and have everything double-checked by others." Afterwards in the evening, after the boy had got what was coming to him, I asked him why he would do such a thing to a good man who acted as his father. "Well, it was not that I was trying to hurt him. I actually thoroughly enjoyed the baffled expressions on the faces of the congregation and the elders' discussion of the importance of fingernails in the strange new religion. Really, several times I saw my own father in contemplation, inspecting his fingernails with great interest. What fun — and what confused ideas must have gone through his head!" I'll conclude this story by saying that we may find similar "fingernails" in the accounts of authors who have not mastered the language of the people they are studying.

Data Gathering

No matter how successful I was in my initial study of the Kapauku language, I was haunted by the possibility that I might never be able to learn this complicated tongue satisfactorily. Despite the fact that I progressed in my daily plodding of ten new Kapauku words, trying to construct in my mind meaningful Kapauku sentences, testing my attempts on my informants, and even eliciting from them a hurrah when I succeeded in forming correct utterances, I knew I was still a long way from mastering the language. As long as I could not understand all of what they were saying to each other, it was nearly impossible to follow a lengthy and involved conversation. Even when my knowledge of the language improved, it bothered me that I was unable to readily recall the right words. Indeed, even in my dreams I would break into a sweat at not being able to recall a particular word while publically addressing a Kapauku gathering. But I constantly bore in mind the precept that guided the ancient Romans through ten centuries of Empire: *per aspera ad astra* (through rough times to the stars!). So, like the Romans, I persisted through my own rough times. I tried to be brave and not give up on my frustrating linguistic endeavours because I was determined to reach my "stars," whatever the difficulties. And finally, on a brisk evening walk to the village of Bunauwobado, my "stars" started to twinkle at me when I began to understand the boys who accompanied me telling each other how they would approach girls at the nightly dance in the dimly-lit dance hall. So that was the beginning of the end of my worries about learning the "unlearnable" language with its thousands of verb conjugations. Unfortunately, my worries were only alleviated during waking hours. At night I was still haunted and continued to sweat when trying to speak the "not so simple" language of my Stone Age companions. Even after all these years (56 to be exact), I still occasionally dream of addressing a large

Kapauku gathering and not being able to find the right word or verb form. I must end this account by disclosing my bravery: I have never attempted to see a psychoanalyst to eradicate that dreadful recurring linguistic nightmare.

With that in mind, I sought out the kind of cultural information that did not require a good command of the language. I took short trips to Botukebo village and its gardens, scattered about the swampy valley floor and the forests of the surrounding mountain slopes, with the aim of drawing maps of the village and its gardens and compiling data on individual houses. By mapping the gardens, recording my observations on the type and quality of the cultivated crops, and eliciting from my companions on the mapping trip information about the titles to particular land areas and garden plots, I constructed a solid foundation for my later quantitative inquiry into the horticulture and economic patterns of the Botukebo community. While measuring the garden plots, I was also able to acquaint myself with the various types of fences, traps, ditches, and cultivation methods used by these mountain Papuans. On many occasions I was able to monitor the performance of individual Kapauku cultivators, recording the time it took them to complete a specific horticultural task.

Since there is no growing season in the Kamu Valley, the climate being characterized as "eternal spring," crops are planted and harvested at any time of year. There are no regular dry and rainy seasons. Thus a large sweet potato garden is harvested gradually, as the need for food requires. When harvesting, the women who cultivate the mountain slopes extract only the ripe and large tubers from the soil, leaving the small sweet potatoes for harvest in the future. Consequently it is not possible to record the amount of harvested sweet potatoes — the staple food of the Kapauku people — from a given area at the same time, the way one can gather such data on other continents such as Europe. So I devised a technique to secure the desired data. I made a deal with several women whose gardens were near my house and who often had to pass my house on their way back to their village: if they stopped at my place, I would reward them with one bead if they let me weigh their net bags of sweet potato. I was thus able to record all the harvests from particular fields and obtain exact harvest figures. For comparison purposes I bought sections of sweet potato gardens with ripe tubers and had all the tubers dug up at the same time. Of course, the harvests from my purchased sections were more meager than those from the more gradually excavated plots. In this way, however, I was able to finish my mapping during the first four months I was in residence, by 15 January 1955. In addition to gathering these quantitative data on the harvesting of crops, I discovered that collecting data on genealogies and kinship terminology required only minimal knowledge of the language. So I started with genealogies on 25 December 1954 and by 25 January 1955 I had finished. Kinship terminology occupied me concurrently from 28 December 1954 to 11 February 1955.

My work on genealogies went slowly, but it was exciting to see how various genealogical segments obtained from different individuals started to fit together. For this research I used twenty-six major informants, whose information was substantiated by statements from an additional thirty-four informants. This procedure resulted in a mosaic-like picture, each informant contributing a single piece to the emerging pattern. I determined the precise location of an individual's genealogical segment in the overall pattern from the overlapping knowledge of several informants. My records included not only the genealogical relationship, sibling affiliation, individual names, domicile, and residence of dead or living individuals, but also their age if living or, if deceased, their approximate age at the time of their death. At the same time, I collected the pertinent kinship terms. This procedure was often redundant, but it provided reliable material for my later terminological analysis (Pospisil 1980). In this way I collected terms for relatives as far removed as five degrees collaterally (fourth cousins). The final result of this effort was a genealogy seven generations deep, composed of about two thousand individuals, dead or alive, which clearly indicated the structure of the Ijaaj-Gepouja lineage and its sub-lineages. This collection also offered a means of testing the accuracy and reliability of my numerous informants. Those whose statements about quite distant relatives were confirmed by informants who were closely related were regarded as reliable. During my subsequent research I trusted these informants more than those who had supplied me with less accurate data on their genealogies.

These extensive genealogies enabled me to identify the exact relationships of individuals to their various economic situations. In this way I could later test my hypotheses that linked economic considerations to social structure. The genealogical data were no less significant when it came to the analysis of the political structure and laws of this community. They enabled me to understand and in many cases even predict the alliances that occurred in legal disputes and political rivalries. The genealogical method proved so important and multifunctional that it came to form one of the pillars on which the economic, legal, and socio-structural analyses of my research rest.

As a bonus, my work on genealogies was not without its entertaining and amusing side. This was especially true when I worked with Ijaaj Awiitigaaj, the elderly headman of the Ijaaj-Enona sub-lineage, who resided in the village of Botukebo. The headman loved to sit in my rattan armchair and lecture me on Kapauku culture. Because of his advanced age and our close friendship (I adopted one of his sons, Pigikiiwode) he treated me as if I were his own son. He mastered my complex genealogical chart and was constantly double-checking and correcting my mistakes. Once when I made the same mistake over again he *gapa tapa* — slapped me goodheartedly. I was receiving an even tougher training than from my professors at Yale. On another occasion he identified a genealogically distant individual as his *oneme*, or cross cousin. I objected, pointing out that the apex in the genealogy that connected him to the man in question was formed by two males, not by individuals of the opposite sex, thus marking them as parallel cousins, as I had been taught at Yale. "No," he insisted. "We are cross cousins. Why do you contest that?" "Because professor Murdock taught me otherwise," I told him. "So tell Murdock," he replied, "that he is wrong." And, indeed, in this way I discovered from him that the difference between cross and parallel cousins was determined not by the sex of those at the top of the genealogical pyramid, but by the sex of the first and last links of their genealogical connection (for example, father's father's brother's daughter's son, is not a parallel cousin but a cross cousin). Independently, the same discovery was made in the same summer by Professor Floyd Lounsbury (1964) working with the Iroquois Indians, and by Van den Leeden (1956), who was studying the Sarmi region of the northern coast of New Guinea. Thus, an ancient headman "beat" a handful of venerable, learned academics.

While doing all this quantitative and genealogical research I became overanxious to record, with my limited knowledge of the Kapauku language, some more sophisticated ethnography. So only one month into my stay, when a native brought me a wooden dart decorated with the bright feathers of a parrot and bird of paradise, I tried to have the man describe the use and function of the object. Of course I could not entirely understand what he was saying, but when he put the wooden point of the dart under his left forefinger and pulled at the long feather on the tail of the specimen while pointing it at another man, I thought I understood his meaning (from my knowledge of Australian aborigine culture). I wrote down in my notes that the dart was used in black magic to kill the victim by secretly pointing it at him and uttering a spell while pulling at the feathered end. As I later found out, this was sheer nonsense. The dart was actually a hairpin used by boys and young men. When the native placed the point under his bent forefinger and pulled at its feathers, he was not talking about the object itself at all, but relating an incident in war when he had to shoot an enemy. He used his hairpin only as a symbol of an arrow, while his action mimicked the discharge from an imaginary bow.

Since Kapauku arrows have no stabilizing feathers at their butts, they have to be guided by the index finger of the left hand, which holds the bow shaft. Thus I realized that in research everything has its time, and I postponed my ethnological enquiry for several months until my command of the language was adequate. I have made many mistakes in my life, and all resulted in some loss or inconvenience — except one. This was the best mistake I could have made, and it proved to be most profitable in my research.

Many boys and young men enthusiastically helped me build my house and other structures. They worked on the construction, split and shaved the planks, cut trees for poles in the forest, and rolled boulders down the mountain to supply me with the necessary materials for my fireplace. For all this arduous work they wanted only one thing: that I give them new names. I thought this was possibly the best deal of my life. In return for the assignment of personal names, I had my house built, a garden planted, fences erected and the ground stripped to expose the beautiful sand layer underneath. Their generosity did not last long, however, once my house was finished. What I did not know at that time was that the Kapauku have a laudable custom by which boys and young men can live with wealthy individuals of their society. If the wealthy man likes them, he adopts them by giving them names. Because I am a white man with (in the Kapauku's eyes) plenty of exotic, expensive objects, I was regarded as particularly wealthy. One morning my many helpers gathered in front of my house and what was the obviously designated speaker stepped forward and addressed me: *Naitai inii igapu*. I rushed indoors to fetch my newly written dictionary (Marion Doble's 1960 work, for the most part translated by knowledgeable local Kapauku from Paniai into the Kamu Valley dialect), and translated the simple sentence as follows: "Our father we are hungry." To my horror I realized that I had become the father of forty-eight boys. As such, I was responsible for their food. I supplied them with food that day, and the same evening wrote a letter to the Ford Foundation apprising them of my precarious position and making them aware of the fact that from now on they were supporting not one student but a family of forty-eight sons and one not-so-happy "father."

There were even problems with the names. The Kapauku disliked the short English ones I had chosen. I realized then that Kapauku personal names are not short like "Frank" or "Steve," but lengthy and more distinguished, like Nakepajokaipougamaga (second-born daughter of the second-born son of the son of Nakemougi). "Steve" was no good, but the long Latin version, "Stephanus," proved terrific. Furthermore, in its inventory of sound the Kapauku language lacks fricatives such as s, sh, z, zh (ž), ts, tsh, and f. Thus the "s" was pronounced as t and f as p. Also, their predilection to end their words with vowels complicated the matter, so that "Stephanus" pronounced in Kapauku became

Etepaanuuti. Their language does not include r but instead a laterally released g (or 1 in g position), so that my "Rudolphus" became "Gudooputi." The boys were also sloppy in their transliteration, so that "Rudolphus" became "Gudaati." Because of this distortion, after three months I could no longer discern the original Latin names. For example, what "Egeneduuti", the name of one of my "sons" originally stood for, is now shrouded in mystery.

While the assignment of names became a problem and worsened with time, the formal aspects of my role as an adoptive father improved remarkably. The Ford Foundation informed me that while they could not give me more money for the current period, they would extend the period of my grant. Thus funds became available for the future. Furthermore, and most importantly, supporting my "super extended family" proved to be no problem. The people were eager to sell me their crops, but only for what they designated as money. Their money was cowry shells, but what they desired from me were large blue glass beads of cylindrical shape. They categorically refused payment in the form of knives, axes, machetes, and blankets. They set the rate of exchange at thirty beads per one cowry shell of their *bomoje* type. I would buy a box of five kilograms of these blue glass beads from Germany via the Dutch administration for $5 per box. And one such box contained enough beads to provide funds to feed my entire extended family for one month! Consequently, I enthusiastically enlarged my family to include girls, who came to help with my household and who also requested Latin names. I refused to adopt any adolescent girls, who were fast becoming young women, deciding instead to adopt five young girls under the age of twelve. Of these, Antonia (Kapauku name Waine Maga) and Veronika (ljaaj Oumau), pronounced by the Kapauku as Peronika, became most loyal and helpful during my original research and all my following fieldwork.

My "mistake" of adopting fifty-three youths proved to be the best help I could have with my research. Without their data collecting, my quantitative analysis of the Kapauku economy (Pospisil 1963b) would have been impossible. Because of the highly developed native mathematical system and a cultural obsession with numerical accuracy, the boys were of invaluable assistance. I was able to draw up a village plan and a map of all the native gardens. I cut two-meter-long rods, and my boys, flipping them over on the ground and counting the turns, measured the natural features, sizes of houses and distances between them, dimensions of the fences surrounding individual gardens, and structures such as drainage ditches, bridges, and the length of streams and native paths. They also brought me exact data on various economic transactions, informing me exactly how my cowry shells were expended or received by individual Kapauku. In return for their daily rations my "sons" served as mail carriers, informants, teachers of the Kamu Kapauku dialect, and especially as invaluable research assistants. Because my presence in people's homes or at secret business meetings tended to interfere with a violent dispute or a business deal, I used the boys to collect much of the data on legal and business cases. Their work proved indispensable to my study of the Papuan communities.

The consequences of my "adoption mistake" were not limited to the gathering of a wealth of data on people's behaviour. It became essential to my communication with the "outer world." I had left my wife at home in the United States, a purely rational and unemotional step though actually an agonizing decision. However, I was informed that I might not survive my adventure because the Papuans of the interior of New Guinea were excessively warlike and most were said to be cannibals. Who would expose his wife to such danger? Only a man indifferent to his wife's safety. Which I was certainly not. My wife was a strong-willed and courageous woman, which she first proved as my girlfriend at the age of sixteen. She was a new date of mine, and she had no idea that I was involved in anti-Nazi resistance. Maybe she could have guessed: my father was in a Nazi concentration camp and three of my uncles were inmates of three different Nazi camps. Because she was so young, the only adventures she had encountered were in her books. We went on a date to the ASO ice rink in my native town of Olomouc. After a prolonged skate, we went inside the lodge to warm up at an open fire burning in the middle of the hall. As we were relaxing at the fire, my old friend Karel Pechoč appeared and whispered to me: "I've been shot in my arm. Get me to your uncle." My uncle Robert Pospíšil was a skilled surgeon who had operated on me several times before (as described elsewhere). I looked at my friend in surprise and noticed blood dripping from his sleeve. "Idiot, hold up your hand with your sleeve," I whispered urgently. If a Nazi spotted the blood we would all be sent to our death. He obeyed immediately and apologized. My stunned date (and future wife) could not have opened her eyes wider. She had probably only seen such a scene in a movie. I turned to her and said: "I have to leave with Karel. You stamp out the blood from the floor." As we were leaving, I saw my date dutifully stamping out the blood stains on the wooden boards. I realized my date was level-headed and someone who would not panic. Her courage was tested several times later, when as a farmer's wife she shared in the risky venture of hiding and feeding member of the resistance, especially a German deserter, Hans Toniuti, whom we hid on our farm for the rest of the war. In spite of her courage and resilience, I could not bring myself to take her with me to the unknown interior of New Guinea.

Every week a couple of my boys, eager to earn more beads, made the four-day trek to Enarotali on the huge Paniai Lake, the only Dutch outpost in the interior of New Guinea, to fetch supplies my Dutch friends would purchase for me there. These consisted chiefly of kerosene in jerry cans, rice, tea, sugar, dried milk, and a cereal called Brinta. The rest of my food I acquired from the Kapauku. The boys also transported my five-pound monthly shipments of blue beads and, crucially, my mail, which meant I received letters from my wife every week! I wonder whether any anthropologist ever had such a mail service during their fieldwork in the wild. Usually two parties of my boys were under way, one traveling to and the other from the distant lake. The two or sometimes three boys would stop in Enarotali overnight and return via Tigi Lake and the Debei Valley, or over a mountain pass called Ijaajdimi, usually meeting a returning party en route. They never stole anything from the supplies they were carrying. Only once did they lose my mail and, sadly, one hundred feet of film depicting a magical ceremony and surgery, when they were attacked by enemies and had to run for their lives. On another occasion my mail delivery was interrupted by the native war at Mujikebo, in the northern part of the Kamu Valley. During two wars that cut off my connection with Enarotali, the district officer dispatched a bush plane to drop my mail near my house and see whether I was still alive and well. While the natives yelled with excitement at the sight of the low-flying plane, I stood in front of my house and waved my shirt, signaling "I'm still alive."

Now this was not the only connection I had with the outside. The Kapauku had, and I still hope they have, a yodelling "telephone" by which a woman yodels a message in falsetto across a valley from a mountain slope or hilltop to someone on the other side, who passes on the message to their neighbour. In this way, I was always informed about a "surprise" visit approaching my house, sometimes even two days prior to its arrival. And all that convenience without any phone bills! I lectured about my stay among the Kapauku at Harvard University and mentioned the Kapauku stone-age telephone. A clever news commentator composed a poem about me and my communication device and printed it in the *New Yorker*. Since his command of the Czech language was non-existant, he had trouble pronouncing our names, so his poem did not sound too poetic:

Oh Leo Leddi
A Papuan climbed a hill
to try to yodel Pospisil.
He succeeded but his wife replied
And Zdenka choked him, and he died

If my wife can kill a man simply with her name, I must be pretty brave to live in such a dangerous marital union. How have I survived these 62 years of marriage? A Roman proverb provides a clue: "Whom the gods love dies young." So they must really hate me "upstairs."

Later in my research, my "sons" accomplished an amazing task. In helping me with ethnobotany, ethnozoology, and especially ethno-entomology, they made it possible for me to cover those fields quite exhaustively in an unbelievably short time. For example, my boys spent twelve days collecting the skeletons of marsupials, from

3 to 15 September, 1955. When I donated this collection to Professor Robinson at Yale University's Peabody Museum, he claimed it was the largest known assemblage of marsupials in the United States. Similarly, I started a herbarium on 5 September, 1955, and within two weeks I had about four hundred culturally important plants, including trees with their flowers, leaves, bark, wood, and, in many cases, seeds. All these were later identified in the United States. By far my most important and extensive collection was insects and spiders. The boys provided me not only with undamaged specimens (which I killed in a cyanide jar provided by Professor Charles Remington of Yale, prior to my departure from the United States), their Kapauku names, and their legendary, culinary, religious, and other cultural significance, but also with information on how to prepare them as food and who should consume them (different insects are eaten by males, females, and children) so that I could write a Kapauku insect cookbook. While I dried most of the insects, especially the beautiful butterflies, I pickled in formaldehyde jars caterpillars, larvae, spiders, reptiles, amphibians, and crustaceans (especially crayfish and land crabs). While I was engaged in this task, my fieldwork had taken a very strange turn. I was simply sitting at my desk in my house as the boys brought me various specimens. These I registered (by their Kapauku names, cultural functions, and habitats), sorted, and placed in cyanide jars and formaldehyde cans. My place became sort of a clearinghouse in this process.

Of course, all my "sons" served as my language teachers and informants. Of my forty-eight boys, one always filled the role of "best boy." He was a sort of personal assistant, helping me with all my chores, especially keeping my household in order, seeing to it that my chicken and pig were regularly fed, helping me to distribute food to my "family" every day and buy supplies from the Papuan women at a small market in front of my house every morning. The women were delighted with this business because they earned hard currency (the blue beads were certainly hard), and with the food they sold me I was actually feeding their own sons and daughters. So everybody was happy: myself with the assistance my "sons and daughters" provided, their mothers with the double profit, the boys and girls with earning a constant income from me by providing information (a report on an economic transaction or a dispute was worth five beads!), insect and plant specimens (two beads apiece, one if I had already collected it), and carrying mail (one tour was worth thirty beads and special gifts, such as a knife, T-shirt, or shorts). There were additional tasks for which they received pay, such as clearing the ground, taking care of the garden, or carrying supplies during my expeditions into the surrounding territory or other valleys.

The adopted young girls usually helped in the household and garden. They washed the dishes, hung my blankets on a pole in the sun, and tried to help with my "cooking." Two of them, Antonia and Peronika, were the most diligent and also lots of fun (Peronika, especially, was a riot) and seemed to be very fond of me. So I was very sad when they both disappeared in late February 1955 and I did not see them for about three weeks. They showed up just as suddenly, greeting me joyously. "Where have you been all this time?" I asked. As it turned out, they had gone to the Paniai Lake region to visit an acquaintance of theirs who worked for an American mission. "Why did you go there?" I persisted. "To get more gifts and fun than you get here?" "No, not at all," was their answer. "But tasting the white man's food you cooked for yourself, which we found almost inedible, we decided that the white man cannot be so dumb to eat such junk. We came to the conclusion that you were a no-good cook who was taken care of in your country by your wife. So we decided to learn *tuanika* (white man's) cooking from our friends and to take proper care of you. Look at yourself. You've become skinny since you came to us!" And they were right. At Yale I was known as the only student who could not even fix himself a cup of instant coffee. And so they started cooking, took over my supplies, and put together my monthly shopping list from Enarotali. They taught me not only how to prepare native food (for example, how to roast sweet potatoes, steam various grasshoppers and crickets, eat live stink bugs and earwigs, make a cooking mound of red-hot stones for mixed pork and vegetables) but also how to prepare Western food, which they had seen for the first time just four months earlier. So this is an answer to my student buddies at Yale who wondered how that Czech fellow would survive a year or more with his nonexistent knowledge of cooking. One has to have either knowledge or luck. I had the latter.

For cooking, the boys built for Antonia and Peronika a *didaapuguu*, a small cooking hut in which the girls prepared the meals. They made soup in a huge pot filled with vegetables and Maggi stock cubes for taste, which I shared every night with my boys and girls and the informants who stayed in my house until late into the night. I found my daily menu quite adequate. It included vegetables like *idaja* (*Amaranthus hybridus*), spinach-like leaves which we first cooked as soup then extracted from the pot and ate like spinach; *pego* (*Saccharum edule*, or reed flower buds), which when steamed tasted like asparagus; leaves of *Solanum nigrum* (a relative of tomatoes, potatoes, and nightshade); leaves of *Hibiscus manihot*, *Setaria palmaefolia* (which reminded me of leeks); several fern leaf varieties; *nakapigu* (a marrow); and steamed unripened bottle gourds. These native vegetables were augmented by my string beans, tomatoes, cucumbers, onions, corn, and parsnips. For starch, like the Kapauku I lived on sweet potatoes. Of these there were twenty-four varieties, differing in taste, size, and color. I preferred the honey-colored *meda*. Peeled and roasted on embers, they were delicious. In addition to this staple I ate taro roots and leaves, roasted and served with the margarine purchased from the Dutch, and my Irish potatoes. The Dutch had introduced manioc (cassava), to which the natives gave the name *pija nota* (wooden sweet potatoes), which I did not like. I used rice, which I purchased from the Enarotali government shop, as a treat for the natives in the evening, when I also fixed myself a dessert of it with sugar and dried milk. Instead of candy I chewed sugar cane (there were sixteen varieties of it) during the day. For fruit I had the three varieties of native bananas; bell-shaped fruits from a tree, white and pink varieties, with an exquisite taste; and the two kinds of citrus fruits mentioned above. I drank ice-cold water and lemonade prepared from native limes.

Although many nutritionists complain about protein deficiency in the native New Guinea diet, our protein supplies in the Kamu Valley were plentiful. Sometimes I consumed as many as thirty delicious crayfish a day, here and there some pork, chicken, and eggs. I tasted the native supplies of marsupials, rats, muskrats, birds, pythons, frogs (even tadpoles!), and an assortment of bugs, including grasshoppers and mole crickets, but I refused to eat living spiders. "Why?" asked my native friends. "They taste very good!" "*Wogaa* [a hairy tarantula-like rusty-colored large spider] makes me scared," I replied. "If it bit you, you might be in serious trouble." "No problem," they assured me. "You just have to be faster with your biting than the spider." Although I enjoyed watching the live spiders disappear into the mouths of the Kapauku, with the legs of the unfortunate arachnids appearing and disappearing between their teeth and parted lips, I never did summon enough courage to imitate them. My few attempts at cooking resulted in some tragic mistakes. When I tried to smoke pork in order to conserve it, the next day it started to smell. My boys consumed it nonetheless. My rice was a burnt brown substance that the Kapauku found unsuitable for human consumption. In order to treat the people to new — and, to them, exotic — white man's food I opened a can of dried milk, added water and sugar, and gave them this "milkshake" to drink. The first who tasted this concoction was Kaadootajbii, the local shaman. After about three swallows he stopped. He turned pale, gave me a bitter smile, held his breath, then jumped up and declared: "Sorry, I am going to vomit!" He ran out of the house into the evening darkness. Upon his return he assured me that I had cleaned him out all right. I was puzzled by the effect of what I had assumed would be a delicious drink. A native aversion to milk? I tasted the drink myself, cautiously, and understood Kaadotajbii's reaction. The drink was horrible nauseating, sour, bitter, and sweet, with a strange "bouquet." After carefully scrutinizing the can, I realized that the shop in Enarotali had sent me by mistake a can of dried sour milk, one of the worst inventions of the food industry I have ever tasted. Although the natives hesitantly accepted my explanation, for weeks they refused to touch powdered milk. I committed yet another faux pas when I tried to share a bottle of champagne I had received from the district officer Den Haan as a gift for a New Year's Eve celebration. The natives swallowed some of the French delicacy, turned red in the face, and started to gasp for air, screaming that they were burning inside. Unbelievably, they labeled this drink *utu-uwo* — "fire water." Unlike the American Indians, they have never (up to my last visit in 1979) picked up the habit of drinking alcohol.

Although my boys helped me in all respects, much of the time they indulged in playing games and having fun. They practiced shooting arrows into ant nests hanging from trees; did gymnastics (which I introduced); engaged in mud ball and, later, tomato warfare; and offered theatrical performances in which the most skillful actor played a mad and hysterical woman, surprisingly enjoyed by the Kapauku girls, who even advised the actor on how to perform the role better. They played a game in which they moved small stones on the ground, and a cradle game with inner-bark strings. They danced, evening and night, and sang the melodic *tuupe* type of songs, which sounded like soft lullabies. These songs often accompanied me to sleep. There was always lots of kicking each other, mock fights, joking, and bursting into *juu tai* — shrill barking in a high-pitched voice, which sounded to me like a horde of attacking Apaches. They also made bonfires at night, fooling around with lit reed torches. Especially enjoyable to them were the nights on which there was a full moon (*agoo ibounu*), when the women would wade into the swamps to catch frogs in scoop nets. They built fires, fitted their arrows with porous pieces of soft wood or reed instead of points, lit them in the fire, and shot them like rockets into the swamps, where their sisters, mothers, and girlfriends were busy collecting frogs. The more cursing and screaming the missiles elicited from the female collectors in the darkness, the greater the joy elicited from my rascals. To me the fireworks were certainly spectacular, and the exchange between the archers and the female missile receivers, I must admit, rather entertaining. To my knowledge, no woman was ever struck by an arrow. Sometimes the boys would set a hollow dead tree on fire. This offered a unique sight at night, looking like a furnace with fire coming out from the hole as if from a gigantic flamethrower. Usually after two or three nights of this activity the tree would collapse.

By far the greatest amusement and entertainment for my boys, and eventually a wider Papuan audience, was European soccer (or, rather "football"), which I introduced. First, in December 1954, they played with a ball of leaves tied together with rattan. Later I secured old tennis balls from Enarotali; kicking these with bare feet was not as painful as making contact with the hard split rattan vine and leaf contraption. The game was a success right away. A soccer field was cleared next to my place, with two "goals" of upright poles. The playground's surface, however, posed a problem. Since it was situated in the dry sandy area on the edge of the swamp, part of it was hard and solid while the other part was soft with muddy puddles, especially after an afternoon rain shower. Also, the rules of this European game were not all acceptable to these natives.

Off-sides were simply ruled out of the game as unnecessary interference with the action; so, also, was the prohibition of any foul, which would have taken all the fun out of the game. This was because, more than kicking the ball with their bare feet, the players kicked each other in the buttocks with gusto, so that the game was accompanied more by the sound of smacking feet hitting rumps than by the usual cheers and screams of a European audience. The conditions of the pitch required a new rule: all hostilities had to stop when the small tennis ball became lost in the mud. Only after its recovery could an honorable Kapauku player kick his opponents' buttocks.

The game spread like wildfire to other localities and pretty soon teams representing local descent groups (lineages and sub-lineages) and political lineage confederacies were formed. The only exception to this team composition was my "sons'" team. They distinguished themselves by another important feature. Since the bottlegourd penis sheaths proved to be clumsy and easily broken in the melee of the game, I provided all my boys with appropriate white trunks. This proved to be of major importance. My boys used the advantage of their dress and sneakily broke the genital coverings of their opponents in premeditated skirmishes, sending the unfortunate players of the opposite team, deprived of their decent coverings, into the adjacent reed areas, whence they pitifully called for help. Not until their friends from the audience supplied them with the proper gourds could they reemerge and join the game. Thus my team easily won the games, and only biased Kapauku from other political confederacies called the whole tactic unfair. As my boys said: "We certainly are not responsible for how our opponents dress." To be sure, I distributed trunks to other Kapauku, but their use of them was astonishing. Since the only thing in their culture which resembled pliable cloth were flexible net bags of bark string suspended by their straps from the people's heads and covering their backs, the recipients of my trunks immediately put them on their heads, with the rubber bands across their foreheads and the rest of the trunks covering their heads and hanging loosely down their necks. The impression was very intriguing: they resembled old Egyptians with their well-known headdresses.

There was one more difference between the typical European soccer tradition and that of the Kapauku. Whereas the Europeans would go to the pub after the match to celebrate their winning or drown the sorrow of losing, both Kapauku teams would take a bath in the nearby Kugumo Lake, not only to cool off, but especially to wash their bodies plastered with mud. I always hoped that soccer would allow the political units represented by the teams to play out their aggression, and thus deprive their endemic warfare of its major function. Reflecting on my experience of the violence of European soccer audiences after some matches, I wonder whether some future wars may not have soccer scores as their obvious cause. I hope the Kapauku prove more "civilized" than Europeans in this respect.

To keep "law and order" in my large family group, and following diligently the precepts of the learning theory of Dollard and Miller (1950), I would reward the boys and girls for good performance and systematically punish mistakes and transgressions. Accordingly, my boys and girls not only received their daily food, but were paid, as indicated above, for performing special services and research assistance. Usually the reward took the form of payment with the much desired large blue beads, occasionally augmented by pieces of clothing, knives, axes, machetes, small scissors, and my used Gillette blades. Upon my return in 1959 and 1962 I brought every son and daughter of mine watches and costume jewelry collected and given to me by my friends in America to help with my research. When I returned again in

1975 and 1979 I was in for a great surprise. Instead of my sixty or so sons and daughters (I later adopted additional children), a multitude of about five hundred youngsters, all calling me muuma "grandfather" and claiming to be the children of my original "adoptive progeny group," greeted my bush plane, which landed on an airstrip built in the Kamu Valley. Luckily I had bags of old watches, rings, earrings, bracelets, and pendants. In 1979 my dear grandchildren requested that next time I return, I should bring them radios, portable television sets, calculators, and radiotelephones. Obviously and luckily I have not returned since. In contrast to those who had behaved well and received rewards, boys who misbehaved had to be punished to deter potential future offenders. Reprimand was the usual sanction administered for the first and second offenses. Habitual offenders were subject to the heaviest penalty — excommunication. Although the natives claimed that *puja peu puja daa*, "lying is bad, lying is taboo," lying to me was the gravest offense, for the sake of my research. They considered me strange because of my exaggerated insistence on exactitude and objectivity. What my boys did not know about was my past experience with notorious and systematic lying to which I had been exposed under the Nazis and communists in Czechoslovakia from 1939 until my escape in 1948. Since I was sixteen years old, people around me had to lie publicly first under the "National Socialist Workers' Party," then under Communism, in order to save themselves. In contrast, during my childhood, I was told to be truthful and sincere. One Czech saying repeated by my parents and my school teacher was *"Co na srdci to na jazyku"* (what's in your heart should be on your tongue). Our national emblem carried the inscription *"Pravda Vitezi"* (the truth wins). And our grade school teacher repeated almost every week: "A man who lies also steals, and he who steals should be hung on the gallows." Suddenly, after the invasion of the Nazis in 1939 everyone (that is, the Czechs) had to lie in order to survive. Those of us who refused to praise Adolf Hitler and Nazism found their way to the concentration camps. Almost all the people whose corpses one can see portrayed in the movies about Nazi concentration camps refused to lie. One of the people who refused to lie was my father. Shortly after the Nazi armies, accompanied by the SS and Gestapo, brought us the "blessings" of National Socialism, he was taken to the concentration camps of Dachau and Buchenwald. Three days after his arrest, the SS and civilians with swastikas on their lapels came to our class in the high school. One of them stopped at my bench and asked me: "How do you like our new socialist order?" What should I have said? The truth would have certainly been my end. I would have probably not even made it to the concentration camp. And so I answered evasively: "You can see how everybody is happy." The fool believed me, but I hated myself. To lie was worse for me than the beating I received a few days before while being questioned where my father was hiding. I did not tell, but it was not due to heroism — I simply did not know. I hated their lies and ours almost as much as the atrocities they committed. These events explain not only my hatred of lying, but also my distrust of statements made by obviously honest Kapauku informants because of their possible unintentional bias. Consequently, my scientific research was without trust; if possible, I tried to double check every statement. Therefore, observations of the same event by several of my boys became mandatory in order for me to formulate correct statements.

I had to penalize only a few of the boys for lying. Accordingly, Etepaanuuti, originally my "best boy," had to be disowned because of periodic lying and arrogance. His substitute became Jogodeeti (original Latin name forgotten), who, shortly after his "promotion," had to be dismissed for stealing. He was replaced by Ijaagodooti, later called, properly, Marius. This boy showed the highest integrity, industry, and dedication to my work, remained my "best son," married my "daughter" Antonia in 1970, and produced five "grandchildren" of mine. In April 1955 Edeneduuti was dismissed with gifts, and the severance of our father-son relationship was amicable (certainly hardly a sanction) and mutually understandable and acceptable. In May of the same year, Antoniuti was excommunicated for stealing, as was Napeetioti. Finally for chronic dissent and quarreling with the rest of the boys, Waine Ibo was sent home, also in May. The vacated places of the dismissed boys were readily filled with many waiting candidates. Generally, however, the boys and girls were and probably still are wonderful.

Although my boys were an excellent source of information immediately upon my arrival, I slowly included other people in my inquiry.
As my knowledge of the language improved I started to ask more and
more questions, received more and more lengthy explanations, until this unorganized but progressively more intensive interrogation
of the people slowly transformed into a more systematic inquiry. Thus
sessions with people who, because of their sophistication and knowledge, could provide specific and general information on their various
actions, happenings, or aspects of their culture, turned into questioning of selected informants. My systematic use of informants started
around mid-February 1955. In so doing I avoided Durkheim's (1893)
misapprehension that in a tribal society all individuals are cognizant of
their whole culture because there is no division of labor and therefore
no special knowledge and specialists. Early during my stay I realized
that different individuals had special knowledge of the various aspects
of their culture, knowledge that certainly was not shared universally.
Thus Kaadotajbii, while an excellent source of information on religion,
magic, legends, philosophy, and *Weltanschauung*, was rather limited
in his understanding of politics, law, and economy. Ijaaj Jokagaibo,
a brilliant politician and economist, was not so keen on types of Kaadotajbii's knowledge, except for legends, of which he supplied me with
several texts. Indeed, when the law, which he had to administer, had
to be applied, he relied heavily on the advice of his paternal grandfather and Ekajewaijokaipouga, his uncle. These older men could be
called Kapauku jurisconsults. Girls, young women, mature and old
women, young men, old men, mature men, and the specialized headmen, traders, matchmakers, and various artisans all had their specialized knowledge. So much for Durkheim and his "De la Division du
Travail Social" (1893). I had to talk to as many informants as possible,
compensating for the gaps in knowledge and biases of individuals.

In ordering the research I distinguished two different types of informants: those who supplied particular case material on law, economy, politics, and social matters, and others who provided information about the Kapauku culture in general. Whereas the former were
numerous (approximately 160 individuals), the latter were relatively

few (eighteen, to be exact) and carefully selected from the multitude. In general, I selected informants on the Kapauku culture according to their reliability, fund of knowledge and intelligence, as well as personal qualities, which I tested in preliminary sessions on genealogies. The large group supplied me with information which I labeled quantitative; the latter well-selected group provided me with valuable qualitative material.

I also distinguished two basically different types of inquiry in terms of their structure and timing. During the day (usually in the afternoon) I questioned numerous informants on case material; in the evening the other type of informants supplied me with a general orientation concerning Kapauku culture. I always made sure that at least three or preferably more of these outstanding men and women were present at a time. They were invariably joined by several other young people, so that the evening sessions consisted of groups ranging from five to as many as twenty at a time. The group always sat in front of my large fireplace and was treated to soup, tea, greens, sugar cane, beans, and, on rare occasions, rice. During these evenings, I collected data which I classified into two broad categories: that pertaining to the ideational Kapauku culture, and others which I regarded as Kapauku opinions and ideas about their behavior. Strictly speaking, then, none of these informants supplied direct information on actual behavior. Both the specific ideals and rules for behavior (moral, legal, religious, what was deemed rational in the native sense, etc.) and the general ideas about actual behavior among members of their society belonged to what may be called "ideational culture." The truly behavioral data had to be secured preferentially through my participant observation or through my collection of quantitative case material during the day. Unless there were some special topics that my evening assembly wanted to talk about, I steered the discussion towards topics I had systematically selected from the most helpful handbooks for such an inquiry — Murdock's Outline of Cultural Material (1961), and Notes and Queries on Anthropology (Royal Anthropological Institute 1929). By following the topics outlined there, I was sure that I would not omit an important category of culture outside my own specialized field. In the case of law and political structure my interest was much more detailed than was outlined in these sources, and I had to work out intensive inquiry procedures myself. In this way the people taught me their ethno-history, philosophy, religion, legal rules, principles of political behavior, rules and proper conduct concerning finances, and so forth. During these meetings I also collected texts of old legends and myths. The presence of several informants at the same time had important advantages. They were able to correct each other's generalizations, fill in gaps in each other's knowledge, and discuss various controversial issues. In this way they provided me with more valuable data, different opinions about the same issue, and variations based on personal perspective, differences in residence, and group affiliation. The results of the evening sessions served as a general orientation for my quantitative inquiry during the day, through which I tried to establish a counterpart to the evening's "ideational" lectures and debates with my outstanding Kapauku "teachers." The evening sessions sometimes dragged on into the night, and I often became tired while sitting among my people on the floor of my house taking notes. Once, early in my research, my back ached and I tried to stretch it to relieve the stress. As usual, the natives were quite considerate and ready to help. Gaamaadii, the sixteen-year-old youngest wife of my then already "best friend" Jokagaibo, who regarded me as her brother, came to my rescue. She sat behind me, embraced me from behind, and leaned me against her body to give me comfort and back support. Although well meant, this good-Samaritan act proved to be a psychological disaster for me. Still suffering from culture shock, I had not yet culturally acclimated to the native behavior and mores. Thus the naked body of a young woman was not by any stretch of the imagination an adequate back rest for me. And certainly not so when my head slipped between her breasts, obscuring my side vision and making it impossible for me to turn my head. I blushed until I was quite red in the face. My best friend, seated opposite me, misinterpreted my appearance completely and asked whether the fire was not too hot because I looked feverish.

I hastily agreed with him to escape his wife's embrace. I learned then that one must lie in certain situations in order to comply with native etiquette and social expectations.

The problem with informants concerned mostly the question of accuracy and only sometimes deliberate lying. Good and reliable informants were "generously rewarded" with five beads per story. Informants and some of my own boys who lied to me were punished with the traditional Kapauku public reprimand. On several occasions the boys and older informants came to me on their own with apologies because they had made mistakes, and corrected their accounts. Of course, for such corrections no extra fee was paid, only an expression of thanks and appreciation for their accuracy. Some of the informants went to great pains to supply me with precise data, as for example, Awiitigaaj, the headman of Botukebo, who went to the Mapia region and brought back several Mapia people to prove the identity of the founder of his lineage, Ijaaj Gepouja. Until then he figured in the Kamu Valley only as a legendary leader of the ancient immigration of the Ijaaj lineage from the Mapia region.

In addition to the general information secured during the evening sessions, I needed to collect very specific and personal data from all the members of the Ijaa-Enona sublineage residing in the village of Botukebo. These I decided to subject to intensive quantitative study. Such information, which I called "personalia," was so personal and delicate that for this purpose a single informant was invited to my house in the afternoon, and as a guest he was served food and tobacco. I steered the discussion toward topics in which I was interested. The informant then spoke about private matters such as his possessions, savings, financial deals, sale and lease contracts, attitude toward specific leaders, loans and credit, and participation in war and trade expeditions and in legal disputes. The questioning was so geared that we avoided generalizations and concentrated upon specific personal information which the informant had, or of which he had firsthand knowledge. It is obvious that complete privacy and discretion, of which every informant was fully assured, were the prerequisites for such sessions. Under such circumstances a promise of a "head pay" of ten glass beads succeeded in making a talker out of the most reluctant Kapauku. Since all adult males and a large number of females of Botukebo were subject to these extensive interrogations, there was no sampling problem. To make sure the information gathered was consistent I proceeded generally along predetermined patterns of questioning. This information was categorized into the informant's life history data, his technological skills and practices, his economic, kinship, and social relationships, political activities and attitudes, and religious and magical experiences. After I had questioned every Botukebo male and most females who were past childhood on all these subjects, I was positive that I had secured an accurate base for my quantitative study of the community. I did not limit myself to a single community. I conducted the same interviews with an additional forty-two Kapauku from outside the villa.

In these sessions I also succeeded in collecting anthropometric measurements from all my male subjects. The women were scared to be touched by the calipers, and so only the more courageous allowed themselves to be subject to this treatment. These measurements, later combined with genetic data derived from blood typing of the individuals, proved most valuable in the accounts of the physical anthropological aspect of my research. Furthermore, there was an unexpected bonus from this procedure. While taking the bodily measurements I could not avoid noticing scars on the bodies of my informants. With every scar came a story of the history of its acquisition, be it in an accident, a brawl, or warfare. Thus I was able to gather valuable case data on personal conflicts, legal cases, and numerous Kapauku wars, with detailed accounts of specific individuals who had inflicted the wounds, the reason and type of the conflicts, the procedures, and the outcomes. Some individuals exhibited quite a collection of scars. For example, on Ijaaj Awiitigaaj, a well-known audacious warrior, I found forty-eight of them, each accompanied by a fascinating story. When I finished with the forty-eighth I sighed with relief and said, "Finally we have finished." Awiitigaaj smiled and said, "Not quite, my friend." To my shock he bent over, pointed at his rectum, and showed me a scar right next to its aperture. "It is most embarrassing," he said, "but to have the complete account I had to show you this. An arrow hit me there while I was bending over to lift a stray arrow from the ground."

A large part of my data was derived from my case study approach. To be sure that the accounts were objective and accurate, I interrogated several of my young "assistants" on different occasions about the same case which they had witnessed. I also talked to the parties to the case and received their stories. Then I recorded accounts of several other observers of the same event. Thus fairly accurate versions of individual transactions were collected. These were used in my publications for my quantitative analyses as well as to illustrate theoretical points. The case method played yet another important role in my research. In family disputes and small quarrels my presence as an outsider and a respected person would have disrupted or at least altered the happenings. Young boys who mixed with the participants and observers of the events, however, went almost unnoticed and the proceedings took their normal course. Thus very often I sacrificed my presence for the sake of accuracy and a normal flow of events. Naturally, one can observe only behavior that takes place in one's presence. However, the case method compensated for situations in which I could not be a participant observer, and my forty-eight adopted "assistants" proved indispensable to this method. For a fee of five beads for a single case they worked like a network of spies, with my house serving as headquarters and a clearinghouse, in which cases were recorded, classified, and filed.

The Participant Observer

Questioning informants gives us only the opinions and recollections of the people. If we eliminate intentional distortions of reality and deliberate lies there still remains the fact that we may receive information on what the reporting individual considers to be reality. This supposed reality may be a story unconsciously distorted by his ideas of what ought to be, or an account warped by his preconceived ideas and ethnocentric biases. In other words, we are getting part of the ideational culture but not necessarily the true account of his actual behaviour. Even the quantitative method described above only approximates the real behaviour of the subjects. In summary, there is no substitute for data based on sensual perception such as seeing or hearing the actual event.

The best way then to record actual behavior is to use the participant observer method, which means direct observation, as long as the presence of the investigator does not affect the proceedings. Consequently as much as possible I stayed with the people in the village, listened to their discussions, partook of their meals in their houses, accepted on several occasions their hospitality and stayed with them overnight, participated in their economic and magical ceremonies and rites connected with life passages, and studied their work in their gardens, on the lakes and rivers, and in the forests.

Whenever invited, I went to the woods to hunt or to watch the construction of a canoe, or to the village to take notes on the building of a house. I delighted at renting a dugout canoe for the purpose of joining the men in diving for crayfish, or the women in their fishing activities. I was often fortunate enough to be able to witness a dispute, a "court in session," or a brawl with sticks. My role as participant observer led me to the battlefield, and I went as a mourner to the freshly dug graves and tree houses constructed for the dead. As much as circumstances allowed, I tried to time behavior and to measure or weigh its tangible results (such as crop yields, structures, artifacts).

Types of behavior which occur almost daily (for example eating, planting, weeding, harvesting, building fences, and digging ditches), or those results of behavior that are sufficiently numerous and observable, may be quantitatively measured. So with the help of my Kapauku "assistants" I measured, inspected, and mapped the gardens of Botukebo, measured and photographed lots of artifacts (many of which I purchased for Yale's Peabody Museum), and observed and timed the performance of numerous planters, woodcutters, weeders, fence builders, ditch diggers, and others. I had no problem measuring the time workers spent on various tasks or the amounts of plant food they consumed, as adequate averages could be compiled. However, some quantitative measurements presented difficulties. For example, the Kapauku are very secretive about consuming animal food — I couldn't weigh all the rats, birds, or marsupials a man, subjected to nutritional observation for several days, ate. I was lucky (and very grateful) to receive honest reports of such consumption. I also had problems determining crop yields. I had to estimate averages of total yields of sweet potatoes on the basis of inspection of different representative harvests and tests of my own design. As I have pointed out, a Kapauku sweet potato garden is harvested slowly as the need arises, and there are often three harvests of the same garden. Since this makes it almost impossible to measure yields accurately, I bought crops in several test regions and harvested the produce myself. Through this procedure I arrived at estimated average yields. When calculating the community gross product I was astonished that my estimates were fairly close to reality.

After acquiring knowledge of the Kapauku language I became a participant observer during the rest of my stay. Toward the end I even had to drop my pretended ignorance of the language when it was spoken quickly. In my many and varied roles (as adoptive father, best friend, son of my best friends' parents, and member of the Ijaaj-Pigome confederacy) I worked, played, participated in political and economic debates, and spent many nights with the people in their houses or on the elevated sprung floor of their dance house. My knowledge of the language made it possible to question informants directly as well as to submit questionnaires to the people of Botukebo and to many members of the extended confederacy. Whenever possible I recorded as precisely as I could songs, political and judicial speeches, debates, rituals, and versions of myths. With my Bell and Howell movie camera I recorded not only horticultural and construction activities and numerous ceremonies and dances (pig feasts, markets, blood reward ceremonies), but also magical rites, wars, disputes, and legal trials. Several times I made a filming expedition in a canoe on the Edege River, nearby lakes and swamps to record and film the natives fishing, collecting amphibians and bugs, and hunting. I also filmed aboriginal games and soccer matches.

One may have several informants for the same event, or even an expert specialist, but one still cannot be sure of obtaining a correct description and understanding of the reality. True empirical knowledge is secured through participant observation. For example, I had inquired about the ownership of virgin forests. Pointing to Kemuge Mountain above my house, I asked who owned the various tracts of wooded areas demarcated by natural features seen from the valley floor where we stood. The explanation came swiftly and in plain Kapauku: from here to there it belongs to the Ijaaj-Enona sub-lineage, from that ridge up to the crevasses the owners are the Pigome Obaaj lineage, and so on. Thus the matter seemed rather simple: tracts of virgin forest were owned collectively by lineages and sub-lineages. In August 1955, I went with several people of Botukebo (Ijaaj-Enona sub-lineage) up the mountain into the forests to take notes and pictures of the construction of a dugout canoe. While two men were hollowing out the trunk of a felled tree, I noticed an even better specimen of the valued *moane* species (a true "canoe tree") standing nearby. I asked why the canoe makers had not selected this tree. I received a surprising answer: "The tree is not mine. You see, I own *buguwa* (virgin forest) only up to the small creek. From there it belongs to my sibmate Pigome Enaago." So even virgin forests were subdivided and individually owned. My former informants were indeed correct in stating that the various forest tracts belonged to that or another sub-lineage or lineage; they failed, however, to elaborate and inform me about an important detail: within these lineage areas forested segments were individually owned. And, of course, I failed to ask. It did not occur to me that individual ownership was extended to more or less untouched forestland.

Similarly I misinterpreted a statement that a large bridge over the Edege River at Degeipige village belonged to the residents of the village. Again, from my Western bias I recorded in my notes a claim that large bridges belonged jointly to the nearby community whose residents had built it. However, fourteen days after my inquiry torrential rains and a severe flood caused the swollen Edege River to tear down the huge structure. When I visited the site of the bridge, I saw individuals fishing out from the floodwaters poles and planks to which they claimed ownership. This was material they had contributed to the building of the bridge. Thus, legally speaking, a Kapauku bridge represents a conglomerate of individual ownership rights to particular poles and planks. It certainly is not communal property, as I erroneously understood. This was a good example of how direct observation — in this case, of canoe building and salvaging of poles from the river — ensures accurate data. In addition to talking to informants, I participated in their community.

Even when the statements of informants are clear and accurate, and the anthropologist understands them correctly, there is still the problem of grasping the particular aspect of the part of the culture under inquiry. Informants tend to provide an idealized perspective of their culture, the correct way things should be done, and what they believe is actually done. But, of course, the reality often differs markedly from the cultural ideal. And that reality can be obtained most often by actual observation and participation in the culture. In my field experience this was especially true in the realm of relations between the sexes and marital affairs. I was told that Kapauku marriages were, if not arranged by the girl's older brothers and father, at least subject to their approval. Thus it would appear that romantic love had little to do with marriage. Indeed, if a girl had sex with her suitor without the consent of her brother or father, then her lover would be brought to the court of the *tonowi*, the headman, and sentenced to pay *pituwo*, a penalty for fornication. Thus non-approved love affairs might be quite expensive. One of my adoptive daughters, Antonia, faced a problem that showed me, in reality, how inaccurate this ideal picture of marriage mores could be. Her brother wanted her to marry a wealthy man from Mapia Valley whom she rejected. Her brother was so enraged that he punished her by shooting her in the thigh with an arrow. Despite this severe punishment the girl resisted. To prevent her brother from forcing her into the marriage she could, according to the Kapauku custom, take refuge with her maternal uncle (her mother's brother), who would hide and protect her against her brother and the unwanted marriage. Instead, however, she ran to me, as her adoptive father, to protect her. This I successfully accomplished without unduly antagonizing her brother and father.

Antonia's troubled love life was not yet over, however. Two of my adoptive sons, Marius and Gudaati, fell in love with her and became rivals. Antonia's brother interfered again, favoring Gudaati over Marius as the former had a wealthy father and thus promised a hefty bride price, while Marius was an orphan. Antonia again thwarted her brother, preferring Marius. Only when Marius's foster father, Pegabii Ipouga, and I reassured Antonia's brother that we would both dig into our net bags (not pockets, because neither he nor I had any) and provide the fellow with the desired funds, did he give his consent. As a matter of fact, the vast majority of first marriages of young men, on which I had accurate data, were based on romance rather than on cool, calculated arrangements. It is interesting to note that by 1979 Marius and Antonia had prospered in the coastal harbor of Nabire, and that even after twenty years of marriage I saw deep affection between these two "children" of mine, which over the years resulted in five offspring.

It may be assumed that the social position of a woman for whom a bride price is paid is of low status, sometimes even approaching chattel. However, in the Kapauku culture this assumption is quite wrong. It is contradicted not only by the actual behaviour of married people, but also by an institutional aspect of the social structure. The fact is that the status of the Kapauku woman is usually very high. This is the result of Kapauku systematic individualism which permeates the whole of Kapauku culture and therefore also the family. Most of property of the husband and wife are kept strictly separate. A married woman keeps her earnings and assets herself, be it part of the bride price for her daughters, income from manufacture of netbags, or sale of crops. If she loves her husband very much, she may loan him some of her assets to help him out in his business. Thus, she becomes the creditor and he the debtor. Since she can retract her loan from the husband anytime, he is indirectly induced to be kind and considerate to his creditor. She therefore wields influence which may even determine whether or whom he marries as a second wife. As we can see from the marital history of my best friend, Jokagaibo (discussed elsewhere), how his wives ganged up against him, went on a strike, and even beat him with sticks (one cannot overpower five furious wives!), Kapauku "gentle women's ways" made him marry his sixth wife against his will. Having witnessed all of this, I was very happy I lived in a monogamous society. Also, a Kapauku woman has a legal right to divorce her husband if she can prove to the court of the headman that there is another girl who wants to marry her spouse, that he has enough money to pay for her and in spite of this stubbornly refuses to enter into a preselected additional marital union. And we think that our women in the West are powerful and a "poor" Kapauku lady in a polygynous marriage is reduced to some sort of harem girl! Maybe it would be advisable not to show this part of my book to our married women. Because of the women's power to preselect additional wives for their husbands, we often find among the Kapauku, "sororal polygyny," that is the marriage of a man to two sisters. In this marital arrangement, the collegium of the co-wives reminded me somehow of a labour union. Yet in spite of the women's power, we sometimes hear complaints about abusive husbands. The Kapauku woman has another way to retaliate other than to retract her loan. In the case of abuse (usually a slap by the palm of the husband's hand) a woman may start crying and turn to her sister co-wife for *ekigei wegii*, to make an incision with a flint chip on her back. The juice of a special plant is rubbed into the wound so that a cicatrix (swelling of scar tissue) is produced, a permanent reminder of the husband's misbehaviour and a testimony to other women to reconsider their affection for a man who has wives with numerous swollen scars decorating their backs. Another interesting aspect of the nature of a husband's cruelty is sometimes its "severity." True enough, there may be some brutes (I have not encountered one), but often it is not so much the painful experience of a slap as the feeling of being offended that matters. I have witnessed one such "cruelty" when in a mild dispute, the husband, impatient with the obstinacy of his wife, took a parrot feather from his hair and struck her on the cheek. Immediately she started to cry and her co-wife fished out from her netbag a flint knife, and made an incision into the back of the crying and insulted wife. I cannot imagine a more gentle physical assault.

The co-wives have to be treated equally. Delicacies from their husband's hunting have to be equally distributed. Sexual relationships are up to the husband (performed in the bush and not at home). The first wife, usually older than subsequent co-spouses, is not usually jealous. It is understood that her husband will spend more time making love with his last and younger wife. However, when the husband gets sick, he is always taken care of by his first wife, often resting in her quarters with his head on her lap. To my amazement, there was no female jealously. I asked my wife what she would do if I came home with a second wife. "I would wring your neck" was her civilized answer. Of course we are no longer "savages."

In a similar way, one can receive an incomplete picture of the power relations within a family if one relies on informants' generalizations and statements of the ideal. I was told, and many of my observations substantiated the claim, that in the Kapauku patrilineal, patrilocal, patriarchal, and polygynous society it is the husband who wields the power and makes his wife or wives conform. This is usually true in cases where the man has a strong will and is in general successful in his horticultural and pig breeding activities and in finance. In these families it is indeed the father and his eldest son whose wills prevail in the marriage arrangements for their daughters and sisters, unless the girl resists and escapes to her maternal uncle. However, this generalization does not necessarily apply in situations where there are only daughters and the father is dominated by his wife. Ijaaj Jikiiwiijaaj and his family gave me an opportunity to observe such a situation, and to be part of the marriage arrangement and settlement of their younger daughter Ijaaj Mabii, sister of my adopted daughter Peronika.

In May 1959, shortly before my second fieldwork stint among the Kapauku, Ijaaj Jikiiwiijaaj and his wife tried to arrange a marriage between their daughter Ijaaj Mabii and a rich man from the Paniai Lake region. A professional Kapauku matchmaker helped close the deal.

The girl at that time was in a missionary school recently opened in the Debei Valley. She rejected the idea of getting married and pleaded with the Catholic catechist in charge of the school to protect her against the forced marriage to a much older man whom she did not know. The catechist was understanding and tried to protect the girl. Some of my informants claimed that his opposition to the marriage emanated mainly from the fact that the prospective groom was associated with the American Protestant missions. The catechist's interference in the relationship between father and daughter, a violation of one of the basic Kapauku legal rules, enraged and insulted good old Jikiiwiijaaj so much that he decided to kill the religious practitioner. This was despite the fact that Jikiiwiijaaj sided with his daughter and was mightily unhappy about the prospective marriage, which had been forced upon them by his strong-willed wife. In family discussions and decision making, he was no match for his forceful, brilliant, but sometimes opinionated spouse. Despite all his opposition to the marriage, the interference was such an insult that in Kapauku eyes it amounted to denying the man his fatherhood. So he grabbed his machete (in 1959 there were already plenty of them around), rushed to the school and into the classroom, and tried to cut off the head of the stunned religious teacher. As Jikiiwiijaaj swung at his neck, the teacher backed off from the blow and the machete crushed his kneecap. Two of my adopted sons who were present restrained Jikiiwiijaaj from further violence.

When I returned to New Guinea and my valley a third time, in 1962, the marriage negotiations were still in progress. One day I heard quite a commotion in front of my house. My boys and others were gathering there, looking toward the village of Botukebo, from where a strange procession was approaching along the trade route that passed in front of my residence. At the head of the crowd walked the matchmaker with the groom, followed by the weeping little girl, Ijaaj Mabii, her mother and mother's sister, and Jikiiwiijaaj. The line ended with some people from Botukebo and a crowd of various spectators from other villages. When the procession neared my house, the girl tore loose from her parents and ran to me, falling on the ground in front of me and embracing my legs while pleading and crying for help. This was a tough moment for me — I had to decide whether to stand by the girl and my Christian upbringing and try to stop the marital procedure, thus obeying my feelings and moral code, or to set my feelings aside and proceed according to Kapauku expectations of proper behavior, using their values rather than mine. Uppermost in my memory was what had happened to the catechist who had interfered previously. Although I did not fear a similar fate, I did realize that I would ruin all the respect and friendship that I had worked hard to secure during my stay with the Kapauku, and would most likely accomplish nothing to help the unfortunate bride-to-be. Thus reason and anthropological knowledge prevailed. Accordingly, I lifted the weeping girl to her feet and told her she must know that the only man who could help her was her father. I had no right to interfere because I had not adopted her as my daughter, as I had done with her sister Peronika. With that I handed her to her father. The multitude screamed their approval. "You are really a Kapauku! You know how to behave!"

Of course, I felt terrible despite all the praise and the hands touching me and slapping my back in approval. I frantically thought how I could be of any help to the girl. Thinking about the rules governing Kapauku marriage I hit upon an idea. I turned to the headmen, Jokagaibo and Amojepa, and stated with a puzzled expression on my face: "I do not understand this marriage arrangement. You must have made a mistake while instructing me in the past." This reproach to my *maagodo noogei* ("real friends," in the sense of best friends) was a serious matter. A best friend may never lie and must be fully trusted. So Jokagaibo exclaimed, "I have never lied to you! Neither have

I suppressed any information important to your questions." I then tactically backed down a little and said: "Maybe I misunderstood, but I do seem to remember that you said that a girl should not be married while her breasts are not yet grown." "That is right," replied my friend. I countered, "But look at the girl. Her breasts have barely started to grow!" Both headmen looked at the girl, who meanwhile had been loaded onto the back of the unhappy matchmaker but was now quickly dropped to the ground. Then her mother and maternal aunt took over, dragging the unfortunate, struggling girl. *"Noukwa bubu"* (by the behind of my mother), swore the headmen, "you are right." They then shouted orders to stop the immoral procedure. All present seemed to be shocked at first, but then happy, except the girl's mother and aunt and, of course, the matchmaker and the groom. The girl looked at me with tears in her eyes and went home. Her father approached me, caught me by the forearm, and thanked me loudly for saving him from being immoral. His unhappiness over the forced marriage of his beloved daughter vanished in a broad smile, and I thought I noticed tears in his eyes — or was it only my ethnocentric imagination? The girl did not say anything, but her long, tearful look at me meant more than any words of thanks. The next morning another procession came to my house. This time it was led by Jikiiwiijaaj, who presented me with a pig as a reward.

The traditional male role in the family, even if manifest in a strong and bossy husband, may be challenged in a polygynous family when the co-wives are all displeased with a specific behavior of his that they consider wrong and offensive. When five co-wives gang up on their husband he has little chance of winning. This was plainly demonstrated to me when my best friend Jokagaibo got into trouble with his five wives.

Toward the end of my first research period among the Kapauku in 1955, the five wives of Jokagaibo, the headman of Aigii, started to spoil me with excellent food, net bags full of crayfish, stalks of bananas, the best kinds of sugar cane and sweet potatoes, and other delicacies. Since I knew that this attention was unusual and unprecedented, I became suspicious. Finally one afternoon Gaamaadii, the youngest of the wives, as always smiling, asked me how I liked the looks of a rather attractive young woman. I readily responded with enthusiasm about her beauty but soon stopped, realizing that I was treading on shaky ground. I then exclaimed: "She is very nice all right, but I cannot marry her. I am already married, and in America we are forbidden to have several wives." All the wives laughed and assured me that they knew that the white man is such an idiot as to be limited to one spouse. No, they reassured me, they did not mean to marry me off to the young woman; it was their husband they had in mind. I was stunned. It was not only the husbands who tried to enlarge their multiple marriages; it was also, and often (as it proved later), the co-wives who selected additional spouses for their husband.

As it turned out, all the food I was receiving was a bribe. I was supposed to persuade my friend to marry the young lady. No question — the food was terrific, so I suggested to Jokagaibo that he marry this beautiful young woman. "No," he exclaimed, "I cannot do it! I have enough wives as it is, and I have saved money to buy myself a sow." So it was no deal, even when the wives offered financial help from their brothers and fathers. Many times they invited the girl into their house to eat together, and then they cleverly disappeared, one by one, leaving their husband alone with her and hoping for the best. But to no avail. When they could not persuade their economy-minded husband in a reasonable and peaceful way, they stopped supplying him with food and they all went "on strike": no food for their spouse and no work in the gardens. Jokagaibo responded in an unemotional and very logical way: he moved in with me. What is a best friend for? But we did not live happily ever after. Pretty soon the wives appeared in full force in front of my house, jeering, screaming, and persuading occasional visitors of mine not to cross their "picket line." So it seems that some of our labor union techniques date back to the Stone Age! In spite of all the nuisance and impediments, we bravely resisted the women's power play. Finally they became impatient, and when Jokagaibo went out at night to relieve himself he was jumped by his spouses and received a persuasive beating. It was very likely that this treatment would be repeated. Even a hero recognizes when a situation is hopeless and further heroism useless. So Jokagaibo succumbed but solemnly proclaimed that he had decided to marry the girl of his "free will" because he found her so attractive. The wives heartily agreed. After all, who would want to be married to a coward? When I saw my friend for the last time in 1979 he was "happily" married to fifteen wives. Privately he complained to me, "Can you imagine how rich I could have been if I did not have to buy so many wives? And look at me. I cannot keep up with them, my *boko peu kai* (vital substance) deteriorates. I am desiccating!" Witnessing all this, I could not have felt more happy and thankful that I lived in a monogamous society.

Although officially the father and brother had ultimate control over an unmarried woman, her mother (as in the case of Jikiiwiijaaj's daughter) has quite a big say and may even override the legal powers of her husband and son. With Jikiiwiijaaj, a dominant wife managed to control her husband and almost force her daughter into a marriage not desired by either the bride-to-be or her father. There the mother had to retreat only because of my argument based on legal and moral grounds. On 20 August 1955, I witnessed another struggle between the socially sanctioned power of a father and his wife over the fate of their unmarried daughter. In this case, the mother's personality and influence prevailed. On that morning in August a loud dispute developed in front of my house, a spot often used for holding native court and political gatherings. Ijaaj Ogiibijokaimopaj was claiming his right to his recently paid-for wife over her loud protests, supported by her mother, Ijaaj Taajwiijokaimaga, and her brother (maternal uncle of the bride), Taajwiijokaipouga. Finally the bride's father, Ijaaj Bunaibomuuma, appeared on the scene and advised the groom to *wakagou*, drag the paid-for girl to his home by force. As the groom complied, the bride's mother attacked both men with her walking stick. Her protests and lamentations centered around the argument that she had not been given enough in the bride price settlement. The two men prevailed in the struggle because the girl did not seem to put up any real resistance.

According to my informants and parties to the dispute previously, Ogiibijokaimopaj, after having paid 300 cowry shells, only part of the bride price, was allowed to sleep in the home of the bride and have sexual intercourse with her. After a while the mother became impatient and urged the groom to pay the rest of the price, which he was unable to do at that time. So the mother induced her daughter not to give food (roasted sweet potatoes) to her husband-to-be. He became infuriated and went back to his home. Later, having amassed the contracted bride price, he paid in full the sum he owed — 420 cowry shells, 300 beads, 1 young pregnant sow, and 4 *dedege* necklaces made of Nassarius shells. The greedy father, however, asked for an additional 10 cowries. When this was refused, the bride escaped into the woods with her mother.

At this point, I was told, Ogiibijokaimopaj sought legal help and asked headman Awiitigaaj (of his Ijaaj-Enona sublineage) to step in. The latter, as the pertinent legal authority, complied with the request and asked Bunaibomuuma to return the bride price, thus annulling the contract. The greedy father, unwilling to return the money and fearful of the legal consequences, proposed to beat his daughter and return her by force to the groom. So he flushed his wife and daughter from the woods. All this had been accomplished just before the scene in front of my house. Naturally, he also dropped his illegitimate request for the ten cowries. On 21 August a formal legal session was held in the clearing in front of my house, where all the parties to the marital dispute were present. The whole case was debated again in front of a large gathering, and a final solution was proposed by the headman and accepted by all those concerned. Accordingly, the groom, along with the father of the bride, took the protesting girl to the groom's house. Her mother did not put up any resistance. When I inquired five days later about the newlyweds I was told that they were getting along very well. The dissatisfied mother, however, did not give up. She made violent scenes at home, attacking her husband with wooden sticks. These family rows were repeated until the tired Bunaibomuuma divorced his wife. She, in turn, convinced her daughter to leave her husband and escape with her to the household of her brother (the bride's maternal uncle). This man could legally provide asylum for both women. Thus, the outcome to this dispute was a double divorce, the obligatory return of the bride price, and unhappiness all around. And all this, as it appears, because of a few extra beads requested by a strong-willed mother — beads which the groom, because of his sense of fair play, refused to pay. He put the law of contractual agreement above his affection for the woman. This is one example of the informal power of the Kapauku women and their ability to successfully challenge male-made law.

Participant observation involves not only looking at people's behavior, listening to their discussions and taking notes when they talk about their experiences and culture; active participation is also required. The anthropologist should become part of the life of the community, preferably adopted into a clan and regarded as a member of the various associations and even secret societies. In other words, he or she should acquire a status ascribed by the natives and is expected to perform faithfully the cultural role pertaining to that status. Native morality and laws apply to him or her as they apply to the studied people. Accordingly, I had to behave as a Kapauku, as a member of the Ijaaj-Pigome confederacy, as the adoptive father of my forty-eight sons and five daughters, as the best friend of several of the local Kapauku, as a relative to the relatives of my best friends, and as a *tonowi*, a Kapauku rich man and political leader, a status bestowed upon me. There I was *nakame* (father), *keneka* (clan member), *nauwa* (older brother), *noogei* (best friend), and *joka* (son), and I had to perform my various roles properly. Of necessity I became an enemy of all the traditional enemies of my confederacy, especially the people of the Waine and Tibaakoto clans. Thus I was also to have the honor to be one of the first of the leaders of my confederacy to be killed in the war with the confederacy of Waine-Tibaakoto. I was in fact informed of this exciting prospect by an emissary prior to the onset of the war.

Thus, any assertion by an anthropologist, that he or she was a participant observer and a friend of everybody is patent nonsense, an impossibility. In my case, roles and behaviors were expected of me that I was quite reluctant to perform because of their incompatibility with the basic moral and legal principles of Western civilization, the Judeo-Christian tradition, and the expectations of my profession, university and sponsoring institution, not to mention the Dutch colonial government. Therefore, I had to skillfully extricate myself from the duty of killing our enemies on the battlefield, of practicing black magic (in which art I have been properly instructed), of dating unmarried girls in order to marry them according to the Kapauku law of polygyny, of following all the totemic taboos of my clan (I loved to eat the tabooed crayfish species), and to partake in foods that were not only strange or distasteful to me, but decidedly shocking.

I managed to avoid some of these role requirements, such as killing an enemy; others I botched on purpose; and a few I exploited as practical jokes. One duty I managed to dodge was that of marrying additional wives as a proper and well-to-do Kapauku should do. By the final month of my first field research, late in 1955, I had participated in many native pig feasts, spending nights in dance houses and swinging on the sprung floors, recording the native songs and dance performances. A Kapauku pig feast is an impressive affair. On such occasions there may be as many as two thousand visitors, and the slaughtered pigs may be counted into the hundreds. This huge ceremony is preceded by a period of about three months, during which men and women from any village or confederacy may visit the site of the future feast on which the necessary dance house and feast houses have been constructed, to spend the night dancing and singing. This practice is called *ema uwii* — "going to the dance house." The dancing period formally begins with *putu duwai naago*, the day during which some pigs are slaughtered and the meat is distributed by the sponsors of the feast to their friends and relatives free of charge, and during which the date of the main and concluding feast is announced.

During these night dances, one or several groups of people — each group representing a lineage, sub-lineage, or even a whole confederacy — arrive at sunset, running, yodeling, and jumping over the puddles dotting the grassy paths. Upon their arrival each group performs *waita tai*, a counterclockwise-running circular dance accompanied by a song that sounds like barking. This performance is followed by *tuupe*, a clockwise trotting dance accompanied by very melodic and, to the Western ear, pleasing songs of different composition. Then the people rush into the dance house to jump onto the springy floor and sing *ugaa* songs. An *ugaa* song starts with barking cheers, while the people, standing on the same spot, bend their knees in rapid rhythm and make the sprung floor go up and down. After a few minutes, the singing subsides and an individual begins a solo song of his composition, which, after a sentence or two, becomes a duet in which a "helper," usually one of his best friends, answers the singer in counterpoint fashion. This duet, lasting only two to three minutes, is followed by a chorus song in which the whole group on the dance floor participates. The *ugaa* song ends with a barking sound while the sprung floor rocks wildly, which introduces yet another solo song with its composer. The solo part of the song is a poem created by the singer, and the duet is usually its repetition in skillful counterpoint fashion. The chorus part of the *ugaa* is a traditional performance of well-defined song types. In his solo performance the singer suggests which of the familiar types he desires the group to sing. Each of these songs has an important meaning that usually has social implications. Accordingly, in an *ugaa* song a man may, for example, mourn his dead relative, ask a friend for a monetary loan or support in an economic venture, challenge a rival to a legal suit, request the authority of his lineage or confederacy to declare or conclude a war, ask a girl for a date, or propose marriage to a young lady who is usually present, walking with a lit torch around the singing group on the sprung floor.

The *ugaa* songs most important for young men and women are those to which a singer proposes marriage to a girl. The composition is usually a nice poem. In it the singer alludes to the beauty of the girl and asks her for a date at a given place, and then to marry her, requesting her to leave with him for his home. The girl to whom the song is addressed is present in the audience or in the group of women who walk around the men in single file as the men dance and sing in the center of the sprung floor, and carry lit torches. If she rejects the proposal she angrily throws away the torch and leaves the dance house. If she continues to carry the torch and *ebobai*, walks with it around the assembly of dancing men, or if she remains in the audience standing among the spectators, she signifies her acceptance of the proposal. Later during the night the two young people steal away, and if marriage was really proposed they run to the boy's village. The close paternal relatives of the couple and the young man's best friends try to make necessary arrangements for an early payment of the bride price.

In my role as participant observer I went to as many pig feasts as I could, and I spent many nights in the dance houses recording the music and the texts of the *ugaa* songs. A participant observer should really participate. Yet, although I swung with the rest on the elevated dance floor and dutifully joined the three hundred to five hundred voices of the chorus, singing the traditional songs (for example, of the "swallow" or the "east wind"), I had not contributed an *ugaa* song of my own composition. On several occasions my best friend Jokagaibo chided me for my abstinence, to the great amusement of the dancers and the rest of the audience. Finally I had had enough. I decided to compose a song which I hoped would put an end to the *gaudium* (fun) and be remembered. A line from Ovid's *Metamorphoses* rang in my ears: *ad mea perpetuum deducite tempora carmen* ("to my times, bring an eternal poem!"). To be lasting, the poem had to be stunning. I had an idea. In those days there was in the Kamu Valley a beautiful young girl named Meekaamude (translation: "man's fallow land") whose fame and popularity, as well as facial features, hair, and figure, gave rise to daily gossip, wide admiration, and, of course, numerous dating and marriage proposals. She had rejected all of these. Her popularity easily matched that of Marilyn Monroe in the United States. There was therefore no better object of poetry and an *ugaa* song than this woman. And what fun it would be to be rejected and join the ever-growing crowd of failed suitors. So I set to work and tried my poetic wit while complying with the native canons of literary goodness and beauty. The resulting poem proposed a date with the beauty at the bend of the Botu River where the reeds whisper the story of eternal love, gently swaying in the soft east wind, and where the *wogio*, a brightly colored warbler, chirps his affections to his spouse as she warms the eggs in a nearby nest. I planned to encourage the multitude in the dance house to follow my poem with their chorus of the traditional *wogio ugaa*, or warbler song. I wrote the text and tried out my singing several times in the seclusion of the nearby forest. There I succeeded only in flushing out some annoyed birds. I hoped for better success during my anticipated night performance.

My day, or rather night, came on 31 May, 1955. My boys and girls, and many people from the Botukebo village, including Obajbegaa, Jagawaugii, and Aigii, traveled with me to the village of Bunauwoba-do for the night dance and pig feast to be held the next day. When we arrived at the ceremonial grounds about six hundred people were already gathered around the dance house, sitting and chatting in the feast houses. As night fell the dances started, and one *ugaa* song followed another. To my satisfaction I noticed Meekaamude in the crowd, so the success of my performance seemed to be at least at that point assured. I was already planning my phony expressions of grief over Meekaamude's rejection of my proposal and how I would join the crowd of rejected suitors, which included most of my confedera-cy's headmen. Certainly, I was in proper and distinguished company. The night was starry and balmy, the singing and dancing were flaw-less, and the girls with lit torches circulated our singing group, among them Meekaamude. My best friend Jokagaibo started an *ugaa* song in which he asked a man to conclude with him a business deal involving the fate of several pigs. His uncle sang the duet with him, and the chorus swung the floor and sang the *ugaa* of the "west wind." Upon finishing, my dear friend turned to me and made everybody laugh by challenging me to a song. Everybody expected me to decline as before. To their amazement I straightened up, gave everybody an offended look, and began my public marriage proposal. The reaction was un-believable. The people burst into laughter and hit each other with fists over the shoulders. Indeed, several of them rolled in convulsions on the dance floor — it was nothing less than a Kapauku riot. They assumed correctly that I was playing a practical joke. But I continued to play my deceitful role, stopped singing, and, seemingly hurt and offended, looked around at the crowd, which was seized in convulsion and laughter. One by one they stopped and, bewildered stood up. Sev-eral apologized for their improper behavior (*ani maagodo ipa* — I am really sorry). Exploiting the resulting quiet, I started my song once more. My best friend, completely flabbergasted, performed his duty and joined me in the duet part of my ugaa. The chorus, having fully recovered from their initial shock, performed magnificently the *wogio ugaa* warbler song I had suggested. As they finished with the barking intermezzo, all eyes turned to Meekaamude, carrying the torch. Everything up to now had followed my plan — I had fooled everybody. But now it was I who got the shock of the day. Instead of throwing away the torch as I had expected, Meekaamude kept walking with properly downcast eyes and a triumphant smile. The resulting silence lasted several seconds, followed by screams, yelling, several people slapping my back, and others congratulating me. I felt like a complete idiot. What now? When Jokagaibo, Awiitigaaj, Ekajewaijokaipouga, and other big shots saw the shock on my face, they interpreted it as financial worries. They surrounded me and assured me of their support and loans for the expected high bride price. It took the congregation another twenty minutes or so to completely recover and resume singing as usual. Luckily the next day was the pig feast, so we all stayed overnight in Bunauwobado in the feast houses. Consequently there was no requirement that I take my "second wife-to-be" to my home.

I realized by then that I had overdone my role of participant observer. Fortunately, being well versed in Kapauku marital proceedings, I assumed the role of the most proper Kapauku gentleman and declared that first I should settle the bride price, which everybody expected to be horrendous, and that only if I succeeded could there be any talk of marrying Meekaamude. I did not rush to collect the bride price and hoped for another successful contender for Meekaamude's favors. But nothing happened. For the rest of my stay the people chided me, made jokes over my alleged affair, and only the clever and sly Awiitigaaj finally understood me. "In due time I shall lead Meekaamude to a decisive fellow." In 1955 I left New Guinea with the Meekaamude business still unsettled.

In 1959 I returned, and the reception was impressive. My adoptive mother, the mother of my best friend Jokagaibo, was the first one to meet me on the trail from Paniai Lake into the Kamu Valley not far from the lofty Ogaajdimi pass. She learned of my coming from the

Kapauku "yodeling telephones", whereby important messages are yodeled in falsetto from one mountain ridge to another. Thus, having traveled two days from Botukebo on the jungle path, she embraced me and surprised me with freshly roasted sweet potatoes of the *meda* kind, my favorite of the twenty-four Kapauku varieties. My subsequent meetings with my friends and adoptive "relations" were similarly touching. Even the witch doctor Kaadootajbii met me on a one-day walk from his village, in the middle of the Kamu swamps.

He became so excited that he wept, caught me by my chin, and shook it back and forth so much that I had trouble chewing for several days. The last five hundred yards I was literally carried by my jubilant adoptive sons and best friends. I did notice that my people were worried about something, keeping something back from me. I feared that there was some serious problem, so I tried to find out whether somebody had died during my four-year absence, but no one had, as far as I could determine. Finally Jokagaibo broke the news to me. "There is something very sad I have to tell you that will make you angry." "Well, let's have it," I encouraged him. "It's Meekaamude! While you were gone she, like many of us, did not believe you would return. So it would have been unreasonable for her to wait." Because it was expected, I swore, showed anger and sorrow, and even smeared my face with the handy yellow clay exposed next to our path. I properly showed my sorrow the whole evening, but in the morning I washed my face. Jokagaibo, my friend, asked me whether I was still mad. I assured him that now I was all right but only a little sad. So everything seemed to be in order. Indeed, in the afternoon Meekaamude appeared at my house with gifts of food. She brought her husband along to present him to me. We *kipo motii*-greeted each other by snapping our index fingers between the fingers of the other man, and became friends — Meekaamude becoming my new classificatory "sister" (as the wife of my new friend). Thus the episode was concluded happily for us both. Since then I have become more careful with my practical jokes.

Although nothing can surpass witnessing a behavior for accuracy, the participant observation method does have several drawbacks. First, it is not possible to participate in or witness every kind of behavior (for example, black magic or sexual behavior), so one must rely on informants. Second, not all the behavior one is permitted to observe and which one needs for an analysis can be recorded first-hand. For example, I could not attend 176 legal disputes, or partici-pate in numerous business transactions, magical performances, and so forth. Third, one can observe only the behavior that takes place. Some ceremonies (feasts, funerals, weddings, and so on) and events (wars, epidemics, starvation, crop failures) do not occur during the period of one's investigation. To compensate for this drawback and still se-cure objective data other than one's impressions and interpretations, one may use the case method, which employs exact and specific data rather than generalities.

Membership

The first important break in my research and contact with the Ka-pauku came when I was adopted into the Ijaaj clan. Jokagaibo and especially Ijaaj Awiitigaaj, the headmen of two of the sublineages of my Ijaaj-Pigome confederacy, were especially proud and glad of my adoption. On one occasion when I was sitting with several people around the fire, Awiitigaaj, looking at me, leaned over to his neighbour and said, "Look at Amerikaibo (the big American), he really looks like an Ijaaj man, like one of us." Needless to say, on returning to my house I carefully examined my face in the mirror. With membership in the Ijaaj clan came all the advantages and restrictions. Thus I became a hereditary enemy of all members of the Waine, Tibaakoto, Jobee, and Anou clans, in addition to others with whom I had had little contact in the past. During times of height-ened animosity I realized than at any time, but especially at night, a sniper could shoot me. If I were to step out of my house at night to relieve myself, appearing in the doorway with a fire burning be-hind me, I would be an easy target. Another drawback was the food restrictions imposed upon me as a member of the totemic Ijaaj clan. Totemic taboos prohibited me from eating fruit bats and a species of crayfish. The prohibition on the fruit bat presented no problem, but I resented the taboo on my beloved crayfish. So I simply broke the ta-boo and continued to eat the forbidden animal. Kapauku believe that violation of a totemic taboo brings deafness to the culprit. When I left Kamu Valley in 1955 my hearing was very good. However, between that departure and my next arrival in 1959 my hearing, especially in my right ear, deteriorated. During the Second World War grenades had exploded near my head on the right side of my body as I lay on the ground, and I had been unable to hear for about twenty-four hours. Then, however, my hearing came back. My partial deafness didn't occur until 1958. Thus the power of the totemic taboo, according to my Kapauku friends, had been validated.

In the years subsequent to my first research, more and more Ijaaj people began eating fruit bats, thus breaking their ancient totemic taboo. They justified this violation by rationalizing that the taboo applied not to the large fruit bat but to a small species of insectivorous bat. This shift in taboo can be explained environmentally. The Kamu Valley was once a lake which gradually dried up as the Edege River cut deeper and deeper into its bed at the outlet of the Kamu Valley in the south. It thus lowered the water level in the valley and drained away the lake, leaving behind some swamps, a series of smaller lakes, and large expanses of dry flatland of extreme fertility. People from the surrounding areas slowly moved in and occupied the exposed lakebed. Kamu Valley became heavily populated with the result that large game, such as marsupials, cassowary birds, pythons, wild boar, and other animals retreated into the forests of the surrounding mountains. The largest remaining animal that could be hunted was the fruit bat. This was obviously why the Ijaaj people began gradually lifting the taboo. Radcliffe-Brown's claim (1952) that economically important animals are assigned totemic status seems not to be correct in all cases. In this case, once the totemic fruit bat assumed a position of economic importance it was dropped from the Ijaaj people's totemic list. The totemic animal, according to the Kapauku, was obviously not pleased with this state of affairs and tried to show its displeasure on several occasions. One night, when I and my people were returning home under a full moon, a giant fruit bat almost dived into my hair. The Kapauku screamed and claimed that the animal was angry that we had broken our totemic taboo.

The advantage of being a clan member was shown quite clearly during my second research in June 1959. The people in the Debei Valley revolted against the white administration and the white man in general. In my neighbouring village of Botukebo I found three Catholic catechists who had fled in a panic from the Valley, claiming that the natives had killed two policemen and were going to kill all the white men and Catholic catechists and missionaries. It was also assumed that all Indonesians would be shot. The catechists urged me to escape, then proceeded to flee north to Jotapuga and Ugapuga villages. However, I decided to stay, especially after the decision of my Ijaaj-Pigome confederacy people to fight the Debei enemy should they come and try to do me or the missionaries any harm. My people had decided to risk their lives for my safety. The next day we met with the Debei people, who complained about police abuse but claimed they had no intention of hurting me or the missionaries. Local Papuans had given similar assurances to American missionaries in Obano in 1956 — and they were subsequently killed by bands of Papuans from other valleys who had revolted against the Dutch administration and drifted into the Obano region. These Papuans were unaware of the local situation and the fact that the missionaries were loved by the Obano people. Here, however, backed by my clan and confederacy fellows, I felt quiet safe. I even managed to negotiate a truce and promised to write up their grievances concerning police brutality and send a memorandum to the Dutch district officer. As a result, the police were publicly disciplined and my prestige in the Kamul Valley rose to the extent that the people regarded me as their advocate.

My greatest insight into Kapauku society occurred when three important headmen of the Ijaaj-Pigome confederacy and a shaman asked me to be their "best friend." A Kapauku may have one or several *maagodo noogei*, or best friends. This relationship is characterized by frequent interactions, unconditional support in financial, legal, and political matters, and extensions of kinship terminology to the primary consanguine relatives. Kapauku best friends are completely open and frank with each other, they have no secrets to hide, and they are expected to present a pig or other valuables to their partners when they suffer a loss of any kind, when a close relative dies, or when for the first time in their lives they become sufficiently excited to perform *wainai*, the mad dance. When two people want to seal the deal on best friendship, one of them, usually the older and richer man, gives his new friend a large pig or sixty or a hundred Kapauku cowries. At the time of the gift transfer the donor asks the recipient to be his best friend and starts to call him *noogei*, my friend. The beneficiary is neither obligated nor expected to reciprocate with a smaller gift immediately. Thus it is up to the recipient to choose the time for proving his affection toward his partner. Subsequently a series of reciprocal gifts is initiated, stopping only when one of the friends dies.

From my new best friends, I secured the most important and intimate information concerning their finances, personal secrets, political deals, and aspirations. Only then did I begin to comprehend Kapauku emotional and economic problems; attitudes toward relatives, outsiders, and business; and their philosophy of life. Since three of these best friends were the richest and most influential men in the confederacy, I received a great deal of information concerning particular business transactions and relationships, as well as an insight into the economic-political power structure of local groupings.

On 21 November 1954 I received a large pig from Ijaaj Jokagaibo, the headman of the Ijaaj Jamaina sublineage. I thanked him and reciprocated with gifts of axes, a machete, and knives. However, it was not until 15 December that the best friendship between us was sealed. On that day he arrived from Enarotali on Lake Paniai, obviously quite sick. I made him a tea and gave him aspirin, which helped. He stayed overnight in the village of Botukebo, but before retiring he embraced me and started to call me *nogei*, my friend. At that time I did not quite understand the meaning of "best friendship" and did not realize how fortunate I had become. As time went on, Ijaaj Jokagaibo became my best and constant teacher of the Kapauku language and culture, and my staunch supporter throughout my research periods. His primary relatives I called by "his" kinship terms, so that his mother became my mother, his father my father; however, his wives I called by their first names and we behaved toward each other as siblings. His mother especially, became quite attached to me, called me "my son," crying and wailing when I left in 1955. She was the first to meet me on the Ogiaajdimi pass when I returned in 1959. She also gave me a family heirloom, a magnificent polished stone machete of green serpentine rock containing iron crystals. When I came down with malaria and later with dengue fever she attended to me and instructed my boys and girls on how to take care of me.

Jokagaibo himself, a true Kapauku gentleman, always behaved as my best friend. Once, for example, while arguing ardently with some people of the southern clans about the divorce case of one of my "sons," and wishing to accentuate my displeasure at my opponent's poor treatment of my boy, I danced the Kapauku mad dance. Jokagaibo, who was squatting nearby, quietly stood up and left. On the following evening I received a small pig from him with the explanation: "I felt very sorry for you, because you became so emotional." On several occasions he stood up for me in various disputes and difficult situations, as, for example, in December 1954. The people had concluded the construction of my house and I had distributed gifts to the multitude. After a while Jokagaibo stood up and made a speech in which he urged his people not to ask for any more gifts; that I had given enough as it was and that eventually I would not be able to buy any products from them because I would not have enough money (beads). Such unsolicited support from my best friend on many occasions steadily increased my esteem for him.

Another best friend of mine was Ijaaj Awiitigaaj of Botukebo, the headman of the Ijaaj-Enona sublineage. He became my "best friend" on 9 December 1954, again when we had finished building my house and I could at last abandon my tent and live more comfortably. My boys and other Ijaaj and Pigome people were enthusiastic about the completion of the building and Awiitigaaj, who asked me for best friendship, gave me a pig. We killed it and I distributed the meat to my boys and friends. I immediately reciprocated with gifts of an iron axe, a machete, steel knives, and other items. On 11 February 1955, Awiitigaaj embraced me in my new house and pleaded with me not to return to America because I was now *keneka*, his clan's mate. This outburst of emotion was prompted by my telling my boys the day before that I would leave for America if they ever told me a lie. On 22 and 24 February, Awiitigaaj planted a whole banana grove next to my house.

Pigome Pegabii, the headman of the Pigome-Obaaj lineage of the village of Obajbegaa, also became my "best friend," presenting me with a small pig on 18 July 1955. Because I decided to keep the pig, he castrated it for me the next day. All I had to do was feed it a few sweet potatoes twice a day. Otherwise it roamed the jungle and the neighbouring swamps to get its nourishment. It became attached to me like a dog to its master. It slept under my bed, or, actually, under the elevated floor of my house. I could call it and it would walk with me like a dog. When I sat down it would come and lie on its side and I had to scratch its belly. Whenever I left my house for one or several days, upon my return it would dash out from the jungle quite a distance from my house to welcome me. I would have to stop, sit down, and scratch its belly, acknowledging its affection and my love.

These best friendships became invaluable for my research because friends never keep secrets from each other, and certainly they do not lie to each other. Accordingly, when Kaadotajbii, the witch doctor, became my "best friend" in June 1955, he came to me and told me that everyone had been lying to me in claiming the Kapauku were not cannibals. This was of great interest to me because when I had come to New Guinea and later to Paniai Lake in the Kapauku territory, I had been told by everyone at Enarotali, the seat of the Dutch administration of that region, that the Kapauku *were* cannibals. This claim was reinforced when I witnessed the trial of an older "cannibal" woman by the administration court of the district officer Den Haan in early November 1954. The woman did not defend herself against the accusation, levelled at her by several native plaintiffs, that she had killed a child and then eaten it. She was duly sentenced to a long jail term. In the Kamu Valley, however, I was told many times that the charge of cannibalism was unfounded. Neither did I find any evidence of it myself. I became convinced that the Kapauku were not cannibals after all. That evening in June when Kaadotajbii entered my hut, he made sure that no one was listening outside. Then he told me that that morning an old local woman, the mother of Ogiibiijokaimopaj, had killed a child who was then buried by his father in a nearby swamp. Then, to my astonishment, he recited a list of names of reputed cannibals and their victims. There were some interesting aspects of Kaadootajbii's claims: all the cannibals were women, all were widows who had not remarried, and all were regarded as misfits in their communities. They were called *meenoo* (a word composed of *me*, meaning men, and *noo* from the verb *nai*, to eat). The witch doctor maintained that all of them, after having killed their victims, let them be buried by their relatives, and only then, the following night, would approach the grave, typically having changed into a dog or a hawk, and feast on the corpse. He insisted that this witch would do the same that night.

So now I was back "among cannibals." Because this information might contain a seed of truth, I decided to put the claim to a test. After nightfall I snuck out of my hut and went to the grave in the swamps to witness the cannibal's work. In order to avoid being betrayed by my tracks in the mud and charged, myself, with cannibalism, I went barefoot into the cold night. Hidden in tall reeds near the grave, I watched throughout the night. The moon was full, the reeds rustled softly in the light breeze, and patches of fog drifted by. I felt like I was watching a Boris Karloff movie. Instead of a walking mummy, however, I expected to see a local woman. The night went by and nothing happened; only a few giant bats and owls flew over my head, and the weird shrieks of animals broke the monotony of an otherwise silent night. Instead of a cannibal, all I caught was a cold. Next morning Kaadootajbii, his eyes wide with excitement, reported important news to me: "The cannibal woman indeed came to the grave, but this time instead of a dog, she changed into an ogre. Her track in the mud showed feet almost twice as large as those of an adult Kapauku." So if anyone comes upon a report from the highlands of New Guinea of a Big Foot sighting, the reader should know his true identity. As it turned out, the Kapauku were not cannibals after all, and all the accusations and wild accounts were actually the result of a belief in witchcraft. I wrote the summary of my findings to the district officer, Den Haan, who promptly released the above-mentioned "cannibal-witch" from jail.

Collecting

Although neither my father nor my mother were collectors of anything, since my childhood I was a compulsive collector. As a four-year-old, I collected toy soldiers with different uniforms supplied by my parents and relatives at Christmas time. Once they discovered my interest in collecting, they started to supply me with troops of different nations. At the age of seven, my interest shifted to more sophisticated matters — to butterflies. I caught these with nets and pinned them down in old cigar boxes. In doing so I learned their specific names and tried to link them with what I thought were corresponding caterpillars. Two years later, I started to collect stamps. This activity taught me geography and developed an interest in foreign countries. I learned not only the names of the various states and their location on the world map in my old atlas, but also the names of the large rivers and mountains ranges that crossed their territories. It was then only logical that I should become focused on various rocks and especially semi-precious stones. Indeed my grandfather, a jeweller and watchmaker, enlarged my mineral collection with scraps of raw emeralds, rubies, and sapphires, augmented with better-looking agates, topazes, quartz, crystals, and amethysts. This interest in collecting has continued with me until the present and my cellar is filled with raw minerals, agates, geodes, and many uncut interesting stones. In biology class at my Czech college, I had to collect and dry plants in order to create a crude herbarium. My marriage brought another collector's item to my inventory. My wife is a painter and sculptor and when she became a professor of Art History, I also became interested in human products — artifacts. While at Yale University, where I studied anthropology, I augmented my scholarship by working in the Peabody Museum. Since I suffer from inertia (I hate to move and change, having stayed at Yale since 1952) I continued my work in the museum after my teaching appointment and, in due course, became curator and later director of the anthropological collection. I love "primitive art" and dislike modern. The name "primitive" assigned to tribal art seems to me to be an anomaly. I find nothing "primitive" in the sophisticated sculpture of New Guinea natives, while I find plenty that is in our modern artistic products, some of which appear unbelievably crude. But my attempt to collect pieces of tribal art hit an "iceberg" in the form of my professor and superior in the museum, Professor Cornelius Osgood (then head of the anthropology section at the Peabody Museum). "Leo," he told me, "since now you are a curator of Anthropology, you cannot collect objects which you are supposed to curate. You may not compete with the museum. Otherwise what will happen is that you will retain the best pieces, and the museum will have to be satisfied with the inferior leftovers. And that would be most unethical." Given my background in law, I clearly saw his point — a vested interest. So out of necessity, I turned my attention to our Western products, of course not to the "modern art" but to the gorgeous Meissen porcelain of Germany. That certainly was no competition to my collecting activity for the museum. The only tribal art objects that I have kept were given to me as presents by my tribal friends and adoptive "relatives," objects which certainly will end up in the Yale Peabody Museum after my soul joins those of my Kapauku friends in New Guinea's tropical forests. Since the Kapauku have no sculpture or painting, my collections for the Peabody Museum consist mainly of utilitarian objects, weapons, dress and body ornaments, a crude herbarium, animal bones, preserved reptiles and amphibians, soil samples, and even human blood (not to be traded to vampires!).

In addition to working with informants and being a participant in the native society, an anthropologist must collect material objects in order to fully comprehend the culture. In describing and analyzing the gathering of material objects it is necessary to include the species of plants the people use as food sources and in the manufacture of other goods. Since in New Guinea many of the plants, insects, and amphibians people use are often scientifically unknown and therefore unidentified, the researcher should create a small herbarium and collect insects and other animals and make sure that experts properly assign them scientific names upon his return from the field. Similarly, when examining the hunting habits of a population under study, one has to assemble the distinguishing parts of those hunted and trapped animals (especially skulls, skins, feathers, etc.). In the study of fishing habits, a similar identification is necessary for the various types of fish, crustaceans, water bugs and insects, their aquatic larvae, and amphibian nymphs.

Properly studying material culture often means assembling a wide collection of artifacts to be studied not only by the research worker, but also by his colleagues and other experts. The history of ethnological theory shows us how important such studies were in determining prehistoric conflicts and genetic relationships between the various cultures. Indeed, in the nineteenth and early twentieth centuries most of the schools of ethnology relied heavily on these studies, which are known as British diffusionist, American diffusionist, and German *Kulturkreislehre*. Since scientifically related evolutions rely exclusively on the empirical evidence drawn from their material collections, the collecting aspect cannot be underestimated. And since documentation through the collection of material objects is especially required for a proper analysis of people's quest for food, let me first describe its three major divisions in Kapauku society: gathering, fishing and hunting, and collection of the documented material itself.

Non-horticultural Food

Gathering

In the anthropological literature, obtaining food by gathering has sometimes been treated qualitatively with superficial generalizations. Yet this activity was an indispensable part of the Kapauku quest for food and, I suspect, that of many other societies. Indeed, even in Western society gathering is important in some regions. In Alpine Central Europe, for example, the harvesting of grass from mountain meadows — where no plowing, manuring or irrigation was done — certainly cannot be classified as agriculture, as it often is. Among the Kapauku, gathering provided not only raw material for construction and manufacture, but an especially important supplement to their diet. Collecting eggs from birds, lizards, snakes, and frogs, as well as insects from among the multitude of species, was important to supply the people with essential proteins. The Kapauku, quite sophisticated linguistically, classified their insects by economic criteria and assigned to the more important among them specific names; they also gave names to their edible larvae. They divided the edible insects into five categories according to consumption: those eaten only by men, only by women, only by children, only by women and children, and by everybody. Various insects, in turn, were prepared for consumption in different ways according to species. Some were eaten raw and alive (for example, spiders, stink bugs); others, especially the larger species, were roasted on embers; and the rest (most of them) were steamed in bamboo containers over a fire. Gathering on a small scale took place almost daily. On the way to their gardens or neighboring villages, the Kapauku would stop at various trees and rotten logs to inspect them for stink bugs, beetles, and grubs. Occasionally they also found birds' nests, an edible large lizard, a wasp or bee hive with delicious larvae, or a few mushrooms.

Many insects and lizards were classified as inedible. I did not test their toxicity, but people assured me that "they are no good for eating." Others were deemed inedible for magical reasons. One evening, for example, when a large lizard called *bego* appeared, crawling between two planks in my home, my boys jumped up and screamed. That lizard was said to possess an evil spirit. I must admit that even to this day I do not know whether it is venomous. In any case, I had to chase the creature out of my house myself.

When a heavy rain transformed the Edege River of the Kamu into a surging torrent that spilled over its banks and inundated the valley, transforming it into a huge lake, the Kapauku women went out in their canoes to collect insects that floated in the water. Wherever there was an island of tall grass, the women stamped down the vegetation in order to force the numerous mole crickets, grasshoppers, stink bugs, roaches, and other species of edible insects into the water, where they were easily caught and placed into bamboo containers the women tucked underneath their belts. Some men disdained this mass collection of insects during a flood. As one unhappy and "starving" husband complained, "I have not seen my wives for three days. I have to go myself and harvest sweet potatoes. All they will bring from their expeditions is a few bugs which will not satisfy my hunger and, of course, heaps of mole crickets which we males do not eat." Yet, far from disliking these times of flood, most men seized this unique opportunity to shoot, catch, or club many flushed-out rats, muskrats, and birds and feast on their delicious meat while their wives were absent and could not claim their share.

Fishing

Fishing was mostly a female activity. A married woman was the owner of her dugout canoe, manufactured for her by her husband. Whenever a woman was present, she was the navigator, pushing and paddling the canoe while the men and children sat in the wobbly craft. Navigating this kind of boat was certainly an art, for one had to balance one's body in order to prevent the boat from overturning. I was always apprehensive in the dugout canoe, not for my own sake (I am a good swimmer) but because of my camera. Luckily the boats I traveled in never capsized, despite the fact that often the boatwoman would stand while pushing the canoe through the reeds and along the streams, typically with her young child sitting on her shoulders holding her by the hair. The children usually watched me closely, so that whenever the canoe suddenly wobbled and I looked terrified, they would burst into laughter.

No fish existed in the lakes and rivers of the mountain region. With their oval nets (sunk with bait, dragged on the bottom of a shallow, or placed at the opening of a reed dam constructed across streams in the swamps) the women would catch crayfish, dragonfly larvae, water bugs, and tadpoles. Another way to fish was to plunge a forked pole into the bottom of the numerous small lakes of the Kamu Valley, which were overgrown with waterweeds. The women would rotate the pole so that a bundle of water plants accumulated on the fork, pull it out, and place it on the side of the boat. By spreading the bundle of weeds over the edge of the canoe, they could locate their prey inside the bundle and place them in bamboo containers tucked under their belts. The men might dive, more as a sport than a serious economic endeavor, and caught large crayfish specimens by hand or spear. Crayfish from rivers and lakes were a delicacy on the European menu. In Paris, crayfish soup was sometimes the most expensive dish, and one would be lucky to locate in one's bowl even a tiny piece of the crustacean. Yet here in the Kamu Valley, I feasted on at least 30 crayfish a day while my wife and friends in the United States worried about my diet. I made many expeditions into the swamps and lakes to film the fishing flotillas of canoes helmed by women. Whenever we approached them through the reeds my Kapauku boys would start to yodel. "Why do you do that?" I asked. "Some of the women take off their *moge* (loin wraps), and both we and they would be very embarrassed if we surprised them naked," came the polite reply.

Hunting

As the Kamu Valley with its rich soil was quite densely settled, the large game had been driven into the surrounding virgin forest and far up the mountain slopes. Unlike in the forested valley of the Pona and Mapia to the south and west of our location, hunting and trapping in the Kamu Valley was practiced more as a sport. Most common was the trapping of rats, whose meat was valued more than pork. The rodents were snared at the openings of their dens or on their trails. Otherwise they were shot with four- or five-pronged arrows on sight, or killed as they tried to escape from grassy areas surrounded by hunters, or stamped down by women. They could be seized alive, a procedure called *pukwamo*, by reaching with bare hands into their burrows. Other animals, such as marsupials, were shot on expeditions to the tropical rain forests during moonlit nights. Often during such expeditions large pythons were killed in a spectacular way. A small boy would walk first as a decoy. When the python slid down from its tree to attack the boy, the hunters following the boy would jump forward, armed with clubs (nowadays also with machetes) and kill the snake by breaking its backbone. Usually a "headman" would try to hit or sever the head of the snake to prevent it from biting the boy; one or several "body men" and a "tail man" would take care of the rest of the reptile. I have never witnessed this activity. But I did once spot a young python about seven feet long in a tree. I called my boys to kill it and have a feast. "No good," they told me. "It is just a child. We let it grow and kill it when it has grown." Another time a giant python was spotted right next to my house. Again I called my boys to kill it. To my surprise they refused again. "No, we cannot kill it. In this particular snake there is a benevolent ancestor's soul which came to your house to visit you." Well, I certainly would not have appreciated any such friendly visit while I was asleep in bed. I did some of my own snake hunting, killing some of the smaller serpents and pickling them in formaldehyde jars for my museum colleagues at Yale. Apparently, unlike in the lowlands of New Guinea, in the highlands none of these snakes were venomous.

I did participate in several hunts for herons, waterfowl, and parakeets. Once I even witnessed a dramatic fight between a man and a wild boar. One evening as a herd of domesticated sows was returning to the village of Botukebo, one could spot among them a large dark animal with tusks — a wild boar that had ventured into that most dangerous of places, a native village. Ijaaj Awiitigaaj was standing next to the path unarmed as the boar passed by. He jumped it from behind, seized it by the ears, and rode it on its rump. Cleverly, like a python, he locked his legs below the thorax of the animal and waited until the beast, turning wildly in circles and trying to bite and shake off the aggressor, exhaled. Then he tightened his leg vice. At the same time he hollered for help, until his son appeared with a bow and arrows and started to circle the wild beast. At an opportune moment he shot it skillfully from behind under its ribcage into the heart, narrowly missing his father's leg. Like Awiitigaaj, who was unprepared for the encounter and weaponless, I was equally surprised, not having my camera ready. What a spectacle it was and what a movie it would have made!

The Kapauku shot birds with bows and arrows. A stalking method was used for large birds such as mud hens, ducks, hawks, and herons. Four- or five-pronged arrows were employed. For small birds such as swallows, finches and parrots, then abundant in the Kamu Valley, pronged or blunt-tipped arrows were used. Not even birds of paradise were spared. Plumage from these birds was used for hair ornaments and hairpins, and the carcasses were roasted or steamed with vegetables or collected greens, wrapped in bundles of reed and heated with red-hot stones extracted from a fire. On a dry and windy day the people surprised me by setting the grassy valley floor on fire, and, following the fire line, they simply collected the roasted animals and birds. Since *daajaaj* — the giant fruit bat — was also called "bird," it was hunted with bow and arrow like any large bird, but only at night. Often I woke up to the loud clapping sound of a bat's wings as it tried to settle on the ripening bananas next to my house. Immediately my alert boys would take up their bows and arrows, and on many occasions they succeeded in shooting the feasting animals. While hunting fruit bats on a moonlit night my friend Kaadotajbii, the witch doctor, was the victim of a freak accident. He spotted a large bat on a banana plant, aimed, and shot the animal dead. But as the dying bat fell, the butt end of the arrow took out the eye of my unfortunate friend. Naturally the accident was interpreted as an evil deed of the dangerous spirit Ukwaanija.

Thorough anthropological research usually includes documentation of the culture and ecology. Accordingly I decided to make an ethnographic collection for the Yale Peabody Museum and augment it with culturally important plant and animal material. Professor Charles Remington was kind enough to equip me with butterfly nets, transparent envelopes, formaldehyde, and a sizable cyanide jar for killing insects and reptiles. The last item caused problems when on my way to New Guinea I stopped in Sydney, Australia. The customs officer declared that I could not import such deadly stuff into the country. The chief of the customs office was called in and told me that the amount of cyanide I was carrying could, if spilled into the city's water supply, kill all of Sydney. My assurances that this was not my intention were brushed aside. So I suggested that I deposit the jar with customs and pick it up upon my departure. After a lengthy debate, the chief, fearing a possible accident, allowed me to take the jar and begged me to be careful with it. I promised that I would.

Later in New Guinea after having settled into my newly built house I started to buy material goods from the natives — nets, net bags, bows, arrows, feather decorations, stone and wooden tools, shell- and tooth-decorated necklaces, and shell money. Some of my collecting followed unconventional paths. For example, in 1959 I traveled with my entourage of Ijaaj clan boys and friends to the Obano flats on the shore of Paniai Lake, where we had to wait for the government boat to ferry us to Enarotali. While waiting in the grassy area we were spotted by members of the local clans, traditional enemies of ours. They screamed insults from the mountain slopes around us and discharged arrows at us. We collected the ammunition, not to shoot back at them but to tie into bundles to be shipped to the Peabody Museum. Whenever they stopped shooting I would step out from behind of our luggage, which had become our buffer, and shout more insults up the mountain slopes. There would come a fresh volley of arrows — all future contributions to the Peabody collection.

Other material collected in this region, whose inhabitants fought the Dutch colonial government in 1956, was more grisly in nature. I bought a pendant — a war trophy — which was actually a dried index finger. Since the finger was well manicured, I presumed it belonged to the local missionary who had been killed during the insurrection. During this military engagement Kapauku troops from other valleys passed through Obano, and on seeing a white man along with his wife and children, killed all of them, not knowing that they were friends of the local people, respected and loved by them — a common error in wartime. I made another such purchase in this region unwittingly. In 1959 I bought lots of shell and tooth necklaces. When my bags were opened at the Peabody Museum one of my graduate students came to me with one of the necklaces, made of netted inner bark string and decorated with what appeared to be slices of polished bailer shell. "What is this material?" he asked pointing to the white slices. "Bailer shell," I explained. "Can't be," he protested and to my amazement bent the white slices like rubber. Slowly, very slowly, I realized what I had purchased. The white pendants on the necklace were made from the keys from the mission's organ — an organ I had played while visiting with the missionaries in the past. The family was survived by one child who had been away at the crucial time with friends in Enarotali, the center of the Dutch administration in the region.

Another item I collected was a beautiful large necklace whose woven base of netted inner bark string was decorated with Nassarius and true cowry shells with a fringe of teeth from a canine. This heirloom had been worn by an old man who had been brought to my house in bad shape, suffering from an abdominal ulceration. Several days before, I had offered to buy this necklace for a large sum, but the man had firmly turned down my offer, explaining that the piece had been passed down in his family from generation to generation and that his son should have it after his death. His sons, who brought the ill man to me several days later, pleaded with me to operate on the abscess. In vain I tried to explain that I did not know anything about surgery. Kapauku operate only on open wounds, usually those made by an arrow, and not something like this — a swollen abdomen which had already turned blue-green. The sons assured me that if their father died I would not be held responsible, that he was expected to die anyway if I could not help him. I could see their point, so I decided to try my luck. I prepared my medical equipment, smeared the man's abdomen with iodine, heated a Gillette blade over the fire, and made a courageous slice into the worst spot on the abdominal wall, praying that the ulcer would be located between the skin and peritoneum. Fortunately for the patient and me, this was the case. A huge amount of exudate poured out of the man's abdomen. After removing as much of it as possible, I cleaned the bleeding wound and dressed it with sterile pads and adhesive tape. The man survived the operation. To improve the man's chances of further recovery (not to say save his life), I gave him a large dose of terramycin antibiotic. I then gave additional pills to the man's son with instructions on how to administer them. Three weeks later, to my amazement, the man came walking to my house, unaided by his accompanying sons. He came to thank me for my performance and, with the enthusiastic agreement of both his sons, gave me his heirloom necklace as a gift. Delighted, I accepted, but reciprocated with gifts of an ax, knife, and machete. Everyone was happy. I have to confess that this was my first and last "fee" for performing surgery. After all, how many anthropologists can boast of having received remuneration for surgery?

In addition to these objects, it was important that I collect samples of plants, marsupials, reptiles, insects, spiders, crustaceans, and birds in order to have their scientific names identified, and to be precise in describing their dietary and technological uses. For this task, my forty-eight adopted sons and five daughters were indispensable. They fanned out into the swamps and forests and brought back many varieties of plants — their stems, blossoms, leaves, and seeds. I would sit in my house and receive the researchers, register the plants, and press them between newspaper pages, thus creating a crude herbarium. From trees, my team collected wood, bark, blossoms, leaves, and fruit. For all these types of vegetation we identified Kapauku names, their uses and their cultural and literary importance. Upon my return to the United States, I sent parts of this large herbarium to different experts at various universities for botanical identification. I employed a similar procedure for collecting insects. The boys and girls roamed the countryside catching specimens by hand or in butterfly nets and brought them to my house, where again I documented their names and cultural significance and killed them in my cyanide jar. Afterwards I dried them in front of my fireplace in the evening and deposited them into various boxes and envelopes. The collectors were rewarded with three beads for each new species, or one if I already had the insect or plant in my collection. This intensive collection process occupied us for four consecutive days in February 1955, then again for three days in 1959, and again in 1962. Throughout my research periods I continued to add to my collections in a nonsystematic way. Special help was provided to me by a visiting entomologist, a Dr. Gressit of the Bernice Bishop Museum, who stayed with me in August 1955, and Dr. Sedláček and Dr. Wilson, who collected around my house in Itoda in August 1962.

Intermittently during my stay I collected and pickled in formaldehyde lizards, frogs, snakes, land crabs, crayfish, bats, aquatic insects and spiders. I caught the spiders in my house. Several times the large hairy spiders called *wogaa* fell on my bed, and I rushed for my cyanide jar. The poor devils had no chance. When I delivered the pickled spiders to Professor Petrunkewitch, a spider specialist at Yale, he was absolutely delighted. In a couple of weeks he called me and told me with great excitement that my collection contained 24 different species of which 18 were previously unknown. I greeted this news with a mixture of delight and frustration, realizing I would not be able to include the names of these species in my new book — Professor Petrunkewitch had to name them all. As compensation for my frustration, I hope Professor Petrunkewitch named at least one of the species "Pospisilensis" or "Leopoldensis" — I have never checked.

In my research on consumption and hunting, I gathered data on the amount and kind of animals hunted. Because trapping rats in snares or catching them by hand in their burrows was a common activity among young men and teenagers and was openly discussed, securing accurate information was no problem. The shooting and trapping of various other animals, however, tended to be kept secret. Some animals were large and meaty and would feed several people; the successful hunter was thus expected not only to share the catch with his relatives and friends but also to give each of his wives an equal share. Because the hunter usually had a favored wife in his polygynous family, or of necessity selected only one wife to share the venison with, he had to keep his hunting success secret. Consumption therefore took place secretively, in the depth of the tropical forest, so that the other wives, relatives, or friends would not know. Consequently, it was difficult for me to get an exact count of animals shot and consumed, and any identification of the species might be inaccurate. I surmounted this difficulty by paying for information and keeping the results secret. I paid extra fees for the bones and especially the skulls of the consumed animals. Professor Robinson then identified the collected bone material for me at Yale. After identification I gave the bone material to the Peabody Museum and to my surprise I found that my collection was the largest in the United States at that time.

As for birds, I collected their names, cultural significance, and artifacts decorated with their feathers. I also collected the whole skins of killed birds. I paid the natives to skin them and then they satisfied themselves with the meat. The feathers of the birds of paradise were magnificent. Eating the meat of these birds seemed to be of equal importance to the natives as using their feathers. The plumage was not only beautiful but also widely varied in shape and size. Thus a small bird might have tail or head feathers that were four times longer than its body. When I first received a couple of feathers of the King of Saxony bird of paradise I returned them, thinking they had been cut from some sort of plastic received from a missionary somewhere. Only subsequently when I received whole skins of these birds did I realize my mistake. When I turned in this collection to Professor Dillon Ripley, an ornithologist and then curator at the Peabody Museum, he surprised me by admitting that he had no skins of the King of Saxony in his inventory of birds of paradise at the museum.

The Kapauku people's knowledge of entomology was encyclopedic. They had names for all the species. They knew about the insect life cycle, from egg to larva, to pupa, and finally to adult. Their knowledge often surpassed my own. For example, I wrongly assumed that dragonfly larvae passed through the pupa stage, which the natives denied. Being arrogant in my ignorance, I was not convinced until Professor Charles Remington at Yale University confirmed what my Papuan friends had insisted on. The Kapauku classification of insects was fascinating. Instead of using genetically based categories, their taxonomy and nomenclature was based on their economic role. Accordingly, a generic name was applied to all small edible insects living near streams and collected together in the same gathering operation. When an adult species became important by virtue of being edible, it was called by a specific name and its larvae named as "child of that particular insect." So a mole cricket was called *ibabi* and its larva *ibabi joka*, "the child of ibabi." If edibility was reversed, the adult form was called "mother of a specified larva" — as was the case with *abuubo*, a large green edible caterpillar, and *abuubo-ukwa*, "mother of abuubo," the huge and spectacular adult moth. If both the adult form and the larva were edible, both had specific unrelated names — for example, an adult dragonfly was known as *kunaajwii* and its larva, *jukuga*. Indeed, if the product of an insect was of major economic importance the adult insect was called "mother of that product." Thus the stingless bee was called *jomi-ikwa*, "mother of wax," because it was its wax that was collected, the honey being considered inedible.

Once, when we were crossing the mountain pass of Ijaajdimi, my boys and other companions on the trip spotted a beehive. Immediately they descended upon it, ripped it apart, and started to smack at the larvae and bees while neglecting the honey. Finally, to my horror they took the honeycombs to a nearby creek and started to wash out the honey to obtain clean wax. I stopped them, took hold of a honeycomb and started to feast on the honey. The people screamed in disgust, "Do you know what you are eating?" "Well, tell me," I replied. "What you're eating is the feces of the bees." "Nonsense," I replied, and then explained to them that the bee swallows the nectar from a blossom, predigests it in its stomach, and then regurgitates it into the comb. I expected that this explanation would be satisfactory and would contribute to the people's diet. To my surprise they replied, "This is even worse than feces! What you're actually eating is the bees' vomit." So I had to eat my honey behind a bush in order not to make my companions sick. While they feasted on the larvae, which were not appetizing to me, I ate my honey, which was nauseating to them. Both types of food were perfect for consumption, but our different cultural values dictated otherwise.

I amassed two additional types of collection. While one was very easy to gather, the other presented a serious logistical problem. The simple one consisted of collecting soil samples from various fields at different depths. The Connecticut Agricultural Station in New Haven subsequently analyzed these samples for me. They revealed the chemical and biotic composition of the soil at different locations within the Botukebo village area. I could then compare these values with the harvest of cultigens in the various gardens. The second collection posed a formidable array of problems. In 1962 I decided to collect samples of human blood so that I could link them to my genealogical and anthropometric data. Blood collection from the Kapauku presented many difficulties. First I had to quell the people's fear of needles, which was actually not too difficult. By the time I planned to do the collecting, during my second research period, in August 1959, I had gained the trust of most of the people. A medical technician came to my residence in Itoda, where I announced that we would help the people medically by injecting them with penicillin against yaws, treating their eye and skin infections, and distributing free aspirin and sulfa drugs to treat various other ailments. Those willing to sell us their blood would be paid. Many people showed up for the treatment, but there was still the problem of collecting blood.

In their society, the Kapauku believe in different types of magic, one of which is the "contagious type." That means that if I am in possession of part of somebody else's body — hair, nail clippings, etc. — or a closely associated object, I could perform sorcery over those objects and thus injure or kill the individual to whom they belong. In other words I would have him or her in my power, at my mercy. Following this reasoning, blood was believed to be more susceptible to manipulation than other less vital items. Fortunately, all my sons and daughters volunteered, along with their close relatives, my friends, and their relatives, so that I ended up with a neat collection of 124 test tubes.

Keeping the blood cool and thus preventing spoilage was another challenge. Anticipating such a problem prior to my departure from the United States, I had purchased several large Thermos flasks with wide openings, into which the test tubes fitted perfectly. I also designed a transport scheme and schedule, which was intended to keep the blood quite cold. Since the American missions on or close to our route back to Enarotali at Paniai Lake had refrigerators, special patrols of boys were dispatched to bring fresh ice to our transport route at various points. So first the collected blood was cooled in the cold brook behind my house, then the test tubes were loaded into the Thermos flasks partially filled with ice, and on the route every night we replaced the old, half-melted ice cubes with fresh ones brought from the missions. When we arrived at Enarotali, the government settlement on Paniai Lake, we deposited the blood in the refrigerator at the local "hospital." The Dutch airline KLM, whose pilots unbelievably picked up fresh ice on the island of Biak and then again in Amsterdam en route to the United States, arranged further transport.

The gravest danger my blood test tubes faced was in New York, where customs would not let them be "imported." They simply had no directives about the import of human blood. At the insistence of the KLM pilots, however, customs did refrigerate the blood and after two days of deliberation and discussions cleared it for transport to Michigan University.

The whole operation, thanks to the KLM pilots and my Papuan friends, was a tremendous success. All the blood samples except for three were good for not only blood group analysis but also the identification of hemoglobin. As I was told at the time, in 1959, this was the largest blood sample ever analyzed for the Pacific. Also, it contained the first Diego positive blood for that area. Since none of the samples belonged to the B blood group, this was further proof of Joseph Birdsell's claim that the Pacific region was free of B-type blood until it was introduced from the Asian mainland to New Guinea (among coastal Papuans, 27 percent were type B in their [1960] samples). Together with Professor Buettner-Janusch (1960) I published a paper on these findings. Unfortunately, my notes were subsequently lost in his laboratory, so I could not link the blood types to my genealogies and anthropometric measurements of individuals. That taught me a lesson for life: never surrender any original data unless you have a duplicate record in your possession.

Kapauku Culture and the Concept of "Primitive Society"

In the nineteenth century anthropologists of various schools of thought (evolutionists, Marxists, diffusionists) created the concept of what they and their followers called primitive society. This concept spread within the discipline almost like an infallible dogma, and some tenets of it persist in the literature to this day. The idea of a "primitive society" (what we now call "tribal society") generally assumes that it is egalitarian, usually collectivistic, lawless and not market-oriented (no laws of supply and demand prevail, and there is no true money). Some claim it is leaderless, and that its members possess pre-logical and so-called "concrete" mentality, that is, a lack of ability to think abstractly. An empirical study of a wild and politically (i.e. colonially) uncontrolled Neolithic tribal society would provide proof of the concept's universal applicability. Since my study of the Kapauku, a non-colonial, politically and legally untouched people, many of whom saw me as their first white man, I feel qualified to check the correctness of this concept and its universal applicability to tribal people. I shall compare the particular tenets of the theory with the facts from the Kapauku society.

1. *Tribal people are collectivists, which means that members of a lineage, sub-lineage, clan, or other type of social segment share the means of production in common ownership* (Llewellen 1983; p. 21, Johnson 1989, p. 50). Rather than being collectivists, the Kapauku are extreme individualists. Everything is owned by individuals, even large drainage ditches, tracts of tropical rain forest, and large or small bridges.

2. *Tribal people possess a simple economy.* On the contrary, the Kapauku economy is a true market economy in which laws of supply and demand determine prices. It employs loans, savings, interest charged on some loans, true money, speculation, investment

trusts, extension of credit, paramount influence in the political sphere, etc.

3. *Exchange is reciprocal.* (Especially Llewellen 1983, p. 20; Polanyi, 1957, p. 43), Marx (1966), Sahins (1972, pp. 300–312). This does not apply to Kapauku society. Prices are determined by supply and demand, fluctuating by as much as 100 percent, and are a dominant factor in Kapauku marketplaces, pig feasts, *dedomai*, and *tapa* ceremonies.

4. *There is no true money.* Kapauku pay with currency consisting of several types of cowry shells (Cuprea moneta) and glass beads (introduced through intertribal trade from the coast). It is not a tribal variety of "special-purpose money" known in Africa, Pacific, or the Americas. It is a universal means of exchange, a measure of value, and medium of payment of fines and compensation.

5. *Economy activity is based on barter.* Barter, the usual exchange of goods in tribal societies, is negligible. Sales account for 90 percent of trade.

6. *Society is egalitarian* (Llewellyn 1983, pp. 22, 25, 93, Marx 1966. Herskowits 1985, Polanyi 1947 and many other anthropologists). In Kapauku society, this is not the case. There are rich people and paupers. While Ekajewaijokaipouja had a fortune amounting to an estimated 250,000 U.S. dollars, Pigikiiwode was severely indebted to the tune of about 30,000 U.S. dollars.

7. *Tribal people are not profit-motivated.* (Polanyl 1947, p. 663, Thurnwald 1932). But the Kapauku certainly are. Most tasks and goods are paid for, such as land, houses, canoes, artifacts, labor, wives, game, pork, pigs, chicken, as well as the services of witch doctors, sorcerers, dentists. One also has to pay for causing somebody grief, which means that if anybody cries at a funeral, the main heir has to pay him compensation. Similarly, if someone becomes so emotional that he starts to perform a mad dance (*wainai*), then his best friend is supposed to pay him with a good-sized pig. Killing an enemy, avenging the death of a relative, losing a relative in war conducted because of an individual — all have to be paid for in monetary compensation.

8. *Primitive society is not wealth-oriented like capitalist societies.* Among the Kapauku, however, the richest man becomes not only a political leader or *tonowi* — he also functions as a judge in his unit and as an economic authority, sponsoring pig feasts and economic ceremonies (markets) *dedomai* and *tapa.* Rich men influence the markets and prices of goods, and they command a fellowship of debtors. If this emphasis on wealth were applied to the United States, then there would be no elections — the richest man would become President, as well as Chief Justice of the Supreme Court.

9. *Primitive societies are leaderless.* Far from being leaderless, all Kapauku societal segments, sub-lineages, lineages, and confederations of lineages have their leaders. There has probably never been a leaderless society in the world.

10. *Absence of law is a feature of all "primitive societies"* (Pershits 1977, Marx 1966, etc.). The Kapauku have a very sophisticated legal system. According to my empirically based theory of law there has never been, and cannot be, a lawless and leaderless functioning human society. Indeed, even a pack of wolves, herds of caribou, and wild horses have their leaders! Law does not emerge as a result of social evolution as, for example, the evolutionists and the Marxists would have it.

11. *Primitive society is static* (Pershits 1977: p. 411). If this were true, civilization could never have emereged. Kapauku society is dynamic; its culture changes with time, sometimes dramatically, as for example my account of incest taboos documents (Pospisil 1958b pp. 832-837).

12. *There is no division of labor in tribal ("primitive") society* (Durkeim 1893: p. 77, also Llewellen 1983, p. 25). Labor is divided among the Kapauku on the basis of sex, age, health, and specialized skills. They have full-time traders, matchmakers, bow makers and net bag manufacturers, as well as part-time witch doctors and dentists (gum cutters, extractionists) — all properly paid for their work.

13. In his book Ancient Law, Sir Henry Maine sees *a universal change in human social evolution from status orientation to a contract-dom-*

inated society (1963: pp. 163, 164 165). Yet the Kapauku economy and other aspects of their social organization are simply ridden with contracts, while emphasis on status was brought to this society by the colonial administration of the Dutch and later by the Indonesians.

14. Pershits (1977: p. 410), Marx (1966), and Lenin *attribute a putative lack of law in "primitive societies" to mononormatism, a concept which asserts that in these societies no distinction is made between morality (preferred behavior) and law (prescribed behavior). Separation of the two is said to have occurred later during the revolution, in what they call the "barbaric stage."* However, the Kapauku, as other well-studied tribal societies (e.g., Max Gluckman's 1967 account of the Lozi), clearly make that distinction. The Kapauku, for example, hold that full payment of the bride price may be requested legally (*kou dani tija*) anytime by the entitled party, i.e. the bride's father or brother, but morally (*kou dani enaa*) only after the bride has borne her first child.

15. *While members of a "primitive society" are supposed to possess a pre-logical (Levy Bruhl 1923) or concrete (Pershits 1977) mentality incapable of logical or abstract thought, this was thought to be a prerogative only of the "advanced" members of that society.* Again, the Kapauku employ a very sophisticated sexagesimal mathematical system in their economy and social life. And what, may I ask, could be more abstract than mathematics?

In conclusion I may say that some tenets of the "primitive society" theory are not to be found in any society. A minority of them may occur in some but certainly not in all, as demonstrated in the case of the Kapauku. Most of the Kapauku cultural characteristics I have enumerated and identified shape the common features of their cultural personality, a discussion of which follows.

Kapauku Personality

The most striking aspect of the Kapauku personality was its individualism. It permeated their culture and their behavior. Their economic undertakings, for example, were all motivated by consideration of self as an independent individual. *Ani beu kai peu* (I need), or "I want to do it for my own benefit," was a commonly heard phrase. I never heard a Kapauku justify an action or argument in terms of social need. Because of this egocentric thinking it was not surprising that all commodities were owned individually; there was no common property. Canoes, houses, pigs and land all had a single owner. As I pointed out in my discussion on being a participant observer, each part of the forest, and each pole constituting the bridge over the Edege River was owned individually. A main drainage ditch conducting surplus water from a large garden area was owned by many different people, yet it was not a communal structure. It had not been excavated by people working together as a team. Indeed, the ditch represented a conglomeration of individual ownership rights to segments of it, determined by ownership of the land that the excavation crossed. These sections had been excavated individually and maintained by their individual owners. Wild animals became individual property as soon as a man or woman killed or caught them. When a man asked somebody to help him or to do a job for him — such as building a fence, digging a ditch, making a garden, keeping his pigs — he was actually proposing a business deal for which the worker would be reimbursed. There might be reciprocation in kind, but again this reflected not a sense of sharing in a common enterprise, but repayment of a debt for past help.

The individualistic orientation of the Kapauku was inculcated at a very early age. A young boy would be given a section of his father's garden, where he would plant and harvest the male-linked cultigens (sugar cane, bananas, amaranthus, green, taro, and so on) while his little sister had a plot of sweet potatoes. This they would work on their own, rather than simply helping their parents. The parents would teach them agronomic skills, but that was all. Kapauku men and women tended to work alone, so that their accomplishments could be clearly distinguished from those of other workers. Young boys and girls often played host to their parents, giving them produce which their proud parents had to reciprocate. A young boy would have his own property and income and sometimes his father would borrow from him in order to teach him the business of loan and credit transactions. In some cases this teaching assumed extraordinary proportions. For example, one day while walking through Botukebo village I heard screaming, loud crying and lamentation. When I discovered the source of the noise I was confronted with an unbelievable scene. An adult man was squatting inside his house and receiving intermittent blows from an infuriated youngster, his own son, about eleven years of age. The father did not put up any resistance and howled with each blow. At my approach the boy stopped and disappeared into the house. When I asked the man for an explanation, he looked warily around to make sure his son was gone, then with a sly smile told me that he had borrowed cowry money from his son but had failed to repay it on demand, as prescribed by custom and law. His son became enraged and hit him. "But why didn't you repay him?" I asked. "My son has to learn business," the father replied. "In business one should not loan money without prior assurance of payment, and so I gave him an exemplary lesson. My boy will be quite a businessman, but he has to learn not to trust anybody. By the way, he flunked the test," he said, smiling. "I made a pretty good deal. By giving way to his emotions and hitting me, he forfeited his right to get the money back. His blows were very weak, so I made a good deal. He has to learn to control his emotions in fiscal matters." From my Western perspective, this behavior was shocking. I could not visualize my own father giving me such a harsh lesson, and even less my beating him in turn. However, I could certainly see the educational value of this lesson, which must have stuck.

Field experiences like this completely shook my trust in the then-fashionable anthropological dogma that tribal people have no laws, and that tribal people, unlike us in the Western capitalist world, share their resources and land and enjoy "primitive collectivism." Certainly Polanyi's categorical claim, based on no personal fieldwork experience, that a tribal community "keeps all its membership from starving unless it is itself borne down by catastrophe, in which case interests are again threatened collectively, not individually" (Polanyi and Arensberg, 1957: 46) sounds to me more like the expression of a creed than a valid scientific generalization. In fact, among the Kapauku, individualism allows natives, particularly children from poor homes, to become malnourished or even to develop kwashiorkor, a lethal protein deficiency, while children from well-off neighboring households are well fed. For example, members of the Kamutaga household of Botukebo village were starving, while their neighbors from the prosperous house of Timajjokainaago lived in plenty. When I asked Timajjokainaago why he did not give some food to his neighbor's children, he replied, surprised by my question; "Why should I? It is the responsibility of the adults there to feed their children, not mine. They all are lazy, do not work much in their gardens and do not hunt and collect insects." Unfortunately, his accusation was true. My distrust of anthropological generalizations about primitive collectivism is also based on the fact that nowhere in the literature have I seen precise accounts of the value of personal property and assets of individuals, a lapse that perpetuates the myth of economic egalitarianism in "primitive" societies. One corollary to this myth is a belief in the absence of wealthy individuals among tribal people. Yet, the Kapauku had their *tonowi* and the Eskimo their *unmealit*. In fact, the disparities in wealth in the Kamu Valley were striking. While Ekajewaijokaipouga had amassed a fortune of about $250,000 in 1955, Ijaaj Pigikiiwode of Botukebo was $30,000 in debt. I calculated the dollar value of their financial status on the basis of the price of a pound of pork, which in 1955 was fifty cents in American currency. Using cowry shell money, I could easily translate all the Kapauku property into pounds of pork.

Kapauku individualism is not limited to their economy. The Kapauku headman, *tonowi*, achieves his position through his own effort and skill in accumulating great wealth and in redistributing it cleverly among his less prosperous tribesmen, who become his debtors and thus dependable supporters in political, legal, and social affairs. Because the assumption of leadership does not follow any rules of inheritance, election, or appointment by a superior, and everything depends on individual effort, most of the political leaders are self-made men. Every *tonowi* decides legal cases himself; consequently there are no formal councils of elders, juries, or governing bodies composed of several members. Since premeditated action and movement were held as basic conditions of life, Kapauku law did not compel people by force or threat of force into a specific desired behavior. Rather, it punished them for their past deeds only. Headmen would try to persuade their constituents to comply with their decision through oratory, or by threatening the withdrawal of credit or refusal to grant any future monetary support. In this way the peoples' individual freedom was preserved; they always had a choice either to comply with the headman's decision and receive his economic support and protection, or to disregard his decision for their immediate benefit but often with disastrous long-term financial consequences. Generally a single influential individual, after pronouncing his verdict, must try through rhetoric to convince his equally individualistic constituency to accept his political and legal decisions. So, for example, my best friend Jokagaibo, the headman of the Ijaaj Jamaina sub-lineage, who in 1955 was about forty years old, was the son of a rather poor man of little importance. His grandfather, although very knowledgeable in native law and lore, had never achieved political, legal, or economic prominence. All Jokagaibo's success in politics and his accumulation of economic assets, as well as five wives, was due to his own initiative, industry, skill in handling his financial affairs, and personal courage in oratory as well as in war. At the same time, he was kind and generous to those who deserved help. It was his shrewd judgment to embrace the opportunity of further success when I appeared — the first white man in the south Kamu Valley. It was his pig that I received as a welcome gift to a stranger, it was his land given to me to build my house on, and it was he who became not only my best informant but also my advocate, supporter, and in times of trouble and war my faithful friend and protector. Although I am convinced Jokagaibo did all this, at least later, altruistically, he did derive benefits from my friendship. On many occasions he induced me to intervene on behalf of the Kapauku with the Dutch government, and since his influence over me was very well known, his prestige soared. In 1956 he refused to fight against the Dutch during the widespread native revolt, and by 1958 he was headman of the whole Ijaaj-Pigome confederacy, gradually replacing his aging second uncle Ekajewaijokaipouga. Due to the presence of the Dutch administration in the Kamu Valley (since 1956), the confederacy system collapsed and the former constituent lineages fused into two large units, one led by a friend of the Dutch local administrator in Moanemani and the other peacefully opposing colonial rule. Jokagaibo became the leader of the latter. On my return visits in 1975 and 1979 I found him to be the leader of all the Kapauku of the vast Kamu Valley, a rich and highly respected man with fifteen wives and numerous children.

For the Kapauku, individualism defined even such typically communal activity as war. Patterns of warfare were shaped along individualistic lines. When I first witnessed the Kapauku in combat, I was surprised to see no phalanxes, no groups of warriors attacking enemy lines in a well-organized way. Instead, the men dispersed so that the success of individuals was well documented and independent. A victory dance identified the successful warriors and marksmen, so that later they could claim their reward from the "owner of the war" for killing individual enemies. For there was always an *ipuwe*, owner of the war, a man for whom the war was being conducted. This *ipuwe* would pay a reward to the killers of his enemy as well as reimburse close paternal relatives for the loss of lives of those fighting on his side. Thus, even war was conceived as primarily an affair of one individual, aided in battle by his patrilineal relatives and other members of his confederacy, as well as allies and personal friends. War also involved snipers, individuals who tried to penetrate enemy battle lines, or at nightfall invade enemy villages, to make a kill.

All Kapauku ceremonies, whether secular or religious, were centered on individualism. For example, an *ipuwe* could be the "owner" of a pig feast, a money-collection ceremony (*tapa*), or a plain market (*dedomai*). He personally derived prestige or blame from the outcomes of these events. His possible co-sponsors always played a secondary role. The socially most important songs, *ugaa*, sung in the dance house during pig feasts or *tapa* ceremonies, were compositions of single individuals who regarded them as their personal property. Accordingly, my own *ugaa*, which I composed as a practical joke, was mine — no one dared to use parts of it to compose songs of their own. Plagiarizing was not only a mark of bad taste but could have legal repercussions. The Kapauku, being basically secular, had shamans conduct their religious ceremonies for particular practical purposes. Again it was an individual shaman and not a group of religious dignitaries who performed healing, money generating, rain-stopping, or enemy-killing ceremonies. The rest of the people present at such occasions were either spectators or passive objects of the performance (as, for example, a patient being cured). In some respects, religious ceremonies were solo acts of a particular witch doctor, a rain-stopping or money-making expert, or a sorcerer.

Kapauku individualism is most pronounced in their economy. Every society places value on some achievement from which an individual can derive prestige. In the United States, it is the accumulation of wealth. In European dictatorships, such as those of the Nazis, fascists, and Communists, prestige was derived from prowess in war. What counted there were the medals on the chests of warriors rather than bank accounts. In contrast, in Chinese civilization, it was knowledge and artisanship that elevated individuals above their peers. While the coastal Papuans emphasized success in war, the Kapauku Papuans lived in a wealth-oriented society. At the time of my research, their shell money represented everything a man could strive for. In this respect, they resembled Americans, yet their emphasis on individual wealth exceeded that of our own.

The Kapauku values of individualism and wealth accumulation extended to war. Many Kapauku went to war almost as mercenaries, helping befriended confederacies even when their own clan was not involved. They did this not only because of loyalty to friends but also because a successful archer who kills an enemy might expect a large monetary payment for his exploit in the form of *dabe uwo*, or blood reward (literally "muddy water"). It often seemed to me that a Kapauku would do almost anything for profit. In war, shell money often solved a difficult strategic problem. Because the Kapauku considered it highly immoral to shoot at a female during battle (even accidentally wounding a woman with a stray arrow could ruin a man's reputation), they not only collected used arrows for their husbands during combat, but also would climb the hills behind enemy lines, watch their movements, and shout advice to their husbands. The most effective way to fend off these women, however, was to throw cowries or beads down the hill. The wives, temporarily forgetting the war, their husbands, and their mission, would follow the cowries and beads, trying to retrieve them from the tall grass at the bottom of the hill. When I first witnessed the Kapauku in combat at Mujikebo, the sight of the women collecting the used arrows, unperturbed by the battle, gave the whole affair a sort of farcical flavor. I learned from this experience, and I used the money-throwing trick any time I wanted to stop my boys from fighting, if I thought there was a danger of serious injury, especially when they used heavy sticks on some outsiders. As soon as my blue beads hit the battleground, all animosity was forgotten and the combatants on both sides would feverishly scramble for the money.

My fifteen-year-old adopted daughter Peronika demonstrated the Kapauku profit motive to me quite convincingly. She was a very intelligent girl. She and Antonia, another of my adopted daughters, cooked for me and kept my household. Toward the end of my stay in 1955 when a Dutch officer visited me and we talked about the intelligence of the natives, I pointed out several individuals whom I regarded as brilliant. The officer was skeptical. Since I had identified Peronika as one of the very bright individuals, I challenged him to test her intelligence. He agreed to conduct an experiment with her. He offered her beads for a performance of a man's mad dance (*waita tai*), which if performed by a woman would look ridiculous. Peronika readily accepted the proposition and acted like a clown as long as the beads kept coming. All the Kapauku who watched the prancing girl laughed, together with the officer. When he thought he had enough proof of the girl's silliness and naïveté he remarked disparagingly: "And this is your clever girl!" I translated his remark to Peronika and reproached her for letting me down. I told her that her buffoonery had convinced the officer that she was silly, even stupid. "I'm not so sure who is actually more stupid," she laughed. "I who performed the silly things or the man who paid for the performance."

To convince this man of how intelligent the Kapauku really were, I told the officer that I had explained to them that earth is like a ball (I used my tennis ball for the demonstration) and spins around its axis as it turns around the sun, a ball of fire. Again the officer was doubtful about the people's ability to understand, claiming they would simply assure me they understood my lecture on the solar system just to make me happy. He said that they might mechanically repeat what I had said, but did not actually comprehend the implications of my statements. To demonstrate his point he asked one of my older boys, "How will your father get to his home in America? Which way will he travel there?" Ijaaj Itoogi, without hesitation pointed to the northeast and said: "He will go this way." Then he stopped, hesitated and said, pointing in the opposite direction; "He could also go this way, but it would take him longer." Both the officer and I were very pleasantly surprised.

The profit motive of the Kapauku in war was well known to all Dutch officers and missionaries. Indeed, it even entered into their dealings with parish priests in already missionized and colonized regions of the Paniai, Tage, and Tigi Lake areas. One story illustrating the people's lust for profit went the rounds in many European outposts and became so notorious that it was even referenced in the title of a book about the Kapauku (Smedts, 1955). In one region of the vast Kapauku territory that had been brought under the control of the Dutch, people regularly visited and enjoyed Sunday services at a Franciscan mission church. Usually after services were over, the kind missionary stood by the church door and distributed tobacco to the men and candy to the women and children as they were leaving the church. The people were regarded as having been already converted to Christianity. The supply of tobacco had begun to run out, however, and the missionary had to wait several weeks for new supplies. As the tobacco distribution dwindled, the church attendance dwindled accordingly, until it stopped altogether. When the unhappy missionary asked the local Kapauku headman the reason for the people's neglect of their spiritual needs, the headman explained the problem briefly and succinctly: "No tobacco, no hallelujah."

The profit-conscious Kapauku and the high value they placed on the accumulation of individual wealth would militate against wasteful expenditures on religious and other ceremonial observances. Accordingly the people were highly secular in their world outlook. Their ceremonial life concerned mainly the realm of economy, largely neglecting the supernatural. Magical elements did feature in some events such as pig feasts, *tapa* (money-collecting ceremonies), pig markets, and wedding and birth ceremonies, but they were all simple and not considered important to the rich sponsors of the events. Many even told me in confidence they were not convinced that magical rites were essential to the success of a feast or other financial transaction. Of paramount importance was the people's own effort and skill. The most elaborate ceremonies were associated with the native economy. Ostensibly religious ceremonies had a secular purpose such as curing a sick man or killing an enemy rather than propitiating a spirit or god. There was a conspicuous absence of life crisis ceremonies, initiation rites, carving of images of supernatural beings, and preoccupation with the dead. This reflects a personal secularism that stands in stark contrast to the Papuan cultures of the New Guinea coastal areas.

In Kapauku culture, the emphasis on individualism and monetary wealth did not preclude principles of morality and justice. The Kapauku would not do anything only for profit. In a sense they were not pragmatists: they had principles and limits to behavior that no profit motive would make them violate. In other words, the American "rugged individual" in business was not a model a decent Kapauku — meaning most Kapauku — would try to emulate. A clash of opinions between Ekajewaijokaipouga and myself illustrates this point. In September, 1955, Ekajewaijokaipouga, the headman of the

Ijaaj-Pigome confederacy, came to my house in Itoda accompanied by many of his constituents and exhorted me, the white man in general, and the Franciscan pastor of Ugapuga in particular, to give presents to his people indiscriminately. He had heard that the first Dutch administrator who entered Kapauku territory in the Paniai Lake region had distributed gifts lavishly. Being a skilled politician, he became quite emotional and started to perform *wainai*, the mad dance. He claimed that a white man did not give to everybody, but only to his friends, that this had been demonstrated over and over again. We, white men, *ba ewo* — were not generous (literally "do not know how to defecate"). I indignantly pointed out how much I had already given to the people, to my friends, most of whom were members of his own confederacy. I turned to him and asked, "What have you given me?" That shocked him quite a bit. He stopped his reproaches, became for some moments pensive, and then declared he was ashamed of himself, and that I was right. To show how sincerely he felt his shame he offered me, as Kapauku morality prescribes, one of his pigs as consolation. I refused the gift on the ground that I did not accept such *jegeka*, a gift given without the duty of immediate reciprocation. Later the same day, in Botukebo village, he told me that he was so ashamed he would not come to Itoda anymore. I objected that this would be wrong, that everybody gets carried away sometimes by their emotions, that now it was as if nothing had been said. I even shared with him an example of how I had became over-emotional while arguing with a Marxist who had insisted that Stalin was indeed "good old Joe," as President Truman put it.

This story made Ekajewaijokaipouga so happy that he embraced me and we were again "best friends." The only after-effect of our clash was that ruthless people were henceforth labeled Stalins (*Talini* in Kapauku pronunciation), and gullible, naively trusting individuals Marxists (*Magekiti* in Kapauku).

I have never seen or heard of a Western (let alone a Marxist) politician who would publicly acknowledge his mistake and propose as penance the voluntary surrender of a large amount of his property. In contrast, Kapauku individualism, competition, market orientation, and profit motivation were checked by moral principles, helping to keep tribal capitalism within the bounds of decency.

Of course, there were immoral individuals within Kapauku society whose lust for easy money made them thieves and embezzlers. Indeed, these two types of offenses were the most common among what we Americans would deem violations of criminal law. Crimes involving physical violence, in comparison, were rare. Robbery involving taking somebody's property by force or under threat was conspicuously absent. On the other hand, theft of pigs, garden produce, building materials, weapons, and other personal possessions was rather frequent. Since the victims, being Kapauku, were remarkably extroverted, one could hear their screams and lamentations over great distances as soon as the theft was discovered. Many days I listened to loud wailing, especially by women standing on elevated ground so that their grief and accusations could be heard far and wide. For example, one morning in June, 1955 when I stepped out of my hut into a beautiful sunny day, I was greeted from the cliff above my house (on the slopes of Kemuge Mountain) by a wailing woman who had just discovered that many poles from the fence she was constructing had disappeared overnight. This public display was not only an emotional outlet to the bereaved person, but also an alert to the general population. A witness might come forward with the identity of the thief, along with evidence to back up his or her accusation.

The secular outlook and emphasis on empiricism of the Kapauku was combined with an insistence on logic. The native religion was a logically consistent system. Once one accepted the basic tenets — for example, the omnipotence, omniscience, and omnipresence of god X — the religious system presented no controversial issues that required resolution by insistence on unquestioned dogmas. Ugatame, the Kapauku Creator, was omnipotent and because he created all existence he did not exist (he did not create himself). Ugatame was beyond existence in another realm of non-phenomenal reality. The Kapauku believed that nothing happens without the will of God, the Creator. The logical consequence of this belief was that man does not have absolutely free will, and therefore there is no place for sin and no reward or punishment after the death of an individual. There is no heaven or hell. The religion rested firmly on their fourfold epistemology whereby phenomenal reality was strictly, by application of the verb "to be" (*tou, topi*), distinguished from non-phenomenal beliefs, mental constructs, philosophical deductions, and speculation.

One could not learn Kapauku epistemology and religious conceptualizations from the questioning of informants. Kapauku epistemology resided deep in their subconscious, covert culture. As an anthropologist, I had to analyze and abstract all this from their beliefs, statements, and behavior. I had to have a thorough command of their language and culture in general, experimenting and frequently testing any abstract generalizations. Ignorance of language and culture precludes proper abstraction. Certainly a short cut by way of some modern and popular "subjective interpretation," coupled with total or partial ignorance of the language, would not do. Often an anthropologist has to go beyond the general statements of informants to get to the real story. So, for example, when I investigated the Kapauku concept of the universe I was told that rain was caused by Ukwanija, the evil water spirit floating in the clouds and urinating down on the people. Similarly, stars, I was told, were the lit butts of Kapauku cigarettes, a concoction of pandanus leaves folded and filled with tobacco, smoked by the evil spirits sitting high on the inverted bowl of the solid sky. Only later my best friends Jokagaibo and Awiitigaaj disclosed the fact that all this was kids' stuff that parents told their children. Then they expounded on their true theory of the universe — a wise and intelligent theory — as described in preceding chapters.

Kapauku Mathematics

The Kapauku emphasis on logical and systematic thinking and on exactitude was no better demonstrated than in their highly sophisticated mathematical system. Their emphasis on quantification was probably unmatched, except in a very few tribal cultures, of which, unfortunately I have no knowledge. Unlike their neighbors, the Kapauku count into the hundreds and even thousands. The importance of counting became clear to me a few days after my arrival at Paniai Lake. Whenever I gave a Papuan a few beads or a cowry shell, he would count them aloud. The Papuans also told me exactly how much they required for carrying my luggage for a day. Their fee, as it was interpreted to me at that time, was precise and uniform as to the number of shells or beads. However, when we arrived at the Debei Valley, with its well-known hostile natives, their fee doubled. So before I could say even a few necessary words, I had to learn to count to sixty. Without counting I would have been lost.

The Kapauku counting system, as it turned out, was of a sexagesimal type known only from Babylonian culture. Like the Babylonians, the Kapauku counted to sixty and then started over again, combining their otherwise decimal system with sixty. The Kapauku numerals from 1 to 10 were simple words: *ena, wija, wido, wee, idibi, benumi, pituwo, waguwo, ije, gaati*. The numerals 11 to 19, 21 to 29, and so on, were formed in a decimal way as 1 and 10 (*ena ma gaati*) 2 and 10 (*wija ma gaati*), and so on. The number 10, *gaati*, was derived from the Kapauku word *gai*, to think. Twenty was *mepiina*, 30 *jokagaati* or *amonaato*, 40 *mepiija*, 50 *gaati beu*, and 60 *bado*. Of these numerals it became clear to me that *amonaato* was derived from the words one half; *gaati beu* meant "10 minus" (therefore 50); and *bado*, a base, foot, or pedestal.

While reading my book on the Kapauku, Professor Derek de Solla Price (1966), a history of science specialist, was fascinated to find these parallels with the Babylonian mathematical system and brought them to my attention. The parallels were certainly striking. In Babylonian the numeral 30 was one half, 50 was minus ten, 60 was a base, and 10 related to the word thought. Only 20 and 40 made no sense to me. De Solla Price urged me to reconsider the two numerals, because the Babylonian 20 means "one third" and 40 "two thirds." So I had another look at my numerals and started to see in them composites of *ena* and *wija* and *mepi*. When I pronounced *mepi ena* — one *mepi* — quickly, I had *mepina*; when I did the same with *mepi wija* — two *mepi*, it came out as *mepiija*. So there it was. What I had failed to detect with my knowledge of the Kapauku, the Babylonian system revealed. The word *mepi* made little sense to me in this context because the only meaning it conveyed to me was "he just arrived." I had no knowledge of any Kapauku word for "one third". Upon my return to the Kapauku in 1962 (my third visit), and also in 1975 and 1979, I inquired in vain about another meaning for *mepi*. They agreed with my notion that it meant only "he just came." Still, the parallels Professor Do Solla Price revealed to me were so convincing that I agreed to publish an article with him, which appeared in the Bulletin of the Indian Academy of Sciences in 1966; however, I did insist that we put a question mark at the end of its title: "Survival of a Babylonian Numerical System in New Guinea?"

Price contended that the Babylonian sexagesimal system had spread to New Guinea and survived in this interior culture until recently. To support his claim he cited such a spread to the Tamil speakers of South India, for which he had hard evidence. Thence, he postulated, the system had somehow crossed the gulf of Bengal, was accepted by some (unknown) Malayo Polynesian speakers in Southeast Asia, and was introduced to the northern shores of New Guinea by Malay fishermen who were known to have traded in that region. I was not so sure of this theory — hence the question mark — because a sexagesimal numerical system had not been (nor has been to this day) discovered in Malaya or Indonesia.

As I mentioned, while the Kapauku could count into the hundreds and thousands, their neighbors of other Papuan Highland tribes possessed numerical systems which ended at 5, 6, or 20. The numerical system was well integrated into Kapauku culture. They counted their possessions and kept track of time (days and moons), especially when they planned a pig feast several years ahead of the agreed time. And, of course, they counted their financial transactions, which involved not only sales and purchases but also the extension of credit and its repayment. The question still arose: how could an ancient tribe like the Kapauku have acquired such a sophisticated mathematical system if it were not by simple diffusion and borrowing from the Malay traders in the north? My informants told me that the system had functioned from time immemorial, that it was of Kapauku origin, and that their neighbors were simply not as smart as they were. Not willing to take that claim at face value, I started to do my own investigation. First, De Solla Price's contention had to be checked out. So I approached my Yale University colleague Harold Conklin and asked him about a possible Malayo-Polynesian origin of some or all of the Kapauku numerals. He readily recognized numerals 7, 8 and 9 — *pituwo, waguwo, ije* — as of Proto-Malay origin. This was the first hard fact I had. It meant, however, that the Kapauku of the interior mountainous New Guinea must have had contact with the Malay, possibly Malay fishermen, in the distant past. That further signified that they must have lived in the coastal lowlands of North New Guinea, somewhere on the shores of Geelvink Bay, in order to come into contact with the Malay people on the coast. The most logical area appeared to me to be the areas around the old villages of the Malay enclaves: Napan and Nabire, with their beaches and tropical rain forests.

Thus I speculated, in 1959 and 1962 during my second and third stays with the Kapauku, that those regions might once have been inhabited by ancestral Kapauku. Indeed, this gave me the idea that this then-unexplored territory could still harbor unknown lowland Kapauku, left behind during the Kapauku migration to the New Guinea Central Highlands. They carried with them the crops introduced by the Portuguese, together with an acquired mathematical knowledge. In 1962, accompanied by several Kapauku and people from the coastal community of Nabire, I made an expedition up the winding Boumi River deep into the lowland virgin forests in the hope of contacting local forest dwellers. This was a fabulous voyage on a winding stream with green walls of tropical trees on both sides, dotted with blooming orchids and other flowers, here and there revealing the bright orange-like fruit of the strychnine plant suspended from long vines. There was constant excitement. Huge parrots, hornbills, white herons and other birds flew over the river; crocodiles showed their heads in the water; and colonies of giant bats (flying foxes) often hung by the thousands from the tall trees. Now and then the peaceful trip was interrupted by a tremendous noise, as if a helicopter were flying overhead. It was the sound produced by large hornbills during flight. Here and there I caught sight of giant butterflies and birds of paradise, their wings and plumage of bright iridescent metallic hues, appearing like gems in the few rays of the sun that penetrated the canopy of dense rain forest.

It was certainly a beautiful and mysterious voyage. I diligently took my 16mm movie camera and recorded in color this spectacular experience. However, from a scientific point of view the expedition proved to be a failure. The only people we came across as we traveled by double outrigger canoe were four Melanesian men and one young woman who had a camp on the bank at a bend in the river. They were collecting the tree resin, called *dammar*, to sell to lacquer and paint companies. They were most friendly, giving us roasted wild boar meat, but they assured me that the whole region seemed to be uninhabited. So I finally gave up, and we returned to Nabire. The Kapauku, however, were intrigued by my crazy idea and did not give up. They started their own exploration on land, down the slopes of their Central Highlands. In 1975, on one of my return visits to my people, I was confronted by some of my Kapauku friends who excitedly reported to me that indeed, lowland Kapauku had been discovered in places where we had searched for them in 1962. Now these people, tucked away in the green sea of lowland tropical rain forest that stretches away to the horizon, have been given the Kapauku name Ogee Bagee, "the hidden people."

With all these new data the mystery of the Kapauku sexagesimal numerical system appeared to be solved. The Kapauku words for 1 to 6, unrelated to Malayo-Polynesian, were old Kapauku words.

Centuries ago, like their neighbors, they used to count only to six. Then, as a result of their contact with the Malay people, they were exposed to their decimal system. This made more sense, for all the fingers could be used for counting. Consequently the Kapauku accepted the Malay words for 7, 8 and 9. The word *gaati* for 10 and the word for 60, *bado*, which in the Kapauku language had their meanings, had been applied, quite coincidentally, in a way parallel to the Babylonian system. Thirty signifying one half (*amonaato*) is logical as half of 60. The idea of one *mepi* and two *mepi* is also logically linked to their sexagesimal counting, and only the word *mepi* itself remains a mystery. Since they had a fraction in their language, "one half," it seems probable that *mepi* once meant "a third" (thus *mepiina*, one third; and *mepiija*, two thirds). But in the Kamu Kapauku dialect its only meaning was "he just came," which in our numerical context makes no sense. It may also be unrelated, or a corrupted foreign word accepted long ago, or it may indeed have once meant "a third," a meaning since forgotten in the Highlands. Hopefully, further inquiry, especially among the newly discovered lowland Kapauku, will provide an answer. It may be that the word for one third is still used among them (Pospisil 1989).

The Kapauku's sophisticated mathematical system, present in an uncolonized ancient society, seems to refute two well-accepted cultural theories. First, it shows the failure of Marxism with its technological determinism. The adoption of the sexagesimal system of counting profoundly affected and changed large parts of Kapauku culture, especially their economy, which resembles Western capitalism. Technology is therefore not necessarily a determinant of any cultural superstructure, as Marxists claim (Pospisil 1989). Although the technology of the Kapauku remained the same as that of their neighbors (stone and bamboo tools), the rest of their culture, especially the economy, changed fundamentally following the adoption of a new system of counting. This radical change among the Kapauku thus occurred in the opposite direction from that anticipated by Marxist dogma. No mental gymnastics on the part of any Marxist anthropologist (if there are any left after the collapse of the Soviet Union) can alter this fact.

The second theory my findings undermine is the contention held by the old school of anthropologists (e.g., Wissler and Kroeber.) that changes in tribal cultures occur in the geographical center of a culture area. In the case of the Kapauku the dramatic shift took place on its periphery, at points of contact with the Malayans. What produces change is the exchange and combination of ideas — not necessarily at the geographic center. According to this theory civilizations rose at the crossroads of the world, where peoples of different cultures and different ideas could come together, rather than in any isolated center. In modern civilizations, of course, capital cities have assumed a pivotal role in the exchange of ideas, facilitated by modern means of communication. When foreigners travel to these capitals, change will and does occur there.

Quantity Obsession

Most likely it was after the appearance of the sexagesimal counting system that the Kapauku became more obsessed with quantification and an emphasis on size. Not only was counting used in their economy and trade but the people showed a peculiar attachment to numbers and a craving for counting in all aspects of their lives. They counted their wives, children, days, visitors, number of people at feasts, and, of course, their shell and glass-bead money. At any feast I attended, or during those pleasant evenings in my house in front of my fireplace, or in the village, there were invariably groups of men squatting over strings of cowry shells, engaged in counting them. Thanks to their pre-occupation with quantity, I was able to secure exact numerical data on trade transactions, credit arrangements, and the wealth of individual Kapauku, which in turn enabled me to analyze the native economy quantitatively, and map their territory and gardens with ease.

In my interactions with the people, I tried to exploit their passion for counting as much as possible. I used to reward my most reliable informants as well as my most industrious boys by granting them per-mission to count glass beads. The honored and "fortunate" individu-al would then squat over my boxes of beads for up to two hours. At the end of his counting he would report the state of my wealth with a victorious smile: "You have six thousand, seven hundred and twen-ty-two beads in your boxes, which means you have spent six hundred and twenty-three beads since Gubeeni counted your money last time (numbers translated from their math systems). I would suggest that at this rate of spending you order more beads in about thirty days so that you do not run out of funds." This financial finding would later be pronounced publicly in front of my house to a multitude of my less fortunate informants and sons. Afterwards the report and my rate of spending would provide a topic for discussion which sometimes lasted long into the night. My finances were never in better shape than during my stay among the Kapauku.

In accord with this quantitative orientation, the Kapauku placed value upon higher numbers and larger volume and size. Thus a tall individual was admired and a weak and small one was regarded as *peu*, "bad." The name for a small child up to about five years of age was *peu joka*, which literally meant "bad child." Most objects that were small were "bad" or at least not as good as larger ones. A female beauty was always judged by her size. Accordingly my "son" Gubeeni came to me one day with great excitement and described to me the beauty of his new girlfriend, hoping I would help buy her for him. "She is fantastically beautiful. She has huge breasts, is tall and quite well fed, and has thighs this thick," and he grasped his blown-up chest with both hands. Naturally, after having heard the description of such a beauty I promised to pay a large part of the conventional bride price. Privately, however, the description evoked in my mind the image of a small elephant. Similarly, one of my best friends, Ijaaj Awiitigaaj, the famous headman of the Ijaaj-Enona sub-lineage of Botukebo village, approached me with a request to help him pay for his hoped-for eleventh wife. He described to me the beauty of his new discovery, a young widow, in similar terms to those employed by Gubeeni. Since I knew that Awiitigaaj was an expert collector of female beauty reposited in his large household, I could safely trust his ecstatic judgment and promised my contribution.

The Kapauku obsession with quantity often assumed forms that came as a shock to me. Once I received from Raphael Den Haan, the district officer of Enarotali on Paniai Lake, a magazine with a cover portrait of the beautifully smiling Gina Lollobrigida. She had a large décolletage, a splendid brunette hairdo, and an attractive gown. I cut out this large picture from the magazine and pinned it to the plank partition wall in the front room of my house. Then I invited my boys and other Papuan friends and showed them the picture, expecting an outburst of enthusiasm over the lady's appearance and also, possibly, because of the décolletage, some sexual comments and jokes. To my great surprise the natives failed completely to react to her beauty. Instead they started to count her teeth, the only quantifiable item in the picture! This "experiment" caused me an additional problem. I left the picture on the wall for more future comments, eventually forgetting that it was there. About three weeks later Father Steltenpool, the Franciscan pastor and Catholic priest of Ugaapuga, visited me on his way to the north. In vain he looked for a cross on my wall, spotting instead the picture of Miss Lollabrigida. Dismayed, he remarked acidly; "I trust she is not your wife." Unwilling to defend my position vis-à-vis the picture and unable to lie and tell him that Gina was my wife, I had to admit sheepishly that my wife was blonde.

The Kapauku reactions to other pictures from my magazines were similar. In a picture of a street in New York they counted the cars and the windows in the skyscrapers. A navy carrier was regarded as an interesting and most rewarding sight because of the numerous planes on its deck. Similarly a picture of spectators watching a football game was a success. In contrast, a dour portrait of Premier Malenkov, the Soviet leader at that time, with his stern look and no trace of a smile and therefore nothing to count — met with a complete lack of interest.

The Kapauku obsession with counting was once again evident during my departure from New Guinea, on the Island of Biak with its international airport. In recognition of the friendship and help with my research of my best friend Ijaaj Jokagaibo, the Dutch Government invited him to accompany me and visit the Island of Biak, its airport, and government establishment there. As the two of us rode in our jeep through the streets of the town of Mokmer, I pointed out to my friend the various buildings such as hotels, hospitals, schools, police headquarters, airport terminal, and military barracks, and lectured on their significance and functions. I observed that my friend was not paying much attention to my explanations. Annoyed, I asked him, "What are you doing? You don't seem to be listening to me." He apologized profusely and admitted hesitantly that he was counting the people on the streets to get an idea of the population size. He wanted to report this to his constituency in the Highlands in order to show them the futility of fighting the white man.

In the mid-fifties, when I was conducting my first fieldwork among the Kapauku, it was common for anthropologists to perform projective tests, whether they related to the topic of their inquiry or not. Just as nowadays it is fashionable, if not mandatory (among postmodernists), to pay homage to anthropological interpretationists, in those days it was the field of "culture and personality" that fascinated many of my colleagues. If one did not acknowledge the brilliance of the psychological insights of people like Margaret Mead, Ruth Benedict, and Geoffrey Gorer — who were ignorant of the languages of the people they studied, and who, in some instances, did their fieldwork for short periods or gathered their knowledge from literature — then one was regarded as an oddball, or incompetent. To avoid this stigma I tried my luck with TAT and Rorschach tests, after having mastered the native tongue and acquired a broad knowledge of the culture. While the TAT test predictably triggered reactions to the size of the figures and items that could be counted, the Rorschach test results were a surprise. Instead of reacting to the number of inkblots on the plates, my Kapauku informants focused on the blots' periphery and gave me their interpretations of their meanings, reacting to the prominences and inlets. There were sometimes as many as 48 reactions to one plate! Even the blot which very convincingly looks like a giant bat did not elicit, as I expected, a spontaneous and enthusiastic exclamation of "*daajaaj*" (the fruit bat or flying fox), so prominent in the game inventory of the Kamu Valley as one of the most hunted animals. They reacted instead to the picture's jagged border. Undoubtedly, this was another manifestation of Kapauku quantitative bias. The tremendous variety of responses precluded trying my luck with many informants, so I became exhausted and satisfied with about a dozen.

This quantitatively and logically conceived universe of the Kapauku was quite realistic. Absolute values are not detached from their relativistic context. As I had learnt, all of what happens has been determined by the Creator, so there could be no sin or postmortem reward. There was also no concept of anything that was absolutely bad or absolutely good. The words *enaa* (good, nice) and *peu* (bad) were used only as adjectives, not as nouns. There was no word in the native vocabulary that could be translated as "evil" or "goodness." Bad and good were only relative ideas that could not be used absolutely, but only in a concrete context. Consequently the question "Is killing a man good or bad?" resulted in surprise and confusion. After some hesitation, the response might be: "Killing of whom?" or "Good for whom?" Naturally, the killing of a man was good for his enemies and bad for his relatives and friends.

Coupled with all this logic, quantification, and relativity was the Kapauku extrovertedness, their free and loud expressions of happiness and sorrow. A typical day in the village was filled with shouting, emotional argument, and at times the free expression of rage and even fighting. My one great advantage was that I knew precisely where I stood with the natives at any time. An extrovert myself, I fit into this society splendidly. Their sense of humor and practical joking delighted me. Every day I tried to invent a new way of pulling somebody's leg, and the people loved it. I must say I had never a dull moment during my stay among the Kapauku, and they could not complain about my participation in their daily life. If nothing else, I enriched their vocabulary by introducing some Dutch and Czech swear words!

In April 1962 a Czech entomologist suddenly appeared at my house and introduced himself as "Sedláček from Vodňany, Bohemia." He told me he had found out about me and my existence in the Kamu Valley by accident. He had been walking with some Kapauku natives in the jungle of the Panai Lake region hunting butterflies for the Bernice Bishop Museum of Hawaii when one of his native assistants, chasing an insect, stumbled over a root and swore in perfect Czech, "*Doprdele!*" (polite translation: "Into my behind!"). "Then," he told me, "I knew right away there must be a Czech around." One never knows when a well-placed swear word might bring about fortunate consequences.

Economy Ceremonies

The tribal territory of the Kapauku formed a mosaic of mutually hostile federations of paternal lineages of people descended from a common paternal ancestor. These federations were intermittently engaged in warfare, usually caused by a failure to meet fiscal obligations originating from the nonpayment of extended loans and required bride price, the theft of pigs, or elopement of married women combined with adultery. Some of these failures to repay monies owed could be regarded as outright fraud or embezzlement. Kapauku ceremonies tended to resolve these conflicts by establishing peaceful regional integration.

The ceremonies provided occasions at which inter-confederational legal problems could be amicably resolved. Even war was usually ended in a formal way with a dance among previously mortal enemies. Although this function alone could be regarded as sufficient justification for the existence of these often elaborate formal gatherings, they in fact accomplished much more. From an economic point of view these were ceremonies at which goods (pigs, pork, salt, artifacts such as bows, necklaces, utilitarian and decorative netted carrying bags, stone axes and adzes, stone knives, tobacco or trade goods from distant coastal areas) and raw materials (shaved wooden planks, sheets of bark for roofing, rattan vines, bailer and other types of shell, plumes of parrots and birds of paradise, serpentine rocks for manufacture of stone axes and adzes, flint nodules for carving tools and surgical instruments, wax, etc.) were widely traded, thus evening out local surpluses and deficiencies. This trading ensured a steady flow of products all over the region, preventing both shortages and overproduction in any of its parts.

The ceremonies were also of paramount importance for intermarriage between members of hostile confederacies. They provided virtually the only opportunity for boys and girls of warring groups to meet and arrange for dates and eventual marriage ceremonies. Even adults used these occasions for matchmaking. These marital ties brought confederacies together, and it was usually the in-laws who served as peace negotiators and formed friendships across traditionally hostile boundaries.

Most importantly, the distribution of pork during these ceremonies allowed people to sell or loan their surpluses of pork to a far wider network of "customers," who would reciprocate in the future after the next slaughter of their own pigs. This enabled people to eat fresh pork for several months while their pigs were growing and slowly maturing. This system of exchange substituted for the service of a deep-freeze or refrigerator in a tropical climate where pork might be rendered inedible in just a couple of days.

The basically secular orientation of the Kapauku culture reflected the fact that all the more important ceremonies were of an economic and not a religious nature, as one might expect in a tribal society. By far the most spectacular was *juwo* — the pig feast. This was a protracted affair comprising several major events and innumerable nights of dancing. The whole cycle of a pig feasts lasted several months. It started with the decision by a rich man, preferably a headman, to sponsor a feast. Having decided to give a feast, he would call on other people to hear their opinions and secure one or several co-sponsors, usually relatives of the main sponsor, who was called *juwo-ipuwe* — the pig feast owner. The reason for giving a feast was not only to make an economic profit by selling quantities of meat and earning the much desired cowry shells, but also to entertain with singing and dancing. The *juwo-ipuwe* also gained prestige from the generous loans of pork, and from the fact that the success of the whole event undermined the popularity of the sponsor's political rivals within and outside of his confederacy. The main pig feast owner with his helpers urged young and poorer people to volunteer for plank-making and collecting rattan, the materials necessary for the construction of the dance and feast houses. A spectacular pig feast also enhanced the reputation of the community and, ultimately, that of the whole confederacy.

In outdoing his enemies the sponsor of a successful pig feast was considered to have done a patriotic and moral deed and often regarded as a sort of tribal hero. Once the building material was gathered, the main sponsor would initiate the construction of the dance house by performing a magical rite, which was expected to assure the success of the feast and bring lots of money to its sponsors. Early in the morning the people would start to build the dance house while the sponsor went to the forest to cut a tall *onage*, a willow-like tree. On the stump of the freshly cut tree the sponsor would pray to the Creator to grant success to the feast. After the prayer was concluded the performer would sacrifice the intestines of a rat by placing them on the stump. Then the sponsor and his aides, shouting and yelling for joy, would run with the cut tree to the building site. There they planted it, together with a ti plant (Cordyline terminalis), next to the place where the main front post which was going to carry the ridge pole of the structure was to be located. When I observed this rite at the Aigii village in September 1955 the sponsor went into a trance in which he placed rat intestines as an offering in a hole dug next to the *onage* while continuously uttering magical spells. The hole was then closed by driving a forked post into it — a post that became the first support for the frame of the sprung floor of the dance house.

After the initial ceremony the Aigii people would start building the walls of the dance house. Typically it had a rectangular floor plan, approximately 5 by 7 meters. It consisted of an elevated sprung floor of long flexible poles, plank walls, and a gabled roof, thatched with a pandanus leaves, with its highest point about 6 meters above ground. An extension of the gabled roof and sidewalls formed a vestibule in front of the structure for the dance audience. It also served as protection from rain, and fires were also lit there to provide light and warmth during the cold night. The dance floor itself was illuminated by small fires burning underneath it in two rows of small openings along the sidewalls. To house the numerous visitors overnight and provide space for cooking facilities, two or more *juwo owa* — feast houses of simple oblong construction with vertical plank walls and a gabled roof thatched with long pandanus leaves — were built next to the dance house. These provided dormitories for guests from distant villages as well as storage room for the owner's pigs tied to poles, a slaughterhouse, and a place where meat was sold, cooked and consumed. After the structure was completed a period of three months began, during which groups of men and women from any village of the confederacy might come and spend a night dancing and singing. The nightly dances were called *ema uwii* — going to the dance house. This dance period was initiated in Aigii on 12 September 1955 with a *putu duwai naago* — a day during which meat was distributed by the sponsors of the pig feast to their relatives and friends without charge. On this occasion the date of the final and most important feast, *juwo degii naago*, was announced. As early as 23 August, Ijaaj Jokagaibo, the nephew of the main sponsor Ijaaj Ekajewaijokaipouga, was asked by his uncle to help him out with the initial feast and kill some of his pigs for the planned distribution. My friend hesitated at first but his uncle was firm, arguing that since Jokagaibo was a rich man and also his nephew he had to offer some pigs, especially since he was also building his own feast house. So on 10 September my friend finally departed for the village of Egebutu to round up some pigs from his debtors. The day before Jokagaibo's departure, my boys and some Botukebo and Obajbegaa villagers went to Aigii to partake in the *putu duwai naago*, the initial feast. I took it easy and traveled there in a dugout canoe on the Edege River. There were at least two thousand people dancing, yodeling, cooking the freely distributed pork, congregating in small groups, discussing political affairs, and making business deals. Young people tried to arrange dates. At one point the multitude stopped dancing, yodeling, and singing and in utter silence looked up at the rooftop of the dance house. There appeared my friend Jokagaibo and his uncle Ekajewaijokaipouga, the first as the headman of the Ijaaj Jamaina sublineage, the second as the headman of the whole Ijaaj-Pigome confederacy. They made speeches to their constituents, urging them to live now in peace with the members of the Waine-Tibaakoto confederacy. Then they started to dance together with their former enemies to ratify the peace agreement and end their ongoing hostilities. Since their demands were accepted and the joint dance was performed, the war was formally ended. I took pictures and filmed this event. The dramatic scene of the multitude listening to the speeches of their leaders should dispel, I hope, all dogmatic notions of leaderless tribal societies.

Thus initiated by the *putu duwai naago* feast, the dancing period formally commenced and people from various confederacies and villages arrived during the evening to spend the night dancing in the dance house, feasting, debating, and sleeping in the feast houses. Only a few young men came there to make formal date and marriage proposals. Most of them came to dance, to get acquainted with girls, and to flirt with them informally. The setting was ideal for such an undertaking. The light was dim, provided by fires burning in the vestibule and underneath the dance floor, and the torch-carrying girls had to push through the dancers on one side and onlookers on the other. As they proceeded in a single or double file the boys would have plenty of opportunity to exchange looks and jokes with the girls. If a girl seemed to be receptive to such approaches, the boy would become encouraged. Next time she passed he would stand in her way so that she had to push him aside in order to keep pace with the rest of the women. This provided the young man with a justification to retaliate with a push on her next turn around the dance floor. He would be delighted if the girl screamed, pushed him away, or even slapped him. However, a rebuke or silence or an unpleasant look from the young lady would be interpreted as displeasure, and the boy would be well advised to try his luck elsewhere. The brightly colored feather hairpins of the boys provided another means for flirtation. The girls, who liked to have such pins as souvenirs and decoration, would snatch them from the boys as they passed. The boys would try to reclaim their ornaments when the girls reappeared in the ever-moving circle. If the torches went out and sudden darkness enveloped the crowd, a few bold men might take the opportunity to grab the passing girls by their breasts. For that the men would be struck with fists, slapped, or sometimes thrown to the floor by the infuriated women. Despite the blows and bruises the boys would feel fine and would be regarded by their friends as the heroes of the evening. Thus successful exploitation of the darkness would constitute a major part of local gossip for the next two weeks. It was not only the boys, however, who initiated advances toward the other sex. Girls desiring a date, accompanied usually by sexual intercourse, could secretly slip a piece of roasted sweet potato into the hand of a selected boy. He would understand the proposal, and when she left the dance house he would follow her inconspicuously into the darkness, to spend the whole or part of the night collecting the highest reward a night dance could offer a young Kapauku.

The night dance would come to a climax on the evening preceding the main and final event of the feast cycle — the *juwo degii naago*, the pig feast proper. In May 1955 I attended a pig feast at Bunauwobado. During that night men danced and sang until about 2 a.m., while the women provided light. In the second half of the night the roles were reversed. Toward morning I tried to get some sleep in the *juwo owa* feast houses but my sleep was constantly interrupted by noise and fleas which seemed to have disregarded even my counterattack with DDT. After sunrise, as soon as the heavy dew on the grass, reeds, and foliage dried, the sponsors slaughtered their pigs by shooting them through the heart with arrows, then tied their legs to a pole. The butchering then began. Pieces of meat and entrails were stored in small compartments at the back wall of the feast house, three in number, where the people went to purchase pork from the pig owners. All morning groups of people came from villages around. Upon their arrival they performed the jumping *waita tai* dance and then the trotting *tuupe* dances, following these with one or two *ugaa* songs on the springy floor of the dance house. Afterwards they dispersed into the multitude to conduct their business transactions. They selected spots in the grass where they slaughtered their pigs, butchered them, and sold the meat. Small or large clusters of buyers gathered around them. Many people were actually not buyers but came to claim repayment for pork they had "loaned" in the past. Others were "borrowing pork" with the promise to repay in kind in the future.

The trading was not limited to meat. Other articles traded that day included salt, bundles of inner bark for making string, artistically netted and decorated carrying bags and purses, bow strings of rattan vine, bamboo containers, bird feathers, and ornaments of various kinds. There was loud arguing and haggling over the prices of the merchandise, but almost everyone seemed to be enjoying the feast. Many people were moving from group to group as onlookers, witnessing the various transactions or seeking out friends to exchange news and gossip. The two co-sponsors of the Bunauwobado feast, the headmen Dou Akoonewiijaaj and Dou Onetaka, held a meeting with other headmen of the Ijaaj-Pigome confederacy to discuss politics, especially whether to pursue a policy of peaceful co-existence or war with the neighboring Waine-Tibaakoto confederacy.

In the late afternoon trading was concluded and most people returned to their homes. Others, especially relatives and friends of the locals, decided to spend the night in Bunauwobado. There they were treated with steamed pork and roasted sweet potatoes and entertained with conversation late into the night. I myself fared very well and received lots of meat and other gifts, especially from three friends of mine. It was afternoon by th time my boys and I left the gathering and set out for home. That night in my house I treated my boys and girls to pork, steamed *idaja* (Amaranthus greens), which tastes like spinach, and soup. None of my boys who had met girlfriends had decided to get married, so there was no threat to my finances.

I have attended other pig feasts, where the pattern of the procedure and events was similar. Many of these were attended by over two thousand participants. Generally speaking, the greater the number of visitors and slaughtered pigs, the greater the prestige of the feast's sponsors. A Kapauku pig feast, although a trading ceremony in nature, transcended its purely economic purpose and constituted a central event around which the public affairs and private lives of the Kapauku were patterned.

In addition to the pig feast, the Kapauku observed two other types of public occasion that related to the economy, albeit far less ritualized, which provided the people with marketplaces. One, called *tapa*, "fund-raising ceremony," preserved one of the ceremonial aspects of the pig feast; the other, *dedomai*, "pig market," involved no ceremonial observances and was thus purely a market for pork, pigs, and other products.

In my monograph Kapauku Papuans and Their Law (1958a) I translated the word *tapa* as "blood reward ceremony," a ceremony at which *dabe uwo*, payment for avenging death by killing an enemy, is transferred to the avenger. During my attendance at *tapa* ceremonies in 1955, the transfer of *dabe uwo* was always the central part of the event. In the course of my subsequent research in 1959 and 1962 it became clear that my translation was incorrect. In my first research in 1954–55 the Kapauku still lived in pure aboriginal conditions in which wars were part of normal life. Consequently, so many people were killed and avenged in those frequent conflicts that at all the *tapa uwo* ceremonies I witnessed the collecting of the blood reward figured as the essential feature of the ceremony. This happened, for example, when I attended the *tapa* at Tuguwaagu. For a *tapa* no special structures are erected and *tuupe* and *waitatai* dances, similar to those performed at the pig feast, take place in the open. From the time of the announcement of the ceremony by its sponsors to the date of the main and final event, there is a period of between 180 and 360 days. However, no *ugaa* songs are sung. The *tapa* superficially resembles a pig feast. People come from all over, kill pigs, and sell the meat. At Tuguwaagu the culmination of the event was the ceremonial payment of the *dabe uwo* by a relative of the slain man (the sponsor of the event) to the man who avenged the death by killing an enemy — though not necessarily the man's actual killer. Prior to the ceremony the sponsor collected the necessary funds not only from his paternal relatives but also from his in-law relatives and maternal cross-cousins. They had traveled ome from various villages, those of the same lineage or confederacy arriving as a group. They came running to the clearing in the village of Tuguwaagu and danced *waita tai*. One of the dancers carried a long pole to which strings of cowry shells were attached — the collected *dabe uwo*. After the dance the money was displayed on mats for the multitude to inspect.

The killer of the enemy, the man to be remunerated, performed *odijaa ugaa*, a dance consisting of tiny jumps performed with bent knees and legs held together, accompanied by a song in which potential donors were asked to be generous. On other occasions I witnessed the money-raising effort, the man's wife and brothers would help him. On the following day a procession of people carried the cowry shells and other contributions to the house of the recipient. On this occasion I had no chance to ascertain the exact amount of money awarded, but displayed on the pole and mats it looked considerable. For example, my friend Jokagaibo collected from Jobee Ibo of Bauwo 60 axes, 60 long strings of beads, 5 *dedege* (Nassarius shell necklaces), 2,400 large trade beads, 240 old Kapauku cowries, and 600 introduced cowries — an amount equal to the purchase price of 31 pigs. In Tuguwaagu, however, the recipient did not keep the money for himself. Part of it he loaned to various individuals, while the rest he handed to the crowd. The crowd threw itself on the largesse and tried to grab whatever they could. Since in such situations one cannot possibly identify the recipients of the monies, there was no obligation to repay the collected amounts. This greatest kind of generosity gave the distributor of the wealth the highest prestige, and for years afterwards the men remembered and talked about the event, and out of gratitude were willing to help the generous donor in his ceremonial, political, and legal affairs. Of course, not all men were so generous. Awiitigaaj, headman of the Botukego Ijaaj-Enona sublineage, told me he would have preferred to collect the money himself and distribute it only to his debtors. He said to me: "I am a headman not because the people like me, but because they owe me money and are afraid I'll ask for repayment."

That ceremony took place at Tuguwaagu. But at the *tapa* ceremonies I attended in 1959 and 1962, no *dabe uwo* was transferred because of the lack of wars under Dutch colonial rule. The ceremony was similar to that described above, only instead of the *dabe uwo*, the blood reward, collections were made for various other purposes determined by the sponsor. He and his close relatives were beneficiaries of the proceeds. It thus became clear that the true essence of the *tapa* ceremony was the collecting of funds for any purpose, rather than solely to pay a blood reward. At the *tapa* at Pouwouda, which I attended in July 1959, the contributions collected for the sponsor's benefit were again strung on a long pole and attached to long strings of inner bark fiber. On arrival, each group of contributors approached the sponsor at a trotting pace, headed by a woman who trotted backwards while facing the bearers of the money. The procession ended with a *waita tai* dance, after which the contributions were ceremonially surrendered to the sponsor. On that occasion the sponsor killed two pigs and distributed some of the meat as gifts. These were given especially to those individuals who came to the ceremony to repay a loan or grant a new one to the sponsor or his co-sponsors. The ceremony was concluded in the afternoon and most contributors returned to their homes in small groups. A few others remained in the village overnight to enjoy freshly steamed pork from the large cooking mounds in the company of their friends.

Although the market economy of the Kapauku benefitted from the ceremonial *juwo* pig feast and *tapa*, trade was so important and intensive that it needed yet another and more flexible vehicle for the mass exchange of goods. This function was filled by *dedomai*, an informal market devoid of all the elaborate structures, involved formalities, and ritual observances of the pig feast and *tapa*. A wealthy man who had several pigs to be slaughtered and did not want to wait for a pig feast or tapa sponsored by others or be bothered by the formalities and social trimmings of those ceremonies, would simply decide to sponsor a *dedomai*, a pig market (the word means "to carve up'). He would announce the place and date to the public and invite everybody to come to the selected place (usually his village) to sell their products and buy goods from others. There was no dancing or singing. Everything was conducted on a purely business basis. When I attended a *dedomai* at the village of Pueta, one of the villages of our arch enemies, the Waine-Tibaakoto confederacy, in April, 1955, I saw not only many pigs slaughtered and their meat sold, but also a variety of manufactured goods and raw material traded by the gathered multitude. Although there were some similarities to the *tapa*, the significance and functions of the *dedomai* are entirely economic, being limited to redistribution of goods and shell money through sales and loan contracts.

The purely economic function was reinforced by the fact that my Kapauku confederates and I went to this enemy village only for trading purposes. It was the headman of the Waine-Tibaakoto confederacy, Tibaakoto Ipouga, who had sent me the message telling me I would be the first of his targets should war erupt between the two confederacies. This precarious situation was resolved when one of my adopted sons, with my financial help, married the daughter of my arch enemy. So at the *dedomai* in Pueta we met again, sat together, ate some pork and sweet potatoes and talked. Since the marriage of our children precluded any violence between us, I was no longer in danger. Indeed, during our conversation Ipouga complained: "I am sorry I cannot kill you anymore." Out of politeness, I commiserated with him on his misfortune. I assured him that I fully shared his sorrow because I also had an arrow reserved for him. Although I had no such weapon or intention, I used this social lie to relieve the man's sorrow and show him that he was not the only one suffering from the friendship forced upon us. When more people share bad luck, the burden seems lighter.

Life Cycle Ceremonies

Birth Ceremony

In addition to ceremonies involving trade and magic, the Kapauku performed two rituals marking the beginning and the end of human life. Their birth ceremony was a simple affair consisting of a feast given by the father to honor the birth of his child. A few days after the child was born the father would host a feast. It was considered appropriate to treat everybody to pork or rats or marsupial meat. The host would typically have at least eight large pieces of pork, each weighing about six pounds, or ten marsupials on hand for the occasion. In March 1955 my son Pigikiiwode announced to me that his wife was shortly to give birth to a child, and that he had to go to the Pona Valley to buy marsupials for the celebration. He had tried before to shoot or trap some but failed. Pona was a region to our south, frequented by some of the Kamu people but unexplored by white men. It was covered by dense forests and, unlike in Kamu Valley, the Kapauku living there kept dogs for hunting the abundant local game. So Pigikiiwode had a good chance of buying the venison he needed. He succeeded, but unfortunately his wife had a stillbirth. Although grief-stricken, he went to look for a pig he could purchase for the planned birth feast. The next day, after the successful purchase of a porker, he gave the sad feast. His father, Awiitigaaj, prepared additional quantities of meat in several *dopo*, cooking mounds made of long pandanus leaves and heated by red hot stones extracted from a nearby fire. He steamed layers of meat between layers of vegetables, especially fern leaves and a spinach-like green (Amaranthus hybridus). The food was prepared in *amaage*, the men's common dormitory at Awiitigaaj's house. The steamed meat was cut into small pieces and distributed to the male guests, who squatted around the cooking mound and, because of lack of space, also gathered around the entrance to the house. To the fe-males who stayed in the women's quarters at the back and side of the building, the food was passed through special openings in the parti-tions between the rooms.

Pigikiiwode was not as sad as I had expected. He bravely distribut-ed the food, squatted among the guests, and discussed serious polit-ical and economic issues. My people stayed long into the night, and some of them stayed and slept in the village of Botukebo. Following Kapauku etiquette I did not see Pigikiiwode's wife that day. She was expected to give, in turn, a similar feast at her parents' house a few days later, at which she would function as hostess. She was expected to prepare the food in the women's quarters and pass it to the males gathered in the men's common dormitory. This event was lower-key than that held by her husband. I failed to attend that feast for senti-mental reasons. I was not a hardboiled scientist oblivious to human feelings. On the night of the birth ceremony I went to my house, where I had supper together with some of my boys and girls. My friend Ijaaj Jokagaibo lectured me on the customs surrounding the birth of a child. One may ask why Pigikiiwode went through with the ceremony al-though he was obviously in deep grief. In fact he had little choice. Not only was he required to follow the Kapauku custom, but since he was the son of Ijaaj Awiitigaaj, the headman of the Ijaaj-Enona sub-lineage and an adoptive son of mine, he could ill afford to skip the ceremo-ny and show unmanly weakness. In addition, by hosting the feast he avoided losing of economic and political prestige.

Death Ceremony

The death of a Kapauku male was always regarded as far more serious and culturally important than the death of a Kapuaku female. As soon as the soul left the body relatives of the deceased started to weep, eat ashes, cut off finger segments, tear their garments and net carry-ing bags, and smear themselves with mud, ash, and yellow clay. The most conspicuous expression of grief was a loud singsong lamentation called *jii-jii tai*. Usually the mourner climbed a cliff where he or she would lament and weep as loudly as his or her vocal cords would allow. The *jii-jii-tai* would carry throughout the valley, announcing the tragedy to friends and relatives. On hearing the message, friends and relatives would smear their faces and bodies with yellow clay, mud, or ashes and hurry to the place of death. There, wailing, they would rush into the men's dormitory of the house where the death occurred and beat the hearth with long sticks. By doing this they believed they were punishing the spirit of the hearth, which lived underneath the fireplace, and which was expected to devour the corpse in the grave, as manifested by its decomposition. In due time one of the best friends or a close patrilineal relative (son, father, brother, etc.) would arrive and present his mourning friend with a large pig. It would be killed later in the afternoon and the meat distributed to the mourners and their friends at the funeral feast, held the same evening.

In the afternoon typically the in-law relatives of the dead would bind the corpse to a pole by its arms and legs and carry it in a procession to the burial place. The disposal of the body was usually a secret affair in which only a few close relatives and friends of the bereaved family participated. Originally I attributed this secrecy to religious taboos and observances. Only much later during my research did the true reason for this secrecy become clear to me. Because everyone who mourned the dead at the grave on the day of the funeral had to be paid by the main heir for their manifestation of grief, the heir, in order not to become bankrupt, would keep the burial site and time secret, inviting only a few trusted friends and relatives to the funeral procession. These precautions were needed because among the Kapauku were professional mourners who participated in as many funerals as they could, collecting handsome payments for their mercenary howling.

On 16 April 1955, my friend Awiitigaaj informed me that his son Mabiipaj was dying because some Kapauku who owed Awiitigaaj blood money had failed to pay on time. I went to see the boy, but it was too late for me to help him and he was dying of bacillary dysentery. I gave him antibiotics, but what he needed at that stage of the disease was a blood transfusion and intravenous fluids. The child died on 18 April, and I was the only man invited to the funeral. Awiitigaaj walked in front of me, carrying the body of his son in his arms. I followed him into the swamps, where he dug a shallow grave and placed the body into it in a squatting position, the head protruding above ground. Over the head he built a thatched roof and around it a wooden fence to prevent pigs from disturbing the burial. When he had finished, he talked to his son for the last time, instructing his soul, and particularly his departed shadow, to take revenge on the irresponsible debtors. The burial ceremony was successfully kept secret and my friend Awiitigaaj, old fox that he was, knew very well that he would not have to pay me "a bead." When Ijaaj Dege, son of Jokagaibo, another of my best friends, died in February 1955, I was invited to the burial and asked to express my grief. I had to give lots of beads, shells and other objects to my friend, as custom required.

In these two cases it was a child who had died. The ceremonies were therefore not elaborate, and the burials were simple affairs. When an old man or woman died the situation was far more complex. Before death claimed the soul of a dying man, he would usually deliver *bogai mana*, a testament in which he not only disposed of his property but gave his fellow Kapauku advice on life, passing on various pieces of wisdom he had acquired during his lifetime. So, for example, when Ijaaj Kamutaga of Botukebo was dying I came to see him and offered to send someone to the Paniai Lake to bring a Dutch doctor to help him. Kamutaga replied: "Son, there will be no use for me to be treated by your doctor, just as there will be no use for white magic. I know I am going to die in about two days, and I want to die. I do not like to sit only in the house and be cared for and fed." Nevertheless, I did give his sons some pills to help their father. That evening the old man called his male relatives and had a long talk with them while the women listened from their quarters. He advised mutual help, assigned his garden plots to individuals, discussed the inheritance, stated his financial obligations, and assigned different amounts of currency to his sons. He was careful to be "just" and to give the largest portion to his oldest son so that his last will would not be invalidated on legal grounds. For the following four days the old man did not talk; he simply contemplated. His sons stood by, and when his soul started to yield its place to the evil spirit they held him in their arms. As soon as this process was concluded the sons started to weep, ate ashes, and smeared their faces with mud, clay, and ash. Their loud wailing could be heard even from my house, which stood outside of Botukebo, close to the village of Kojogeepa. The old man received an honorable burial. His sons built a tree house in which they laid their father's body with his net bag, rain mat, and penis sheath. For quite a while afterwards they would return to the grave to talk to their father.

In June 1955 I went with Pigome Pegabii and his brother to visit the tree house of their deceased father, erected in the forest near the village of Obajbegaa. As we approached the burial site the brothers smeared their faces with yellow clay. The structure appeared suddenly over a cliff and was quite impressive, built in a tree whose branches were half cut off and completely defoliated. The edifice consisted of a solid platform on which a "house" of bent branches was built, with a window situated in such a way that the dead man, bound in a squatting position, could look down the mountain upon his children's house. Pegabii declared: "We loved him very much. His soul is going to come to our house and stay with us and help." The two men climbed the tree and spent some time wailing while holding their father's hand. When I asked how long they would be coming back to the tree to mourn, they replied that as the leaves and new branches grew back and covered the burial site with their foliage, so their grief would slowly disappear. When the younger brother and I were leaving, the older brother, the eldest son of the deceased, stayed behind, squatting on the edge of the cliff, his eyes turned to the setting sun as he talked silently with his father.

The Kapauku built various kinds of burial structures, depending upon the status of the individual and the way he or she died. People killed in war or executed by being shot with arrows were buried with the arrows in their wounds, stretched out on an elevated platform where they were exposed to the elements and birds of prey. A drowned person was laid in the same extended position on the bank of the stream where he was found with a fence built around him, and left there exposed. When a known witch died she was left in a squatting position in her house, which was abandoned, as happened to the mother of one of my sons, Ijaaj Ogiibiijokaimopaj of Botukebo. For a rich man a wooden house was built on stilts. His body was left there in a squatting position, with his eyes facing a small window. The body was mummified, having been pierced with arrows to release the fluids. The tropical heat desiccated the body and prevented it from decomposing. When a grave or burial structure rotted and collapsed, the skull would usually be cleaned and put on a pole near the house of his or her patrilineal descendants, where it was believed to guard the inhabitants against evil spirits.

Marriage

When I attended a Kapauku marriage for the first time, I recalled my own. Though it had been very different, some features were surprisingly similar. Like the Kapauku, I have not divorced my wife. Indeed, I have been married to her since 1945! Has it been a deep love for her that kept me in that relationship for my whole life? Well, there was one important ingredient in my personality that kept me going. I have to confess that I suffer from inertia. I do not like change. Accordingly, I kept my wife my whole life and I drove my Corvair for 47 years, only selling it because I have to use pills that make me dizzy and unsteady. In old Czechoslovakia, I lived in the same house for 25 years, and in the U.S. I have been in my "new home" since 1957! Furthermore, I came to Yale University as a student in 1952, and I am still there (now as Emeritus). This is in spite of having received many offers from other universities, indeed even twice from Harvard, with much better pay. Has it been my loyalty to Yale, as several provosts and two Yale presidents claimed? I wonder. I did my research among the Kapauku Papuans and returned "only" four times because of the difficult political situation in West New Guinea. But I spent at least three years of my life there. In my other long-term research in Tirol, Austria, I have been diligently returning since my initial year in 1962 until now (having spent about seven years of my life there — living in the same farm and sleeping in the same bed). I was brought up in Masaryk's democratic

Czechoslovakia as a democratically-minded, independently-thinking individual, and no Nazism, Fascism, or Communism could make me change. When the Communist take-over in Czechoslovakia forced me to escape, I found a new home in the United States with a similar democratic, political, and economic system (Czechoslovakian President Masaryk was a University of Chicago professor and his wife Charlotte Garrigue, our first Czech First Lady, was an American lady from Illinois). I like to wear my old clothes, and I still have the old briefcase with which I escaped from Czechoslovakia in 1948. I have kept the only possession I took with me during my escape for the past 62 years! So what is it that has dominated my life? Love, loyalty, or simply general inertia? But in most of this I resemble my Kapauku people: we keep our wives, our culture, and our dedication to democracy and independent thinking. Even politically, I have remained "independent" in all the American elections.

But the process of dating my wife and marrying her was quite different from the Kapauku — and probably from most people. There was no pig feast to bring us together, and there was no requirement that I should pay a lofty bride price for her. Indeed, the reverse happened. Instead of paying for her, I received a large sum of money as a dowry from her father. Definitely a better arrangement than that of the Kapauku. When I told them, the Kapauku simply could not comprehend the logic of our behaviour. My reason for marrying at the early age of 22 may sound quite peculiar. I had a girlfriend who was a wise and strong-willed young woman. She disapproved of my phony smoking (I did not like it, but I tried to keep up with the Jonese — or rather the Nováks). When I wanted to show off by smoking my valuable imported cigarettes (swiped from my father's supply for important guests, since he himself did not smoke) on a date, she became angry and trampled my Turkish cigarette box to pieces. Furious, I stopped talking to her and dutifully escorted her home. My friend Dohnal was waiting in front of her house and asked my girlfriend to fix up a double date for the next day with a girl he fancied. "Sure," she said. Then, looking at my face which resembled the black clouds of an approaching storm, she spitefully asked: "How many girls should I bring for you?" "Seven is the lucky number," I snapped back. And so it happened. My friend got the girl of his desire, and I got "stuck" with seven girls who expected to be entertained. What vicious revenge! Among these seven falsely-lured girls was my wife. I had not even noticed her and fixed my attention on another beautiful college girl named Liba. I had dated her several times when she surprised me by revealing that her best friend had a crush on me, and so, as a faithful friend, she surrendered me to her affection. So these two friends treated me like the young woman who was traded in the famous opera by Smetana, "The Bartered Bride." Fortunately there was no composer on hand to write an opera entitled "The Bartered Boyfriend." Needless to say, my wife does not like me repeating that story. As for me, I accepted the inevitable. So we started dating, and I hoped she would shape up as she grew older (she was 14 years old at that time, all bones and long legs and arms). And then in 1939, the Nazis entered our country. To avoid having to do forced labour in heavily bombed Germany, I became a farmer. My date, who after her graduation from college duly became my wife, was employed by my uncle who was a surgeon and the owner of a sanatorium. It was not long before our luck ran out. I was called to the Nazi agricultural office (Oberlandrat) and firmly told that Nazi law did not permit a farm to be run by a single male, only by an "orderly" family. At about the same time, my uncle told me that my girlfriend, as a nurse, was in danger of being transported by the German army to the Russian front. So to avoid those two unpleasant outcomes and escape our fate of becoming slaves to the Third Reich, we got married. Strange as it may seem, we have Adolf Hitler and his laws to thank for that. Prior to our marriage, I had had to think very hard whether to take that fateful step. But finally, I concluded that marriage could not be worse than slavery in a German factory, visited nightly by U.S. and British bombers, or for her the risk of getting caught up in the fighting on the Eastern (Russian) front. So I must conclude that no Kapauku could match my experience of marriage. The only situation that comes close to it is when a young Kapauku girl is induced by her father or brother to marry against her will. There is also another difference. When a Kapauku man has marital troubles he screams at his wife. When I have marital troubles, I curse Adolf Hitler.

Although many Kapauku marriages started with a love affair — the bride would accept the marriage proposal (as described above) or elope if she feared her family's opposition — a normal and proper marriage procedure was expected to begin officially with a contract. It would start with a conference between the groom, who was usually supported by some of his patrilineal relatives, and the bride's kinsmen. The primary objective of this conference was to agree on a mutually acceptable bride price. The well-being of the bride and her desire to marry the suitor were taken for granted. If the girl's aversion to the man was well known and manifested by her explicit refusal, means would be discussed to overcome her resistance. In such instances the bride price would usually increase. Although such difficulties did occur, they were rare and the price and date of payment were usually agreed upon. The Kapauku bride price consisted of two parts: the main payment, composed of the oldest Kapauku cowry shells and pigs; and a supplementary payment known as *kade*. *Kade* consisted of inexpensive, introduced fresh cowries, *dedege* (Nassarius shell) necklaces, net bags, glass beads, and (formerly) stone axes. While the one part of the bride price was paid out of the groom's own resources and contributions from his patrilineal relatives, the *kade* payment represented numerous small gifts donated by all the groom's relatives — both patrilineal and matrilineal, as well as cross relatives — and by his friends. The contributions to the main price were regarded as loans, to be repaid in the distant future. The donations to *kade* were considered gifts which ought to be reciprocated, not usually at the request of the donor but in the form of *kade* when the donors or their close relatives got married.

The *kade* gifts were payable ceremonially on a specified day called *kade makii naago* ("the day when the kade is put down"). On that day the already collected price would be publicly displayed on pandanus rain mats before being formally surrendered to the bride's relatives. An average bride price usually consisted of 120 old Kapauku cowries,

120 introduced cowries, 300 glass beads, 3 shell necklaces, and one large male pig. Of course, the price varied with the age and beauty of the bride, importance of her father and brothers, and wealth of the groom. During my subsequent stays (1959, 1962, 1975, 1979) I noted sharp increases in bride prices.

I witnessed my first ceremony of *kade makii naago* on 1 March 1955. It was one of my adoptive sons Tibooti (the Kapauku version of the Czech name, Ctibor, I had given him) who was marrying Pigome Maga of Botukebo. The main recipients of bride wealth were Pigome Naago and his brother. The contributors to the bride price were Tibooti's Ijaaj bilateral relatives and friends, which category included especially me, as the groom's adoptive father. The ceremony started in the village of Botukebo at approximately ten o'clock in the morning. The groom and his close relatives placed two rain mats in front of their house on which the already collected main part of the bride price was laid out. It consisted of the handsome sum of 180 old Kapauku cowries, plus an additional 120 cowries contributed by me. A male pig, an important part of the transaction, was kept tied nearby. People started to arrive in the morning from all directions to act either as contributors to the ceremony or simply as spectators. The bride's relatives, some of whom resided in the same village, appeared at the scene in one group. The gathering was augmented by many of their distant relatives and friends who were prepared to support the bride's kin in case a dispute arose over the amount to be paid.

At the gathering the bride's and groom's relatives formed two separate groups, squatting on opposite sides of the two mats where the bride wealth was displayed. The bride's party intermittently inspected the shells, passing them to each other and whispering comments. Mostly they failed to meet their expectations — but this did not necessarily mean the price was too low. Indeed, when augmented by my contribution of 120 shells, it was a handsome sum. Rather, it was a cue for the contributors to *kade*, the minor part of the price, to come forward and deposit their shells and necklaces on the two mats. Male and female relatives rose from the various squatting groups and silently approached the displayed bride price in order to add their own treasures. I could not sit still, and rose on several occasions to place 180 cylindrical blue glass beads, an iron axe, a machete, and two T-shirts on the mats. The bride's relatives were satisfied. It was not necessary for the headman to intervene and make long appeals to the relatives of the groom to solicit more contributions. He did not have to play on the feelings of the bride's party toward the "poor worried groom", or appeal to their pride as generous and well regarded individuals. Typically, in order to make this appeal more dramatic, a headmen might start *wainai*, a mad dance, by stamping the ground with his feet and extending his left arm, the index finger pointing, and the right arms bent at the elbow, as if he were about to discharge an imaginary arrow. As he stamped the ground in a furiously fast rhythm, he would yell and scream his demands to the gathered audience. Usually the father, brother, and paternal uncles and cousins of the bride would join in the tumult with reproaches and insults, hurled not so much at the already insolvent groom and his close paternal relatives as at their more distant kin and friends, trying to make them ashamed of their lack of generosity. If the bride's relatives were forced into a mad dance, the wedding might break up and physical violence might follow. None of this occurred on this occasion due to the generosity of Tibooti's relatives and friends. The bride's relatives seemed to be happy right from the beginning (in itself very unusual) not only due to the generous price offered but also because both of the bride's brothers resided in the same village as the groom. The ceremony was concluded at about three o'clock in the afternoon, at which time Tibooti presented the bride's party with the pig. Everybody was happy, and so was I, taking movies and pictures of the proceedings. In the evening, in front of the fireplace in my house, I discussed the wedding with my best friend Jokagaibo and several other friends and "children" of mine.

I have been present at many Kapauku weddings, most of which involved violent disputes. Tibooti's was the quietest and most pleasant of them all. Indeed, during the wedding of my own adoptive daughter Peronika (in 1959), I myself had to dance a mad dance, screaming insults and reproaches at the groom's party. Not enough had been paid for the daughter of an American Yale University alumnus! Although they could not understand the meaning of all this, they felt the gravity of the situation and accordingly increased their contributions. Finally even the biological father of Peronika, Ijaaj Jikiiwiijaaj, was satisfied with the price and complimented me on my performance. The two of us, being fathers, and in the absence of brothers, split the profits fairly. Jijiiwiijaaj kept six-sevenths of the price while I claimed the remaining seventh. This division was determined by the amount of time we had supported Peronika prior to her marriage. He had taken care of her for twelve years, while she had lived with me for two. My performance must have been regarded as a great success, because I was asked on several subsequent occasions to participate in a wedding in order to raise the bride price.

Law

Innovations in My Theory of Law

Theories of law of the nineteenth and early twentieth centuries defined the concept non-empirically, usually on the basis of then prevailing philosophies (so-called -isms, such as Marxism, evolutionism, functionalism, structuralism, etc.) or sheer speculation. Other scholars based their theories on their experiences of one particular society, but even then they were influenced by the prevailing "-isms" of the time.

I wanted to create a theory of law based on, or at least supported by, the available accumulated evidence from studies of specific legal systems. From the sociological and social psychological literature, I knew that every functioning social group had to have leaders whose major task was to eliminate internal conflicts by passing binding decisions. In many books and monographs, anthropologists distinguish preferred behavior (morality) from prescribed behavior (law). Prescribed behavior must exist within any social institution, which sees to it that decisions are followed and often necessarily enforced. This is the role of legal authority, be it a judge, king, tribal headman, chief, or council of elders. From the available literature and my four field experiences, I found that legal decisions must always be pronounced by an authority, thus distinguishing them from mere customs — an authority who intends to apply the principles they embody to all "same" cases in the future (intention of universal application.) This intention distinguishes laws from political decisions passed ad hoc. Furthermore, this authority has to give right to one party to the dispute and duty to the other, a criterion I call "obligatia." Legal decisions are different from religious ones, where the party may be God or another kind of spirit unrepresented by a priest, shaman, or other type of religious personality. Finally, a legal decision must be provided with a sanction, which would make it different from a moral decision. Unfortunately in the past, the literature recognized and described sanction only in the physical realm: execution, jail term, fine, torture, etc. I noticed that this left out an important form of sanction, the psychological, which includes public reprimand, public shaming, derisive song, assigning the culprit a derogatory new name (Eskimo), a formal declaration of ostracism or excommunication. Part of my legal theory is that a society does not possess one single prevailing legal system, but as many systems as it has social subgroups. Thus even a family, clan, or any association has its own legal system, which notion makes law universal, leaving no tribal society lawless. This idea, called "legal pluralism," is now widely accepted. Among the Kapauku I found the most convincing verification of my theory (Pospisil 1971).

Two Kapauku
Legal Cases

When I first traveled to New Guinea in 1954, my purpose was to study native law and use the collected data as a basis for my Ph.D. dissertation on a comparative theory of law. Prior to my departure I had studied 50 societies as library research, the results of which I used in my master's thesis at the University of Oregon (on the "Nature of Law"). I also had a law degree from the Charles University of Prague and done fieldwork research on law and social control among the Tewa-Hopi of the Hano village on the First Mesa in Arizona in 1952. Thus I had formulated some tentative ideas about a generally valid legal theory. To test them I had to study a genuine tribal system of law and social control, a system unpolluted by exposure to Western civilization and colonial suppression and destruction, which many of my colleagues in the field of anthropology of law had studied. Even back then the idea of leaderless and lawless societies, perpetuated as faddy dogma, appeared to me to be nonsense. I asked myself: Is it possible that tribal people, who originated the world's civilizations, could be more primitive than, say, a pack of wolves, a herd of wild horses, or a troop of baboons, all of which are social animals and have a leadership structure? Most of the so-called theories of the 19th century were accepted as infallible dogmas (e.g., Marxism, evolutionism, diffusionism), despite being based on speculation rather than on data derived from solid empirical research. Thus when I came to New Guinea I decided to study the Kapauku because they were regarded by the Dutch administration and missionaries as having no leadership system and laws. For the same reason, I declined to study the Dani Papuans, who were supposed to be politically well organized, governed by a leadership with what appeared to be a system of laws.

When I arrived in the Kamu Valley I was gratified not only to find a hierarchy of native leaders called *tonowi* but also to witness native gatherings at which local conflicts were adjudicated. They were not being "resolved" as was usually the case in areas dominated by colonial governments, where the native leadership was forced to surrender its adjudicatory powers. When I approached the Dutch administrators with my findings, I came up against their long-held dogma of a leaderless, primitive society. They claimed that the *tonowi* were not actually leaders but *primi inter pares* — first among equals, which meant that in a society of equals somebody had to be first in any group action. Of course, I countered, if somebody is always or nearly always the "first," then an egalitarian society is simply an illusion of Western conservative thinking (the dogmas of the 19th century). Indeed, I found that the *tonowi* had quite a bit of power over their constituents; they even sentenced people to death! A *tonowi* was an informal leader, a man of wealth who was at the same time generous in distributing his shell money as loans to his followers and who had the verbal courage to speak his opinion publicly. Wealth and generosity were not enough because, as I'd seen, Ijaaj Timaajjokainaago, a wealthy and generous man could not be a leader of his lineage because of his shy personality. These *tonowi* formed a hierarchy of which those of the sub-lineages were the lowest, those of the lineages occupied the middle, and those of entire confederacies were the highest. I have shown that all of them had adjudicatory powers not only through my descriptions of warfare and peace-making, but also with my documentation on film and my collection of evidence from many dozens of legal cases which even a hardboiled dogmatist would have difficulty challenging (Pospisil 1958a).

Thus the *tonowi*'s decisions concerning disputes were based on all the criteria of law that we find in civilized societies. The decisions were made by individuals wielding the authority to adjudicate; they were based on a general principle which the authority intended to apply to the "same" or similar cases in the future; they incorporated the attribute of obligation — that is, the decisions gave rights to one party and assigned duty to another; and they carried sanctions of an economic, corporal (physical), and psychological nature. They certainly were not negotiations in which the accused was one of the negotiating parties.

Thus we have tribal law *par excellence*. Although I expected to find these phenomena in Kapauku society, I was shocked to find something else: a whole legal code composed of numerous abstract legal rules (*leges*, pl. of *lex* — rule or statute) which the headmen and their legal advisors had memorized. Indeed, these rules were repeated to me by different individuals at different times almost verbatim — a true mental legal codification. I was able to record and publish 121 of these statutes. My surprise increased as I learned more about Kapauku law. These people lived according to a series of sophisticated legal concepts. So, for example, they made a distinction that even the English language does not make (although all other languages that I know do make it), between the abstract explicit rule — as, for example, statute, in Kapauku *daa mana* (in Latin *lex*, in German *Gesetz*, in French *loi*, in Spanish *ley*, etc.) — and law proper (in Latin *ius*, in German *Recht*, in French *droit*, in Spanish *derecho*), in Kapauku *bogo duwai mana*. A precedent, which they also used in their legal argumentation, is called *me etita mana*.

The most spectacular legal case I witnessed and filmed, during my first research, concerned the notorious embezzler Ijaaj Bunaibomuuma of Botukebo. He was known in the southern Kamu Valley for his fraudulent activity and quarrelsome temperament. He did not work his gardens, neither did he breed pigs. He traveled around buying and selling pigs, and was also a good bow maker. Borrowing shell money seemed to be his major enterprise. From the fact that he had been able to feed three wives and half a dozen children, it was apparent that his business transactions were profitable. He was a specialist in trade, which contradicts Durkheim's theory of the absence of specialization of labor (and division of labor) in "primitive society." If asked, the people in the Kamu Valley would agree with the statement that most of his deals were frauds or outright theft. Members of his Ijaaj-Enona sublineage had become weary of the incessant complaints from his creditors, and of the constant fear of losing their own pigs or other property during a raid by those he had cheated, because they shared common responsibility for the crimes of Bonaibomuuma.

In March 1955 Bunaibomuuma was traveling through the Tigi Lake region. In Tuwaago village he found a trusting individual who, after Bunaibomuuma had promised three large pigs, loaned him 2,880 beads, 20 Kapauku old cowries, and 30 introduced cowries. Four months later the Tigi people came to Botukebo to collect the pigs. To their surprise, they found that the culprit had none. Moreover, their money had been spent some time ago. They realized that the only way to recover their property would be through forceful seizure of pigs belonging to Bunaibomuuma's cousins or other clansmen. And they threatened to do just that. The people of Botukebo pleaded with them and declared that they should take revenge rather than deplete their livestock. The defendant, who at that time was visiting some friend in the northern part of the Kamu Valley, was incommunicado. A member of Bunaibomuuma's household was dispatched to the north to fetch him, but he refused to return. At a large gathering of important men from Botukebo, long speeches were made in which many of the speakers asked for the death penalty for the culprit.

On 29 July, I was alerted to the fact that the creditors had returned to Botukebo. This time, however, many armed people accompanied them from the Debei Valley. Long negotiations started between the war party and the culprit's people. At this point Bunaibomuuma, who had returned to the village, was brought to the scene of negotiation, where he promised to collect money and repay the debt within two days. After assurances from the culprit's relatives as well as the *tonowi* Awiitigaaj, the Ijaaj-Enona sublineage headman of Botukebo, the Debei people left.

As soon as the creditors had departed, the trial of the Bunaibomuuma began. The headmen, especially Awitiigaaj and Ekajewaijokaipouga (the confederacy's authority), started the process of *book petai* ("to seek vital substance") to secure a solid account of the evidence in the case. They questioned the culprit and various witnesses in order to obtain all the pertinent facts. For about a week afterward the headmen kept publicly reprimanding the culprit, who squatted at the entrance to his house, looking at the ground. Jikiiwiijaaj, an old man from Botukebo who had injured his leg while escaping from the village with his pigs to save them from confiscation by the creditors, beat Bunaibomuuma with a stick. Detailed accusations and demands for the man's execution were heard. The headmen performed a mad dance and started on the second part of the procedure, called *book duwai* ("to cut vital substance"), to formulate the judgment and sentence. They held a council in which the death sentence was discussed at length. The various speakers, in order to lend importance to their oratory, not only danced, gesticulated, and shouted but also wept skillfully at important moments during their speeches. Most of the younger members of the council, such as my friends Jokagaibo (headman of Ijaaj Jamaina sublineage) and Ekajewaijokaipouge (headman of the whole confederacy), opposed execution and asked for leniency in the hope that Bunaibomuuma might become honest. Finally they decided to take a collection among Bunaibomuuma's relatives to pay his debt, and to give him one last warning.

The old headman of the Ijaaj-Enona sublineage, Awiitigaaj, delivered the following concluding reprimand: "You are a very bad thief. You simply travel and think how to steal something. You have forgotten how to make gardens, and how to build houses. You simply exploit all of us by eating from our bags. You raise no pigs; you make no gardens; you have no cowries, no beads, and no houses. Your creditors will take our pigs away and burn our houses. You really are a burden to us all, a bad man in our community. If the creditors take our pigs or burn our houses, we will kill you with a *pogo* arrow (usually used for killing pigs — a bamboo-tipped missile). If Jikiiwiijaaj had sons they would have beaten you to death or shot you because Jikiiwiijaaj injured himself so badly while escaping with his pigs for fear of your creditors. If you wish to have money, work your gardens and raise pigs. If you go on stealing like this you will end up like Dimiidakebo, who was stealing from people and raping other men's wives." Dimiidakebo died of disease, probably pneumonia, but people believed he was bewitched by sorcerers and killed by their evil spirit helpers.

I heard several times of people fearing their creditors. They feared not only being forced to sacrifice their pigs for compensation for debt, but also the creditors burning their houses, a fear which was not imagined but very realistic. Kapauku creditors did burn down houses as, for example, the brother of my adopted son Jagodooti experienced. In August 1955 his brothers' two houses at Pueta village were burned down by frustrated creditors whose demands for repayment had not been met. All these cases show profit motivation.

When I started to systematically investigate the legal system of the Kapauku I immediately ran into a problem. While working with genealogies I noticed that several marriages were between clan members despite the fact that there was a legal rule against it: *keneka bukii daa*, it is forbidden to marry one's sibmate. Even worse, that rule demanded the death penalty for both the transgressors. Yet these marriages existed; indeed, even the headmen of my confederacy married women from their own clan. I found out that in some cases intra-clan marriage was not only tolerated but also even preferred, while in other confederacies and lineages the culprits were punished by death. The whole legal picture of incest prohibitions appeared to be quite chaotic, so much so that I started to wish I had selected another place for my research. However, as soon as I identified the persons involved in these marriages genealogically the chaos started to vanish, and a precise pattern emerged.

The law of a primitive society has traditionally been portrayed as a single well-integrated legal system with preferably no judicial deviations from the prevailing rule. However, such a smooth, relatively static and simple picture of "primitive" law is definitely unrealistic in any functioning society because it fails to take into consideration one of the most important functions of law: any system of law necessarily reflects a particular societal structure, the segmentation pattern of the society in which it exists. There is no social group or subgroup that does not possess leadership and regulatory mechanisms to induce good conduct from its members. Thus societal structure not only determines the rank of the various leaders (authorities) but also creates a configuration of legal systems of the society's subgroups. Legal systems of subgroups of the same membership and type form a legal level. Accordingly, I found in Kapauku society levels of confederacies, lineages, sub-lineages, households and families. Laws or prescribed behavior varied within a legal level (different families had different sets of rule for behavior), and sometimes different, even contradictory precepts existed in legal systems at different legal levels. Since a Kapauku individual was simultaneously a member of several subgroups of different inclusiveness (such as family, household, sublineage, lineage, and confederacy) he was subject to all the various legal systems of these groupings, as an American citizen is subject to at least state and federal laws. Consequently, he might be ruled, and often actually was, by several legal systems that differed to the point of contradiction.

When I went to do my research in New Guinea I knew all of this already and had included it in my tentative theory of law for my master's thesis. However, I was surprised to find that in this community of only 650, four different legal systems coexisted that were marked by basic and profound differences, such as radically different incest taboos and reasons for the death penalty. So, indeed, in the Ijaaj-Enona sub-lineage intra-clan marriages were not only allowed but preferred, with the provision that second paternal parallel cousins (father's father's brother's son's daughters) would be eligible spouses while marriage between first cousins was punishable as incest. In the related Jamaina and Nibakago sublineages of the same lineage only a fourth patrilineal cousin was permitted to be a spouse. In the Ijaaj-Pigome lineage clan exogamy was upheld and marriage within the clan broken up and punished by severe beating. An extreme of orthodoxy was reached in the Dou Buna lineage, where intra-clan sex was punished by death.

The breaking down of the intra-clan marriage taboo, punishable by death in all the numerous confederacies of the Kamu Valley, had been initiated by Ijaaj Awiitigaaj himself, who, thanks to his trickery, not only escaped punishment for his initial incest but as a headman was able to inaugurate a new legal rule (lex) which allowed the formerly incestuous marriage. Later this had profound residential and social consequences, including the splitting up of Awiitigaaj's sublineage into two subgroups. I described this cataclysmic rift in an article in 1958. However, in 1958 my explanation of social change not as the work of Durkheimean mystical social forces but as the result of an act by a specific individual was heresy. I was immediately attacked by Edmund Leach. In my reply I not only challenged his sociologically conformist view but also predicted further changes, which my subsequent research in 1959 and 1962 upheld and documented empirically. This subsequent argument against Leach remained unanswered by my learned colleague (Pospisil 1960b).

Theft of Pigs and Embezzlement

The theft of a pig, economically the most valuable property of the Kapauku, was regarded as a grave crime, and it occurred quite frequently. I recorded many instances, nine of which I described in detail in my book on Kapauku law (1959). During one of my stays from 1954 to 1955, ten such crimes were committed against my adopted son Dou Itoogi and my best friend Ijaaj Jokagaibo. In one such case involving Itoogi, the thief did not succeed in carrying away his loot. One March morning in 1955 Itoogi appeared at my house smeared with ashes and dirt, a symbol of grief and utmost anger. He told me, his eyes full of tears, that his only pig had been shot and killed by a thief. The next day he started an investigation, asking for help with his search for the thief and for justice from the headman of Botukebo, Awiitigaaj, and from the confederacy's headman Ijaaj Ekajewaijokaipouga. The next day he appeared again at my house in a much happier state of mind. His pig, although shot in the chest with an arrow and taken for dead, had come almost miraculously back to life and had even started to eat sweet potatoes. Indeed, after a week the animal was back on its feet and searching for its food in the nearby swamps. Itoogi was so happy that he did not bother to proceed with the investigation.

Much more serious was the case of pig theft affecting my friend Ijaaj Jokagaibo. In June 1954 two men from the village of Degeipige stole his pig. After a few days a woman approached Jokagaibo and offered to disclose the identity of the criminals for a fee of 60 beads. My anxious friend paid the price. After having heard the names of the culprits — Edowai Mabii and Ijowau Imaatobii, both men from Degeipige — he led an expedition of men from his Ijaaj-Pigome confederacy to Degeipige to demand justice. The two men denied the deed and a fight almost started. However, the headman of Degeipige, Edowai Pejabii, sided with Jokagaibo and urged the culprits to pay an indemnity. He lectured the suspects: "Jokagaibo is a really rich man and has many wives. Therefore I am very much ashamed (because of you two). You repay him with a pig, or I shall feel embarrassed even to look at him." The two thieves, having been moved by the speech and possible repercussions if they did not comply, gave Jokagaipo a pig worth 12 cowries (in 1954 worth about $60).

Interestingly all the thefts of pigs I recorded, except two, involved parties from different confederacies. In the two cases which did occur within the same confederacy no punishment was administered to the culprits. With the rest, none of the punishments were heavier than those for other types of theft, while some were even lighter, and most involved no corporal punishment whatsoever. Therefore, it is safe to say that though pigs were the basis of the Kapauku economy, the primary source of wealth, and the most precious possession a Kapauku could have, the stealing of a pig did not elicit punishment commensurate with the animal's importance.

As in American society, theft was not the only way to acquire other people's property illegally. Embezzlement and fraud were also quite frequent offenses, reflecting in a way the people's desire to make a profit. In one case of fraud my own well-being and the future of my research was endangered. On 23 January 1955, Ijaaj Auwejokaamoje of Jawaugii village, one of the constituent villages of my Ijaaj-Pigome confederacy, went to Pueta, a village of the hostile Waine-Tibaakoto federation, our arch enemy, to claim a "stolen" bride price: that is, shell money which the groom's party had agreed to pay for a bride but which, after the consummation of the marriage, they refused to pay. Ijaaj Awiitigaaj, the headman of the Ijaaj-Enona sublineage of our Ijaaj-Pigome confederacy, accused his confederate co-member Auwejokaamoje of lying and trying to extort a sum of money that had not been agreed upon at all. By this act, he claimed, he had not only committed fraud (in Kapauku society, theft is not distinguished from fraud), but he enraged our traditional enemy to the south to such an extent that war might have resulted. On the 25 January, Ijaaj Auwe-jookaamoje returned from the south with Ijaaj Debabega and victoriously announced that he had succeeded in collecting the supposedly owed bride price because of the justice of his demand. However, we soon found out that he had threatened the Waine people by invoking my own influence in our confederacy and the Dutch administration of the distant Paniai Lake region. He claimed that I had ordered the payment. This lie enraged me, because it could have ruined my position as an impartial observer and made me not only a sort of judge and politician but also a crook. I castigated him publicly, and in this I was joined by the most important headmen of our confederacy Ekajew-aijokaipouga, Awiitigaaj, and Jokagaibo. They accused him of lying, of constantly begging other people for their property: beads, shell money, necklaces, and other items. Some of the people got quite worked up and Jokagaibo, Amojepa (the strong man of the Kojogeepa village), and even a man from outside our confederacy started the *wainai*, the mad dance, by which they signified that they might take violent action against the swindler. They piled new accusations on the head of the culprit. Ijaaj Jokagaibo prefaced his dance performance with an inflammatory speech as the headman of the culprit's sub-lineage. As a legal authority, he condemned the accused man to the dreaded public reprimand of which the mad dance of the three men was just the beginning. Of course Auwejokaamoje had to return the embezzled and extorted "bride price." Thus justice was done, peace with our traditional enemy restored, and excessive greed and cupidity curbed.

Rape and Adultery

One crime frequently committed in Kapauku society was rape. This typically meant the rape of a married woman. Rape of an unmarried girl was always considered problematic and usually treated as fornication, for which the offender had to pay *pituwo*, a certain amount of shell money depending on the degree of force he had used, the status and reputation of the girl, and his own past conduct and financial situation. During my prolonged stay this second type of offense was rare and represented a small part of the Kapauku adjudication process. The rape of a married woman was different. Exclusive sexual rights to a woman belong to her husband who had paid the requested bride price for her. Since the economic aspect of this crime was the dominant one, rape as well as adultery was called *oma magi*, "to steal sexual intercourse." Kapauku legal rules required the death penalty for the culprit, and in cases of voluntary adultery, death for both partners. An attempted rape would be punishable only by public reprimand.

The actual administration of justice was different, however. Almost invariably an adulterous woman was not killed but only publicly reprimanded and beaten by the infuriated husband. In the case of rape her husband, relatives, and the authorities pitied her and would not consider it adultery. That act, which had to involve force and overpowering, was called *pukwamo oma magi*, "to steal sex by force" (literally, overpowering the woman by forceful embracing). The male adulterer or rapist could escape the death penalty by generously compensating the husband, often as much as an average bride price. If payment was refused, killing, or even a war might be the consequence. Of the sixteen wars I recorded in the Kamu Valley, six were caused by adultery and a refusal to pay compensation. On 4 February 1955 my research became compromised by an act of adultery committed by Damianuuti, a native member of the Dutch colonial police who had been left with me to provide me with "protection." Instead, he might have had both of us killed. To counter the rage of the husband, Ijaaj Auwejokaamoje, I immediately offered him a knife and some beads as consolation. This made him friendly toward me and he dissociated me from the culprit, whom I sent away and who was later thrown out of the police and severely fined by the district officer, Raphael Den Haan. His dishonorable discharge from the force and the payment of the indemnity were publicly and ceremonially conducted at a large gathering on 19 February 1955.

The payment went to the "financially cheated husband." Had Damianuuti otherwise injured the raped woman in any way, he would have faced an additional charge and payment, and the money would have been given to the injured woman. In cases of adultery and elopement with a lover, the pair would be pursued by the lineage members of the offended husband. Many other people would join in, combing the forests to flush out and apprehend the two offenders. So it happened in my household when, in August 1955, Pegomuumaibo's wife escaped with her lover and all my forty-eight sons joined the excitement of the pursuit. The Kapauku search for offenders had a similar function to their public court hearings, almost as an entertainment would in American culture, with the exception that there was no charge for admission.

The most fascinating case of adultery I witnessed was that of Goo Amaadii, then the youngest wife of Ijaaj Jokagaibo, my best friend. In January 1955 a general alarm was sounded in our Ijaaj-Pigome confederacy. Goo Amadii was said to have run off with a man from the southern Waine-Tibaakoto confederacy, our traditional enemy. All my forty-eight sons went to help catch the culprits. Before leaving they promised me they would not kill either of the fugitives but would bring them back alive to face justice administered by the *tonowi*(s). Ijaaj Jokagaibo himself went to the village of Bibigi, the home of his unfaithful wife, in the hope of getting some information about her whereabouts and to enlist help in his search from her relatives, especially her brothers. He knew very well that his wife's brothers would support him because in the case of a broken marriage they might face the sad prospect of having to return the whole bride price. Jokagaibo's search was successful. He brought his wife back to Itoda with her hands tied, her *moge* (skirt, actually a loin wrap) torn, and the obvious marks of a beating.

The court was held right away. Since she had been caught *in flagrante delicto* there was no need for further evidence and the plea and sentencing could take place right away. A large number of spectators gathered around the "court in session." The enraged husband, supported by his brothers and those of his wife, demanded the death penalty for her and her seducer from the village of Mogokotu, who was still at large. There were no people on the defense side except, surprisingly, the mother of Jokagaibo (my classificatory mother), the mother-in-law of the guilty wife. In the Western tradition she would probably have been the last person to protect her adulterous daughter-in-law. She pleaded with her son and with the headman of the confederacy, Ijaaj Ekajewaijokaipouga, for leniency. In her plea she did not try to deny the guilt of the young woman or the seriousness of the crime. Very ingeniously she emphasized the extenuating circumstances, such as the young age of the woman (sixteen), her childlike and carefree personality, her industry and obedience, and her compulsion to please. Indeed, it was because of these good qualities that she had not tried to oppose her seducer. The only trouble was, as she rightly pointed out, she had made a mistake and pleased the wrong man. Jokagaibo quieted down a bit, intrigued by the eloquence of his mother and her unexpected arguments. Then she turned on him and started to castigate him saying that he would be a fool to kill such a beautiful woman and lose all the money he had paid for her. She said she had always regarded her son as a clever man and a good businessman, led by dispassionate reasoning rather than by blind emotions. Now he was acting like a romantically disillusioned *agaana*, a teenager. Her plea worked marvelously on the audience, the authorities, and especially the plaintiff — her son. He dropped the request for execution, but to save his reputation as a forceful leader, he furiously demanded death to the seducer. Goo Amaadii was untied, wrapped in a new *moge* supplied by her mother in-law, and led away by her to her husband's home. I was spellbound by her lecture and was only sorry I had not tape-recorded it. What a defense! What a clever argumentation using reasoning and logic, and at the same time playing cleverly on the emotions and pride of the plaintiff, the authorities, and her audience! I was proud of her, especially because she was my classificatory mother, the mother of my best friend.

The conclusion of the affair came only one day after Goo Amaadii's trial, when Jokagaibo led a war party to Mogokotu to kill the adulterer or obtain an adequate settlement. The Mogokotu people, frightened by such a show of force (my forty-eight sons, for example, all showed up in arms), pressed the culprit for settlement. Under pressure from his own headman he gave Jokagaibo a huge pig, which settled the affair peacefully. Goo Amaadii became a faithful wife to my friend, and a year afterwards she gave him a baby boy and they have lived "happily ever after" — along with Jokagaibo's fourteen other wives.

Overview
of Kapauku Law

Logic and empiricism permeate the Kapauku legal system. Their legal procedures characterized by a gathering of people; the presence of *tonowi*, an actual authority adjudicating cases; testimonies of witnesses; statements from the defense; the subdued attitude of the accused; the gathering and presenting of the evidence — all this reminded me of our own courts. How could it be claimed that these people had neither law nor leadership? The answer was obvious: those administrators and anthropologists working in colonized areas who had not lived among the natives for a prolonged time in an "uncontrolled" territory — an area not "pacified" by colonial powers — tended to take authority and power away from the native headmen or chiefs, either totally or partially. Very often these people did not speak the native tongue, relying on lingua franca or interpreters: they were not participant observers in any sense of the word. It was after such wholly inadequate experience that they claimed the role of the native headmen and chiefs was mainly conciliatory, and their solutions to problems invariably compromises.

Among the Kapauku, the *tonowi*'s ruling had to be justified: at sentencing, he would summarize the relevant evidence and refer to precedent and existing abstract rules. Indeed, the Kapauku, to my great surprise, had a very sophisticated codification of law, deposited in the minds of the old and knowledgeable men, who could recite excerpts verbatim, each man's version being virtually identical to the others'. These rules formed a beautifully logical, consistent whole, in which I could find little contradiction. How different from American law, in which our plethora of statutes often contradict each other, in which our lawyers have to search among old books and compilations of precedents rather than knowing their essence by heart. The Kapauku sanctions were reasonable; one could not find among them the absurdity that a man could be sentenced to several hundred or even a thousand years in prison. And most importantly, the plain truth and nothing but the truth was the main objective of legal procedure. There were no exclusionary rules, by which truth can be suppressed and jeopardized by technicalities, such as the inadmissibility evidence gathered in an illegal way. In Kapauku society, if such a violation occurred and the culprit was sentenced on the basis of illegally collected evidence, the collector himself would be sentenced in a separate hearing and punished. In such situations in American society, the obvious criminal as well as the irresponsible police officer often go unpunished.

The elaborate concepts of Kapauku law belied the commonly held notions among anthropologists regarding tribal "primitiveness" and "concrete thought." In at least one major respect they were more refined than is the case in America. So, as I stated above, while English does not distinguish between *ius* (law proper) and *lex* (abstract, usually written and codified rule, or statute), calling both concepts by the same term, "law" (which no other language to my knowledge does), the Kapauku language contrasts *boko duwai mana* (law proper) and *daa mana* (abstract rules, statutes). Precedent is called *me etita mania*, and dispute *mana koto*. Kapauku legal experts, be it the *tonowi*, the prosecutor, or the defense council, strive for their concept of justice, and since none of them receive any pay, they are not interested in getting as much as they can for their client. Certainly they are not perceived as parasites within their community. As Llewellyn and Hoebel did in the case of the Cheyenne Indians (1941). I cannot help but compare in its excellence Kapauku law to Old Roman Law.

War

War can be defined as an armed conflict between two politically autonomous social groups that are not parts of a larger, more inclusive political organization. Wars among the Kapauku Papuans may be considered endemic. I took detailed notes on fourteen such conflicts and have partial accounts of an additional eight. The recorded wars cover a span of twenty years preceding and during my first research period (1935–1955). In these wars a total of 359 men were killed, with casualties ranging from none to 140 (Pospisil 1993).

Although war between two confederacies of patrilineal lineages exacts the lives of people on both sides and sometimes results in considerable destruction of property, it also has a positive function. Unlike in our world, the Kapauku wars I observed were not fought because of racial or political intolerance, or because of different religious or philosophical beliefs. They all aimed to redress a crime, a refusal of payment of money owed, or rejection of a request for compensation for suffering or harm. Sometimes it even appeared to be an extension of justice where law was absent. One might even speculate that inter-confederational justice was helped by the threat of a possible war and its negative human and economic consequences.

My research in the Kamu Valley was conducted in an uncontrolled territory — the Dutch administration had not pacified it by extending their police control over it. So I was warned by the Dutch government that I might be in danger, that native warfare was endemic in my area. Indeed, during my stay in 1954–1955, I was exposed to two wars that involved me personally and a third that did not affect me directly. Because the Kapauku are economically oriented and prestige derives from economic success, fighting skill and exploits in war are not particularly valued, as is the case in the coastal area of New Guinea. In fact, no Kapauku seemed to like war. "War is bad and nobody likes it," observed Jokagaibo. "Sweet potatoes disappear, pigs disappear, gardens deteriorate, and relatives and friends get killed. But one cannot help it. A man starts a fight and no matter how much one despises him, one has to go and help him because he may be one's relative and one feels sorry for him." A war might last only a few days, claiming few or no casualties, or it might be a protracted affair that continued for a month or more and may account for the deaths of several hundred warriors. Indeed one war in Egebutu, part of the Kamu Valley, lasted over a year; the number of dead exceeded 140, leaving one community, Degeipige, practically without any adult male inhabitants. The number of participants also varied. In one of the fourteen engagements I recorded, only about 110 warriors were involved, while in another they numbered over 500. My Ijaaj-Pigome confederacy could mobilize about 600 warriors, men ranging in age from fourteen to about fifty years (the number includes not only confederacy members but also their in-laws, friends, and maternal relatives from villages outside of the confederacy). The confederacy headman was the most influential figure in starting a war, but also in stopping it and negotiating peace. If he was not a brave man and a skilled warrior himself, however, he would be limited in making decisions concerning war or peace. The conduct of the war would in that case be delegated to an expert war commander. This was not necessary in our own confederation because the sublineage, lineage, and confederacy headmen of the Ijaaj-Pigome confederacy (Ijaaj Jokagaibo, Awiitigaaj, Auwejokaamoje, Pegabii, Akoonewiijaaj, Onetaka Amojepa, and Ekajewaijokaipouga) were all brave and renowned warriors.

In the Kamu Valley, war was typically triggered by the elopement of a married woman with a man from another confederacy who subsequently refused to pay indemnity. Of the fourteen wars I recorded, three occurred during my fieldwork. Six had as their cause elopement (desertion of a wife), two occurred because of killing by sorcery, one because of an accidental killing, and one started as a game of arrow shooting. Stealing or reneging on a monetary obligation accounted for the last four. The man whose wife eloped, who was swindled, whose relative was killed, or whose property (mostly pigs) was stolen tried to initiate war by pleading his case with the *tonowi* and demanding action. If his case was ethical and justified the authorities would support him and call for their constituents to go to war. The man on whose behalf the war was fought was called *jape ipuwe* — the owner of the enemy — and was basically held responsible for the consequences of the conflict. If he started the conflict without the approval of his headman and his reason for fighting was regarded as unethical, he might risk capital punishment passed upon him in a secret council of the *tonowi*. His close patrilineal relatives might then try to shoot him in an ambush, or he might be extradited to the enemy who did the killing. If, however, his cause was just and the war was officially sanctioned, a secret attack on the enemy villages would be planned. In practice, no such plan could ever be kept completely secret because people talk, and married women who were born in the enemy confederacy and moved to their husbands' village would warn their fathers, brothers, and patri-parallel cousins (such as their father's brother's son, father's father's brother's son's son, etc.) of the imminent danger. Sometimes the intention to go to war was made public, and an emissary might even be dispatched to warn about the ensuing armed conflict.

Two Wars Witnessed

This was the case in the war between the Ijaaj-Pigome and Waine-Tibaakoto confederacies during my research in 1955. Actually, the emissary also came to me and told me that I was regarded as one of the most important leaders of the Ijaaj-Pigome people and that the Waine-Tibaakoto people would try to shoot me first. The threat was very real, so when writing my diary before I retired that night I explained in it the reason for my death, should I be killed. Of course I did not like the idea of being the first target to be hit by the enemy snipers. That night I did not sleep well and tried to figure out how I could get out of this unenviable situation. I remembered University of Oregon Professor Cressman's lecture on an Inca emperor, how he skillfully pacified his beaten enemy by adopting sons of the enemy leaders and bringing them to his capital, Cuzco, for schooling. "That's it!" I yelled, waking up my pig, which was sleeping underneath my bed. It grunted as if in approval. At sun-up I got hold of the emissary, who had slept in Botukebo (he was "immune" because he was only an in-law of the enemy — a go-between). I told him I wanted to adopt several boys, sons of the headmen of our enemy confederacy. He was skeptical about the possibility of success, because, as he said, there was little time to do that. Hostilities could erupt at any time. After this not very reassuring comment he left. That same evening I was amazed to see five sons of our enemy's ringleaders coming to be adopted. I gave them proper names and my sons accepted them quite willingly into their midst.

Although the animosity between the two confederacies grew, there was no war until one day the boys from both confederacies began playing a war game shooting blunt-tipped arrows at each other (the tips were blunted by a fresh, soft segment of reed). The game was called *kimuutii* and was usually lots of fun. However, some infuriated rascals who had been hit by the blunt arrows and had drawn laughter from onlookers started to shoot war arrows. Real war, which had been simmering for quite a time, erupted in earnest. Being father to boys on both sides, I was necessarily not only neutral but also immune to their arrows. To exploit this fortunate situation, I put on my raincoat (to buffer any stray arrows should they hit me), took my movie and Leica cameras, and went to the battlefield. My first walk between the battle lines was not too comfortable because some arrows came disagreeably close to me. But soon, realizing that my neutrality was really respected, I walked freely between the two lines of warriors fighting on the grassy flatland bordering the large swampy area of the Kamu Valley. Adults and headmen had joined both sides, and a real fight was in progress. Arrows were whizzing back and forth, and people were yelling, hiding in the tall grass then suddenly reappearing to discharge their missiles. If they were really brave they would jump back and forth to dodge incoming arrows and shoot without taking cover at all. Snipers circled the area, and I succeeded in taking some good shots of them. All went well for me until some of my boys started to take cover behind me. I had to chase them away and asked them to go home — of course, to no avail. Several of my boys tried to protect me from the flying arrows with their naked bodies. I had to dissuade them from their valiant efforts by claiming that I had to take my own risks, just as they did. Several warriors were dancing *ukwa-wakii-tai,* a victory dance, by running round in circles yelling *wuii wuii* in high-pitched voices and holding their bows by one end in an upright position and twisting them left and right by turning their wrists — a gesture indicating that they had hit an enemy. As the day came to its close the hostilities stopped and people disengaged and went home to manufacture more war arrows or to dress their wounds. Fortunately there were no fatalities, only wounded people, whose wounds I helped to dress. That night in my role as a go-between related to both sides I succeeded, with the help of my friend-headman Jokagaibo, to negotiate peace.

This brief engagement was not typical of a Kapauku war. I had witnessed one before at a place called Mujikebo, on the far northern fringe of the Kamu Valley. A war broke out there between confederacies of the Pekej and Pigaaj clans. My people joined the Pigaaj side. In this case, the war started as a planned attack against a Pigaaj village. The approach of the war party was discovered in time, so that the two battle lines met before the village came under attack. My boys and friends urged me to go see the fighting. This was my first real experience of war among the Kapauku. The fighting presented a very strange sight. Since the Kapauku fought exclusively with bows and arrows and did not use stabbing or crushing weapons, their warfare resembled our modern wars. The people did not mass themselves in fighting formations but fought almost individually, dodging the flying arrows, disappearing in the tall grass and reappearing to shoot. As in the war described above, the bravest did not take cover, but instead skipped from side to side facing the enemy missiles. However, between the lines of warriors and behind them I observed women unperturbed by the fighting, peacefully collecting stray arrows as if they were harvesting potatoes. To accomplish this task they had a generally accepted immunity that protected them from the enemy. Much as I had witnessed in previous battles, the bolder members of the "weaker" sex climbed a hill behind enemy lines and, from there, shouted advice concerning the enemy's movements to their fighting husbands. The annoyed and embarrassed enemy could do nothing other than chase the women away by pushing them or beating them with their fists or bows, but because the women wielded walking sticks, which were usually much longer than the bows, I saw some men receive a good thrashing. During this particular war no side was winning, so even after several days there were no clear victors who could invade and plunder the gardens of the enemy, burn their houses, and kill their pigs.

In addition to this type of combat, snipers would usually try to penetrate deep into the enemy's territory and shoot from ambush. Often the sniper would be accompanied by several of his relatives who would then let him go alone the last few hundred yards into the enemy village to make the kill. This was done not to prove the skill and courage of the sniper, but because it was easier for an individual to penetrate an enemy village alone than for a whole group of warriors who might be easily spotted. I was able to film only one sniper expedition, which tried to circle the enemy's battle line and shoot the enemy from behind. However, they were detected and a brief exchange of arrows followed.

The Mujikebo war started to become really bloody. In the first three days one man died, four were very seriously wounded, and many others were hurt. As I was taking pictures and filming, a man nearby was shot by a lean (unbarbed) arrow called a *matii* through the back of his neck. The arrow pierced the trapezoid muscle cleanly and protruded from the other side. I tried to take his picture, but my film was finished and I had to reload my camera. The fellow grabbed the wooden point of the arrow with the rattan wrapping which fastened it to the reed shaft and wanted to break it off. I pleaded with him to wait until I could take his picture. He, ignorant of picture-taking and cameras, screamed at me, "*Noukwa bubu* (a profanity meaning 'by the behind of my mother') will I wait!" broke the tip, and pulled the shaft from his neck. What a pity! What a spectacular shot it would have been. In 1959 when I returned for my second research to the Kapauku I ran into the man at a gathering. By that time the people had been exposed to Dutch control and the inventions of civilization. He smiled at me and said, "How stupid I was not to wait for your picture-taking. How I would appreciate it now to be able to show off with it!" Thus there were at least two people sorry for his impatience. "Of course," he said, "it hurt pretty bad."

The war dragged on, and my Ijaaj-Pigome people, being allies of the Pigaaj clansmen, were brought into the conflict. So I had to worry that a Pekej sniper might take a shot at me. While this and other wars were raging in the Kamu region and between it and the Paniai Lake and the Dutch outpost at Enarotali, Mr. Lewis, a tough pilot of the American Christian Mission Alliance, flew once a week over my valley dropping me my mail and looking from his Cessna plane to see if I was still alive. The Dutch side made two attempts to end the conflict. The first was undertaken by Father Steltenpool of the Catholic Mission at Ugapuga, who went to the battle lines and tried to stop the shooting. In his effort he was almost shot himself, an arrow barely missing his chest. The second was a police expedition organized by my friend the District Officer Raphael Den Haan. Although the territory was not yet under Dutch colonial control, he interfered because he feared for my well-being. His policemen, armed with rifles and submachine guns, moved in, stopped the fighting, and arrested twenty-seven of the warriors. Prior to this police action I had received a "formal ultimatum" on a scroll from Mr. Den Haan, requesting that I withdraw from the battle lines to avoid being arrested together with the rest of the Kapauku war leaders. Later, after writing a number of letters, I managed to get the twenty-seven men out of jail. Raphael Den Haan was quite a sport.

Aftermath

Peace was usually negotiated by in-laws of the combatants who were central to the conflict. The prerequisite for an easy conclusion of war was that the number of people killed on both sides should be the same. Any discrepancy in the numbers would either preclude a peace agreement or would require monetary compensation, called me mere ("human cowries"), a sort of blood money that would even out the balance. My records show that the payments were quite onerous, consisting of at least 180 old cowries, 180 introduced cowries, and two fully grown pigs for the death of a single man. The money was paid by the *jape ipuwe* ("owner of the enemy") of the side that had fewer men killed to the father and brothers of an enemy whose death had not been avenged. Establishing death totals might be complicated by the fact that any individual who died of a wound received in the war after the peace was concluded upset the so-called *uta-uta,* or balance ("half-half," like our fifty-fifty), thus requiring a new payment in order to reestablish the equilibrium. Even after many years, if a previously wounded man died and the progeny could prove that a sliver of the arrow or a piece of the orchid-wrapping that held the arrowhead had been left in the wound, blood money had to be paid. If payment was not made the refusal might cause another war. In 1962, during my third research visit, Keija Ipouga of Bunauwobado died, supposedly from the splinter of an arrow left in the wound by his surgeon about 25 years earlier. The relatives of the deceased man, led by Ijaaj Maatabii of Aigii, the son of Keija's father's mother's brother, requested blood money payment from Tagi Tagikabii of Tuguteke, the son of the late Tagi Kumeebo, the man credited with injuring Keija originally. Tagi, however, refused to pay, claiming that there was no proof that Keija had died of the injury inflicted on him in the war. Indeed, he challenged Maatabii and his relatives to conduct an autopsy to prove whether a splinter had actually been left in Keija's body. At the time of my departure the problem was still being negotiated, and it appeared that the incoming Indonesian government would have to adjudicate this difficult dispute.

The financial aspect of a Kapauku war involved more than only blood money. *Uwataa,* or blood compensation, had to be paid by the *jape ipuwe* to the relatives of a man who died while fighting on his side. Furthermore, *dabe uwo* ("mud water"), the blood reward discussed above, had to be paid to an avenger of one's patrilineal relative. Indeed, even a man in whose arms a man died has to be paid *emoo mana* ("blood words") by the deceased man's relatives. Thus Kapauku warfare was for many a very serious financial burden, and it was for this reason as well as the loss of lives that war was generally hated.

This is therefore a summary of Kapauku warfare for the twenty years preceding and including my first research. According to the Dutch colonial administration I was putting my life at risk — a risk I could have easily avoided by studying a Papuan society in a so-called "pacified territory." But, as I explained above, such a study would not have revealed an aboriginal legal system unpolluted by the white man's law and administrative colonial regulations. It would have been simply another study of colonized people, obscuring their original administration of justice. So I had to face the danger of being killed "in the line of scientific research." As it turned out, the presumed danger to my person, although real, was not so dramatic. When compared with wars in our civilized society, the native war causalities of 359 deaths over a span of 22 recorded years was unbelievably low. So I was justified in not being afraid and facing the possible danger. After all, I had already lived through the Second World War, in which SS troops killed millions of civilians, the front went right through my village, three of my schoolmates were brutally murdered, I was interrogated several times by the Gestapo (an interrogation that many did not survive), and I harboured an anti-Nazi military deserter in the loft of my farm. With my past, who would be afraid of tribal warfare?

And Kapauki warfare, it turned out, was governed by unwritten laws and rules of engagement. Kapauku did not kill the wives of their enemies or old men. They did not take prisoners of war and hostages to be traded with the enemy after the conflict, or eventually killed. Even when an old man or woman refused to leave their home in a conquered village, the houses were not set on fire. How does this supposed "savagery" compare with our "total warfare"? When my village was strafed by fighter-bombers and bombs were exploding all around me, a piece of shrapnel hit the pavement two yards from me (I kept it as a souvenir). I somehow had no fear of war. I was much more worried about the atrocities of modern dictatorships, be it German National Socialism (the Nazis) who murdered 20 million people in their concentration camps; Soviet Union Communists with a record of more than sixty million victims in the "Gulag Archipelago" in Russia and Siberia; Red China and Cambodia competing with these numbers in the "political cleansing" of their populations. So having these thoughts and memories, I would be a strange fellow indeed to be afraid of Kapauku warfare and hostilities. I have learned from experience and from recent history that war, horrible as it is, is not the worst thing that can happen to a man or woman. Modern dictatorship is."

Magic and Religion

Religion may be defined as a system of belief in a non-phenomenal (not empirically verifiable) superior power vested in a supernatural theory (philosophy). In other words, it is non-empirical because it does not require verification by sensual perception. It is a non-rational, essentially emotional, attachment to a creed. Usually it is intolerant of other views. Humans have no control over this power, their contact with it is prayer, and their attitude is one of humility. Its practitioner is an intermediary — usually a priest, prophet, shaman, or other personality with knowledge of the particular religious doctrine — but he or she has no special powers of his or her own.

Magic, in comparison, is also non-empirical. It is also based in the realm of emotion. However, unlike religion, it is a belief in a nexus between a formula or a specific act and a desired result. Therefore, unlike religion, it is practical. Like science, it operates on the basis of principles, rules, and formulas, albeit empirically non-verifiable ones. Unlike religion and unlike science, its practitioners, be they magicians, shamans, sorcerers or witchdoctors, are believed to possess powers of a supernatural nature. Unlike in religion but like in science, these practitioners are in control of the outcome. As in religion, the practitioner's emotional bond with the magical procedure is expressed through a ritual. These practitioners, especially magicians, must be distinguished from witches, who are believed to be malevolent individuals. The supernatural powers of witches are not acquired through learning, as are those of the magician — they are inborn. Far from being practitioners like magicians, they are scapegoats, nonconformists, or social misfits. In the Kapauku repertory of belief in the supernatural, I found that both the shamans (magicians, *kamu epi me*) and witches (*meenoo*) played important roles.

My plan was to analyze the magic, religion, and philosophy of the Kapauku people as late in my research as possible, knowing that

I would need a good command of their language and knowledge of their culture. As for my own culture, I violated it as soon as I came to the Kamu Valley. Three days after my arrival some of the Kapauku tried to stop the rain so that we could proceed with clearing the ground to build my house. Thus I was exposed to Kapauku magic almost immediately. Although at that time I was not able to record the words and magical formulas, I did take notes about the behavior of the magicians and the reactions of the bystanders. The performer used words to address the approaching clouds then spit three times in the direction of the rain, and occasionally threw ashes from the fireplace into the rainy weather. Later I learned the formula. *Idi damo uwo damo kamunimak-eega geepii, geekii katijawega*: "Gates of rain, gates of water I have shut them because of you, I have told you *geepii, geekii* [to reproduce the sounds of dry leaves and reeds swung in the wind)." Although some of my students at Yale pronounced the formula and tried to stop the rain in New Haven, they had no success, obviously because they failed to spit into the rain. Connecticut law prohibits spitting since the time of the Spanish flu epidemic after World War I. So we have the law to blame for the terrible weather in New Haven.

Another not so commonly practiced magic was of the curative type. Every magical procedure that I witnessed started with the shaman's prayer to the sun and moon god (i.e. creator) and to his own guardian spirits. During the performance the shaman would invariably use a magically powerful plant. Its selection often depended on the type of disease diagnosed. As a rule, the evil spirits causing a disease were associated with specific plants. However, the most commonly used remedy was the green variety of the ti plant (Cordyline terminalis), a repellent of most evil spirits. The shaman would carry it around his patient, touch the head and other parts of the body with it, shake it frequently, and thus expel the spirit causing the disease. Very often the plants were used together with glowing embers. A bundle consisting of both of these ingredients would be moved counterclockwise around the patient's head, followed immediately by clockwise circles. The ritual was accompanied by repetitive spells, uttered rapidly by the shaman, and by his spitting on the embers as well as around the patient. Since water is believed to have a purifying force, both shaman and patient would apply it frequently to different parts of their bodies. Indeed, during one performance I filmed the shaman Kaadoot-ajbii, who in his ecstasy jumped periodically into the adjacent creek on whose bank the ceremony was being performed. This could have been a magnificent piece of documentation, complete with beautiful scenery and setting sun, and a shaman in full trance. Unfortunately, the film was lost when my boys, transporting it to Paniai Lake, were attacked by enemies and threw away everything they were carrying, including my movie.

The spirits were always "bribed" to leave the patient's body with the plants and glowing embers, often augmented by small birds and sacrificial rats and the intestines of some larger animals. Toward the end of the ritual the offerings would be hung on a pole or thrown by the shaman behind his back into the bush. The procedure might be combined with activities in which the shaman would extract by sleight of hand an evil object from the patient's body. The practitioner might also try to recapture the patient's soul on the end of his ti plant broom and reintroduce it into the patient's body. The magician's trance, as well as his dreams, might also be employed in the cure. Through these the shaman might claim to have learned the cause of the illness as well as the remedy for it. At the end of the magical ceremony he would suggest some special observances that the patient must follow as a continuation of his cure. For a period of time, or for the rest of his or her life, he or she might have to refrain from eating certain kinds of food (plant or animal). As a condition for a complete cure the patient might be requested to manifest his or her generosity. This usually consisted of killing a pig and distributing the meat free of charge to the public. Sometimes an adult patient might also be asked to set aside a certain quantity of cowries for his or her son's inheritance in the form of a trust deposited in a cache in a cave, or entrusted to the custody of one of his wives.

In July 1959, I observed a special type of curative magic performed by Ijaaj Ekajewaijokaipouga, the headman of the Ijaaj-Pigome confederacy, on my best friend Ijaaj Jokagaibo. This was of the *kego ekigai* (literally, "to untie sorcery") type, a preventive magic employed when a man suspected an enemy of having sent an evil spirit upon him (having performed *kego tai*, black magic). In such a case the endangered individual would not wait until the onset of the affliction but would seek shamanistic help in advance. In this counter-magic, the shaman would employ the curative magical procedure just described, except that the ceremony would be more elaborate and the bribes more numerous, and greater generosity would generally be required from the patient. This was necessary because the evil spirit that caused the disease would not only be asked to leave the patient's body, but would actually be bribed into attacking the sick man's enemy, the sorcerer himself. It stands to reason that for such an amount of work the evil spirit would have to be offered more than he usually received for simply refraining from killing his designated victim.

There were other types of *kamu tai* (white magic), such as that used for economic gain performed especially during the pig feast ceremony, or for winning a war and killing many enemies, or to prevent a man from dying of arrow wounds by eliminating the evil spirit that might cause infection and "blood poisoning." This ritual was very simple, consisting of either licking a *jape daagu*, a small highly polished black stone with white veins, or using green branches of the ti tree and rubbing them in slow motion over one's body. All of these magical rites might be employed to treat not only an individual but a group of people. In this kind of group magic, many people would be treated at the same time — some of the rites had to be modified to adapt them to this different situation.

Unlike the various magical rites described above, which I not only observed but also filmed, the sorcery was the strictly private affair of an individual and kept rigorously secret. Consequently I witnessed none of these performances, deriving my data only from interviews with my informants. The Kapauku sorcerer was a specialist in his art, for which he was paid a fee. His rites, which took place in the secrecy of the jungle, varied in complexity from an "evil eye," accompanied by a magical formula, to contagious magic in which a spell was cast upon something belonging to the intended victim (e.g. a hair clipping, pieces of clothing, bodily excretions, or a footprint in the mud), to a complex rite of imitative magic. In the latter performance the sorcerer would use the magical plant associated with a particular evil spirit, which was then asked to be the sorcerer's executioner. For example, a cut *otikai* tree stem would be planted in the ground, spells uttered, and offerings given to Tege, an evil spirit who was believed to be magically associated with the *otikai* tree. Then, with a single blow of an ax or machete, the *otikai* stem would be cut in half. Tege was supposed to kill the victim magically in the same way that the tree was cut down.

As in the case of white magic, the sorcerer would also employ a plant that was generally applicable in all his rites. This was the *jukune*, the red variety of the ti plant. Fear of the *jukune* and its use was indeed real. Once in 1955 I visited the mission in Ugapuga and was surprised to see that the church, whose walls were made of an Indonesian type of matting, were torn and the whole structure damaged. Part of it looked as if a bulldozer had gone through it. Father Steltenpool explained to me that for a mysterious reason his congregation had suddenly become panicky during his service and tore through the walls and door in order to escape from the structure. Since the missionary had conducted services in that village for many months without any such incident, the sudden violent behavior of the people seemed inexplicable. On further inquiry, I found that the Kapauku houseboy of the missionary, the rascal who had pulled the practical joke I described earlier by translating the word "soul" as *kedi*, "nails", and who helped the clergyman with his services, had substituted *jukune*, the red variety of the ti plant, for the green variety normally used for blessing the congregation with holy water. When the unfortunate Father Steltenpool started to swing the plant associated with sorcery, the frantic worshippers, desperate to avoid death from the missionary's supposed "black magic," escaped wherever there was an opening in the walls of the structure. The effect was the same as if a gangster had sprayed an audience in our city with submachine gun fire. Needless to say, when I unraveled the mystery of his congregation's strange behavior to the missionary, the young rascal took a swift leave.

The ability to perform white magic was always an asset to a Kapauku, especially to a headman. In order to partake in this source of prestige I used my supplies of aspirin to cure headaches and sulfa drugs to save people who had bacillary dysentery. I would point to the heavens and predict that a headache would cease when the sun reached a certain point on its route. Saving children from dysentery was of course the most spectacular and rewarding task. In serious cases I used penicillin and Terramycin. However, my "magical" abilities received the highest recognition in an unexpected way. Since distribution of food to my boys and girls would have been quite time consuming if it occurred throughout the day, I instituted a rule that the boys and girls would have to get their daily provisions at the time when *tege mana tidaa* — when the cicada started to hum. This occurred almost exactly and regularly around six o'clock in the evening. All went well until one evening when I was waiting behind the heaps of food supplies and my adopted progeny were seated in a semicircle in front of me, awaiting their daily rations and showing their impatience ... and the darned insects would not start their evening concert. To help the situation I took a blade of grass, put it between the thumbs of both my hands, and blew on it, producing a sharp, shrill sound. The whole valley started to resound with a magnificent chorus of cicadas. The boys and girls rolled about in laughter, and I brazenly claimed credit for that entomological feat.

What did I think of Kapauku magic when I witnessed the various observances? Did I regard their actions as hopelessly primitive or silly? No, not with my knowledge of their culture and life. In the absence of microscopes and other medical technology, their performances seemed quite natural to me. In situations where reason and knowledge cannot help, the emotional part of the human mind takes over. Are we really so rational when faced with problems like an incurable disease, financial ruin, or the loss of our child? Most of us would pray, but some might resort to a magical observations. A magical utterance learned from friends or relatives might escape my lips, a curse might be uttered, and the "magically significant and dangerous" situation might even be avoided. Personally, I do not believe in magic, but when escaping from Communist Czechoslovakia through the "Iron Curtain" on Friday the thirteenth of March 1948, the traditionally inauspicious date caused a peculiar uneasiness in the back of my mind about our future in the strange foreign world. Was it a subconscious regression into primitiveness? Well, I didn't care then and I still don't care today, but thanks to that experience, I understand the Kapauku reaction to any similar problematic situation. After all, I have read that some hotels do not have a thirteenth floor or a room with the number thirteen. When we react with a bias against the number thirteen, are we so different from tribal people?

Religion

Generally speaking, and especially in comparison with the lowlands of New Guinea, the Kapauku were basically secular in orientation. Their ceremonial life, unlike that of their lowland neighbors, was characterized by simplicity, lack of conformity to a rigid pattern, and a marked stress on secularity and sobriety. Whereas the ceremonial events of many coastal tribes were mainly concerned with the supernatural and occult, almost all Kapauku ceremonies were connected with their economy. Their religion was based on the concept of a supreme deity and a set of spirits that fell into several categories. Most of these were regarded as evil (*enija*, evil spirit; *tene*, departed shade; *meeno*, ghouls; etc.), while only some were beneficent (*ani ipuwe enija* — the soul of a deceased relative).

The whole universe, according to Kapauku belief, was designed and created by Ugatame, the creator of men (*ugai* — to create; *me* — man). He was supposed to be masculine and feminine at the same time, and was referred to in dual number as if two entities — a duality manifest to men as the sun and the moon. These were only manifestations, not God him- or herself. The sun was regarded as a hot fireball, while the moon was compared to the light of a firefly or foxfire in rotting wood. Ugatame was omniscient, omnipotent, credited with the creation of all existence, and responsible for all future happenings. Logically then, he himself did not exist (he "was not") because he/she created all existence — he/she was beyond it. Because he/she existed in a kind of fifth dimension and was not of a phenomenal nature, he/

she was able to be omnipresent. From this basic premise the rest of the Kapauku religion was logically derived, not exhibiting the inconsistencies and contradictions so evident in some religions. Because Ugatame created all existence, he himself necessarily was responsible not only for the good things (*enaa*), but also for the evil (*peu*). And because Ugatame determined everything, there could be no sin as man had no free will. There was no concept of hell and heaven; neither reward for good behavior nor punishment for bad after death. After all, the Creator created good as well as evil, so why should he punish man for executing his/her own will?

In their religious beliefs, the Kapauku were basically logical. They refused to accept dogmas that either opposed empirical evidence or contradicted each other. The logical thinking of the Kapauku was revealed to me in 1955, when a very old man from the Mapia region, supported by his two sons, managed to come to see me in the Kamu Valley. His main purpose in seeking me out was to clarify a problem he thought existed in the religious thought of the white man, as he had heard about it from people who traveled to Paniai Lake and were exposed to the white man's religion. He simply could not understand how it was possible that the white man could be so clever and ingenious in designing such contrivances as airplanes (which he had seen flying over his valley), clothing, medicine, guns, and steel tools and, at the same time, be so illogical in his religion. "How can you think that a man can sin and can have free will, and at the same time believe that his God is omnipotent, that he created the world and determined all that happens in it? If he determined all that happens, including bad deeds, how can a man be held responsible? Why, if he is omnipotent, did he have to change into a man and allow himself to be killed (crucified) when it would have been enough for him just to order men to behave?" The notion that some deeds could be absolutely bad or good or that God could resemble man in appearance seemed to him utterly wrong.

Because of their conception of God and the universe and their insistence on logic, the Kapauku misinterpreted the Christian ideas of hell and heaven. The missionaries certainly were not responsible for their understanding of these ideas and reactions to them. My friend Awiitigaaj, the old headman of the Ijaaj-Enona sub-lineage of Botukebo, once told me something truly surprising. He stated flatly that if Christianity reflected the true nature of the world, as the newly arrived Catholic catechist preached, then he wanted to go to hell. The reason was quite obvious, as he explained: "In hell there is an eternal fire. One does not have to worry about fuel, which is generously supplied by devils. In hell it must be warm and cozy, while it stands to reason that up in the heaven, above the clouds, it must be dreadfully cold. You can feel it when you climb the high mountains how cold it must be up there." However, the advantage of having an eternal fire did not strike me as the real reason Awiitigaaj wished to go to hell. So I kept questioning him until I finally learned the true reason. Since Awiitigaaj had 10 wives, he argued, he would have to surrender nine of them if he went into the cold heavens. On the contrary, in hell he could keep all of them and stay there happily in a warm environment. He then smiled at me and asked, "You realize what kind of women will be up there? All the women I am interested in will be down in hell." This was a most convincing argument that, if publicly pronounced, would be unlikely to make the Franciscan missionaries happy.

As I tried to be as scientific in my study as possible, I wanted to make some experiments to verify certain of my conclusions. For example, it was not clear to me how real the fear of evil spirits was. So when my boys and some people from Botukebo village went to Egebutu, located across the swamps and river on the other side of the Kamu Valley, I decided to conduct an experiment. At night on their way back through the swamps they would have to pass a tree with dense foliage that stood alone on a small island in the middle of the swamp and was credited with housing Ukwaanija, an abominable water spirit. That night, long after their departure, I went to the tree, climbed into its crown, and waited for my people. Around midnight I heard them approaching in the semidarkness of a starry night. As they drew close to the tree I started shaking the branches and producing frightening sounds in a deep voice: "whoo-whoo!" I expected screams and running in panic. To my amazement the first boy Jaagodooti lifted his head and called, "Our father, climb down, we know it is you up there." I was flabbergasted. "How did you know?" I inquired. I can best translate their answer as, "Very elementary, our father. An evil spirit does not say 'whoo-whoo' in a low voice but makes a high-pitched 'yee-yee'." My experiment was a dismal failure, but I did enlarge my knowledge of the vocal behavior of Kapauku supernatural beings.

So this is an account of the religion of a tribal people whom many of our theoreticians and even social scientists (especially Marxists) have called "primitive" or, in the not distant past, "savage." If we consider the Kapauku religion, what do we find that is primitive? The belief in an omnipotent, omniscient, and omnipresent supreme being called "Ugatame," creator of men? It is actually a type of monotheism, the belief in a single god, a similar belief to Christianity. Since their belief parallels Christianity, Judaism, Islam, and other "civilized" religions, it seems naïve to call it primitive. It is complex and imbued with so-phisticated concepts, and actually surpasses Christianity, Judaism, and Islam in its systematic logical construction, devoid of self-con-tradictory dogmas. In calling it "primitive" or even "savage" and our own religion "civilized," we are treading on very shaky ground. What about members of a society who are atheists, who deny the existence of god or any other supernatural being, and even religion itself? Is their system of believing in the various "-isms" (Marxism, Nazism, Fascism) not also a belief in a philosophy which is non-empirical and which they consider infallible? In their worldview, religion is actually any belief in a specific infallible doctrine. Thus, in a way our modern political systems are indeed religions because their essence is a blind belief in a political ideology. Strangely enough, these political systems parallel religions, especially Christianity, since they too originated in our Western civilization. As in Christianity, such "-isms" are believed by their followers to be infallible. Just as Christianity has its Bible, they have their own holy texts (e.g. Das Kapital, Mein Kampf, etc.). In both Christianity and the political "-isms," there are prophets (Marx, Lenin, Hitler, Mussolini), with their "holy" tombs (Lenin embalmed like an Egyptian pharaoh, for example); "pilgrimages" to sacred places (Red Square, Walhalla, etc.); and processions in which portraits of the saints and prophets are carried. Deviants from these creeds are not regarded as common criminals but as heretics who, prior to their execution, should be forced to admit their "sins," like John Hus who was burnt at the stake for his beliefs, many so-called medieval witches, and modern political heretics such as, in Communism, Zinoviev, Kamenev, Trotsky, Bukharin, and, in Nazism, Röhm and others. Shockingly, even the official emblems of the "-isms" resemble the cross in Christianity: the swastika (*Hakenkreuz* or "cross of hooks" and *Kruckenkreuz* or cross of crutches) of the fascists; the crossed hammer and sickle of the communists. These political religions murdered millions of people in prisons and concentration camps set up for the purpose (Nazi Dachau and Auschwitz, to name only two, and the multitude of concentration and extermination camps of the Gulag Archipelago in the Soviet Union) and killing fields (as in Cambodia). Men, women, and children were sent to their death under unbelievably horrible conditions. How true remains the old Roman saying *homo homini lupus* ("Man is to man a wolf"). These are the real savages, not the far more humane tribal peoples such as the Kapauku. These comparisons haunted me during my stay in New Guinea. In the Kamu Valley I was not living among "savages." It took no courage to stay among those Stone Age people; but I would not have the courage to cross Central Park alone at night. In comparison with my past in Europe, among the Kapauku I felt like I was in heaven. Was I in danger of my life there? No. The danger was in my old home — Europe.

Tabooed Mt. Deijai

In another incident involving Kapauku evil spirits, my participation was not voluntary.

Over the Kamu Valley towered a monumental mountain, Mount Deijai, its peak about 13,000 feet high. Together with the surrounding forest it was a tabooed place. As I was told, the forests and the mountain were haunted by various evil spirits, of which Madou, the terrible mountain and water demon, was the most feared. People avoided the area, no one had ever climbed the peak, and the people spoke about the territory with reverence and in a subdued voice. Unfortunately, I decided to climb it and take pictures of the Kamu Valley and the mountainous terrain. But before I set out I had to determine what kind of taboo had been imposed on the area. The Kapauku had two types of taboo. One type was imposed upon actions which were believed to hurt individuals other than the actor. Such taboos were provided not only with sanctions from the supernatural, but since their violation caused, according to their belief, harm or even death to other people, the perpetrator was also charged with a crime and brought to trial. The sentencing always fitted the believed consequence of the violation. So, for example, in around 1940 Dou Maga of Jotapuga, a woman of child-bearing age, violated a taboo and ate *apuu*, a type of yam. It was believed that eating *apuu* — or *teto*, a red variety of sugar cane; *kugou* and *jigikago*, two types of plantain; *wiijaaj* and *pugaago*, two types of parrot; or *agou*, a marsupial species — by an adult woman prior to menopause would cause the death of the woman's husband, for which she should be punished by death. Indeed, Maga ate the fruit and her husband died a few days later. Ijaaj Tideemabii of Kojogee-pa — the son of the dead man — and one of his co-wives heard about the wife's misbehavior from people who had seen the woman eat the forbidden fruit. He reported the act to Ijaaj Ekajewaijokaipouga of Aigii, the headman of his lineage and also of the whole Ijaaj-Pigome confederacy. On the basis of the evidence Ekajewaijokaipouga was convinced of the woman's guilt and decided on execution. Tideemabii then waited for the woman to return from her garden and shot her from ambush. After her execution the people, as custom commanded, erected a *keage*, a wooden platform on which the corpse was laid out and abandoned.

The second type of taboo was a violation that caused harm only to the violator of the taboo and was not subject to legal regulation. On the contrary, breaking these taboos, were regarded as a folly of the violator, or sometimes even as a heroic deed — a challenge to the evil spirit and as such to be admired. Luckily for me the taboo imposed on Mount Deijai was of this second type. So I decided to try my luck and announced my intention to the Kapauku. While my adopted sons were undecided but intrigued by the idea and the possibility of becoming heroes, my adult friends, especially Kaadootajbii, the shaman and a best friend of mine, were appalled and tried to dissuade me from the venture. But I would not give in. Like Sir Edmund Hilary I had to attempt it "because it was there." So on 18 September 1955, in the company of nine of my boys and the shaman (who insisted on protecting me) we went to Ugapuga. There my people heard dissuading arguments that the Agapaa and Pekej people, clans whose members lived around the holy mountain and the tabooed area, would be mad at us and shoot us if we tried to break the supernatural prohibition. However, this proved to be a false rumor, so I decided to start immediately and make a night camp in the forbidden forest. My boys, however, were by now so scared of the supernatural that they would not follow me. Instead of trying to argue with them I used an effective Kapauku ploy: I stood up, picked up my pack and bid them goodbye — a final goodbye because alone, I claimed, I stood no chance of survival. Without waiting for the effect of my speech, I turned and set off into the forest in the direction of the mountain. Without turning my head I knew that my boys, one by one, had started to follow me. Even the unhappy witch doctor joined the single-file procession. The forest was a tangle of giant trees and rotting fallen trunks. We went over a small hill, cutting our way with machetes, then on through unbelievably dense brush and wooded swamps. We finally arrived at a creek where in heavy rain we made our first camp. In the evening I found out that expedition had been sabotaged by the witch doctor, who had thrown away our supplies of sweet potato. I decided we would continue nonetheless. As we settled down to sleep around our fires I heard footsteps and alerted my companions. At first they heard nothing. Finally they too heard the movement and became frightened. An evil spirit, maybe even Madou herself, was coming to kill us all. Instead, from the trees around us emerged two other Papuans who had decided, after we had left Ugapuga, to join us.

The next day we continued over two mountains, deep canyons, and dense jungle which slowly gave way to true tropical rain forest. Finally we came to a clearing made by a giant fallen tree. The whole time I had been leading the party, I had not been able to see the sky, let alone Mount Deijai. Although my orientation was usually good, I was not sure after all this climbing, descending, and wading in small streams and swamps where we were, and whether we had been going in the right direction. Then, in the clearing, I looked up and there it was. In front of us towered Mount Deijai. After shouting for joy we crossed the last valley, at an elevation of about two thousand meters (six thousand feet), and started to climb the mountain proper. On its slopes we found drinkable water, a good camping ground, and pandanus trees whose leaves we used to thatch our rain hut. The forest was really spectacular with its unbelievable vegetation and magnificent giant trees, but most amazing of all were the birds. Not having experienced the danger of man, they sat on branches so close that I could almost pick up the bright parrots with my hand. Magnificent birds of paradise flew around us, displaying their brilliant plumage in the dim yet glittering light of the forest. This was a true paradise, as depicted in European art, a true Eden. The natives, hungry because of the loss of our sweet potatoes, killed and ate several of these trusting birds. Then something amazing happened. I almost stumbled over the dancing ground of *odijaaj*, the bower bird. Here we found an exquisitely intricate structure of twigs that resembled a spectacular house with a roof, surrounded by several rows of fences. We watched as the male appeared and started to prance in the structure in order to lure a female for mating. We were witnessing a truly unique experience, as Professor Dillon Ripley of Yale later testified. I was delighted and prepared my food while the boys feasted on the slaughtered birds. To my horror, however, I discovered that they had killed (and my friend Jokagaibo had eaten) the male bower bird I had admired only an hour before. At that point I felt God had been right to expel Man from Paradise. It was with sadness that I salvaged the plumes for my Peabody Museum collection.

Then came the night, with the weird shrieks of birds and marsupials all around us. Suddenly a gust of wind brought an unbelievably sweet smell resembling that of trumpet lilies. "What is it?" I asked the natives. They had never smelled anything like it and claimed that it was a lure of Madou, the evil spirit. I enjoyed this lure and wished for more. The next morning it was drizzling, but later on the sun showed through the trees, which had ceased to form a dense canopy and now stood farther apart from each other. Most of these trees were tropical oaks. From their branches hung lichens, and cold drops of water dripped onto us. We climbed through the zone of moss (or cloud) forest. Then the climbing became steep and rugged, over precipitous walls and into deep ravines which we crossed on sometimes dangerous rotten logs. This zone eventually gave way to dense brush where I had to cut a path with my machete for two and a half hours. We scrambled up rock faces, numb with cold, drenched by rain, and suffering from exposure. All the brush was soaking so there was no hope of making a fire. At one point, on a steep ascent, my numb hand finally gave way and I fell ten meters into a crevasse. Luckily, I slid down the mossy surface of the rock into a deep sediment of rotten leaves. Actually it was like landing on cushions. But the natives, to whom my fall appeared spectacular, screamed in horror: "Madou pushed you off the cliff, we saw her hairy hand." There was no point blaming my fall on my numb hands; they knew better. We gave up for the day. However, at the upper end of the brush zone I discovered the source of the magnificent fragrance: a species of pink rhododendron — indeed, an exquisite plant. We returned through our cut path to our camp. There the situation became hopeless — the boys were starving from lack of sweet potatoes and terrified by the evil Madou pushing me off the cliff. Because of this and the continuing bad weather I decided to beat a retreat. The next day we descended along our old path all the way to Ugapuga. There I found out that two Dutch gentlemen, members of the administration, had also gone up the mountain to join me. We had missed them in the vastness of the forest. Since I could not find companions the next day to try my luck again, I gave up and, angry at the witch doctor — the saboteur — I traveled on through the forests and mountain passes to Enarotali on Paniai Lake. This experience taught me not to trust shamans — and not to underestimate the power of the native evil spirits!

Health, Sickness
and Medicine

Most Kapauku magical rites and ceremonies pertained to the problems of health and curing various diseases and afflictions. Indeed, a Kapauku shaman functioned not only as a magician but also as some sort of a psychoanalyst and physician. It therefore seems appropriate to discuss health, sickness and medicine in this chapter, in juxtaposition to the previous chapter, on magic and religion.

Since this book is about my personal experiences and research methods, only secondarily providing glimpses of the native culture as they related to my life in the Kamu Valley, I shall focus first on my own health, safety, and medical problems, and only afterward describe the diseases and medical art of the Kapauku. My safety was not much endangered by the local conflicts and wars described above. The environment presented similarly small risks, but the danger of contracting disease was the worst. The climate was wonderful, and the area devoid of malaria, mosquitoes, and most of the deadly tropical diseases of the New Guinea lowlands. Indeed, there were no venomous snakes (at least to my knowledge), no deadly spiders or scorpions, and even the honeybees did not sting. The days were mostly sunny with a brief afternoon tropical rain, clear air, beautiful starry or moonlit nights, the daily temperatures rising in the afternoon to the mid-twenties Centigrade in the shade. The nights were cool; one might even say a bit cold.

Yet nature was not completely docile. Periodically we received torrential rains lasting one or more days. During such times the Kamu Valley, which had inadequate drainage thanks to its narrow neck in the south, flooded and became a lake, the waters reaching to within ten feet of the entrance of my house. Although prolonged flooding destroyed crops of sweet potatoes cultivated on the valley floor, it left those on the mountain slopes untouched. Floods were generally accepted as welcome changes from routine life. Women went into the flooded valley and collected floating insects, and men hunted marsupials and rats stranded on small grassy islands protruding from the waters.

I would take a canoe and paddle through the flooded reeds and grass, filming the gathering and hunting activities. In contrast, I lived through only one drought, lasting about 14 days, when I witnessed extensive burning of the valley's grasslands and its reed floor during the Kapauku grass fire hunting and gathering enterprise. Far more exciting were earthquakes. When I started to build my house the natives stopped me and persuaded me to build it on a nice sandy spot. At that time my command of the Kapauku language was almost nonexistent. The natives seemed to object to the site I had originally selected, screaming at me *maki-pigi* (earthquake), which I did not understand. So they shook their torsos and arms, pointing at the towering cliffs above and to several huge boulders lying around and in the nearby jungle. I slowly started to comprehend, abandoned my choice, and let the people select the site of my future home. I lived through two earthquakes one severe, one mild. The strong one came at 8 o'clock in the morning on 1 May 1955. My house began shaking and rocking and was on the point of collapse. I fled outside, where my boys and friends had gathered, and looked up in amazement as huge boulders peeled off the cliffs above my house and, like bulldozers rolling down the steep slopes, tore paths through the tropical rain forest, felling trees and flattening the rest of the vegetation. One of these boulders came close to my house, stopping at the spot I had originally selected as the site for my dwelling. If the people had not warned me there would have been one flattened anthropologist, probably to the delight of scholars whose theories my research data damaged or undermined.

Worse than the danger from earthquakes, floods, and droughts were diseases. I suffered periodically from tonsillitis and strep throat, which I tried to cure, rather successfully, by gargling salt water, taking aspirin and Terramycin, and smearing my tonsils with tincture of iodine. The cure helped temporarily, but the disease kept coming back. Additionally I had periodic backaches in the lumbar region. Bacillary dysentery visited me three times, and I treated it each time with Ter-ramycin. I also had a bout with malaria "tropica", and another time I experienced an absurdly high fever and terrific pain in all my joints. The fever was so intense that my jaw rattled and I was afraid I would break my teeth. The last thing I remember I was holding the clenched fist of my right hand against my jaw, and then I passed out. When I woke up the next day I found myself swimming in sweat and being attended by my boys and girls. I was so weak I could hardly move. Because of the high fever combined with ache joints I thought I had rheumatic fever and feared that my research was finished. I managed to scribble a note to the doctor in Enarotali on Paniai Lake describing my symptoms. One of my boys carried it on the long trip to the lake, only to return eleven days later with the doctor's diagnosis, which read something like this: "If you are still alive you had an attack of dengue fever. In that case, as a consolation, you should enjoy immu-nity from this disease for the rest of your life." But my trouble with dengue fever was far from over. When I returned to Yale and made it known that I had had dengue, I was mercilessly drained of my blood by some doctors at the Yale New Haven Hospital who were conduct-ing research on this ailment. They badly needed the antibodies from my blood.

My last bout with a tropical disease was in 1979 at Port Moresby, where I contracted bacillary dysentery. Not yet knowing about my infection I departed on a small plane via Wewak to Jayapura in Irian Jaya (West New Guinea). In Wewak my old friend Dr. Gajdusek (M.D.) joined me. While flying to Jayapura I noticed the first telltale cramps in my abdomen and told my friend. There was a serious problem: the plane had no toilet. So I bravely struggled to compose myself. I man-aged with great difficulty until we landed in the capital of West New Guinea. There I ran out of the plane and through the line of startled customs officers, while my friend followed me and loudly announced to the surrounding crowd that I had a bad case of diarrhea. So, instead of checking me out, a customs officer led the sprint through the halls, opening doors as required, until he landed me on the toilet. Just in time. When I emerged from my seclusion, a gathering of customs officers and passengers applauded and broke into cheers as if I were an Olympic medalist. It had, after all, been a heroic run.

In addition to all these troubles I contracted several types of skin disease, so that when my dermatologist in New Haven examined me upon my return from the Pacific he said with delight: "I always look forward to seeing you back from your trips. You never come with only one skin disease; you always bring a whole collection."

My last disease account is the perhaps the most alarming. When in 1955 I climbed Kenuge Mountain I scratched my right leg. I had forgotten to take any iodine with me and so was not able to disinfect the wound. My right lower leg became infected and my lymphatic gland swelled up. Next morning my leg was so swollen that I decided to cut open the infected wound. My boys watched me with great interest as I heated a Gillette blade over fire and prepared to make the first incision. At that moment Marius, my best assistant, grabbed my hand. "You cannot cut it like this, you shall bleed profusely." Then in disbelief he asked: "Do you not know how to cut your leg?" I ashamedly admitted my utter ignorance. On hearing my admission, the boys exclaimed that it was foolish of me to try when they could get a skilled witch doctor surgeon. "Well," I reflected, "in these matters the witch doctor cannot be dumber than I am." So I agreed.

The witch doctor (not a local practitioner) arrived later in the day with two attendants. He planned to cut my leg with a flint knife. "What an anthropological experience," I thought, "if I only survive to tell the tale!" And so we started. Like in any decent U.S. hospital, the first thing we had to settle was how and how much I should pay. The fee of three cowries of the precious old type was reasonable. However, there was a catch. "If you should die your boys and best friends have to pay double the price," the distinguished surgeon announced. This demand disquieted me a little. But I calmed down when I learned that this charge was customary and most reasonable in light of the fact that if I died after the surgery my departed shadow would change into an evil spirit who take revenge on the unfortunate doctor. So the double charge seemed to be justified to compensate him for the risk. Then came the problem of anesthesia. This took the form of two chunky doctor's assistants. One sat down on the floor of my house, while I sat between his legs and leaned against his body, which provided a semblance of an armchair. The other fellow sat on my thighs so that I was fully immobilized, being sandwiched between the two men and leaning against the first one who, apparently to protect the surgeon from any possible blows from my hands, gently embraced me. My legs rested on spread banana leaves. The doctor extracted from his net bag a flint nodule and another stone and started to strike off chips onto a leaf. I asked him why he had to do this, since he had old chips in his net carrying bag. The reply astonished me and dispelled some of my worries: "The old ones are no good. There is an evil spirit sitting on them." It seemed to me that the fellow knew what he was doing, using fresh and sterile chips. Then I had another concern. When I was about twenty years of age my uncle, a skilled surgeon, had to extract a flattened ricochet bullet from my knee without anesthesia (the Nazis' dogs would otherwise sniff me out). It was the most excruciating pain I had ever suffered, as my uncle cut deeper and deeper into the joint, using a scalpel and some kind of scissors and finally tweezers to extract the projectile. So I was prepared for the worst. Yet it never came. The native surgeon held his *ekigei*, the stone "scalpel," between the thumb and index finger of his right hand, making tiny and swift incisions. It felt as if a needle had pricked me. When I wanted to scream the pain was gone because the knife had been withdrawn. The fellow on my thighs kept the incision open, spreading the cut with his thumbs. After a while the doctor stopped and asked me if I felt tired (not if I was in pain, mind you). I said yes. So he stopped the operation and gave me a piece of peeled sugar cane to chew. Sweet potatoes were not suitable for the occasion, he assured me. After this refreshment he finished his cutting, peeled off a piece of liana, and inserted it into the wound as a drain. He crushed some leaves of a certain shrub and pressed them into the wound, which he then closed tight with rattan vines fastened over a bandage of ti plant leaves (*Cordyline terminalis*). When he was finished he instructed my sons that I should not put any pressure on that leg and that they should carry me even to the toilet.

And so it was. The next day and six days afterward the doctor came in the morning, took off the bandage, extracted the leaves and the drain, and smelled the latter. "No good," he exclaimed, "it still stinks." And he would put fresh crushed leaves into the wound, insert a new drain, and apply the bandage. On the seventh day he was satisfied, closing the wound without inserting any drain or leaves. I paid my fee and a few days afterward I was walking again. If I had had what was usually called a "tropical ulcer," the witch doctor's performance would have been considered a feat. My friends Victor De Bruijn and Dr. Galis were incapacitated with this affliction for months in the modern Dutch hospital. I must admit, though, that to be sure of the cure I swallowed terramycine tablets secretly. After my successful recuperation from the affliction, I collected the leaves and stems of the shrub that seemed to have cured me and sent them to the doctor in Enarotali for analysis. What happened to that sample, I am ashamed to admit, I do not know.

To my knowledge, the Kapauku only operated on infected wounds or extracted war arrows. At both procedures they seemed to be masters. If there was no wound, as in case of an abscess, ulcer, or appendicitis, they refrained from opening the body. The only exception was the practice of gum-cutting. There were specialists in this art who operated with bamboo knives. Another case seemed to be more problematic. I saw a man at the tapa ceremony in Pueta with a deep, perfectly rounded scar in the middle of his forehead. To me it looked like a consequence of a trephining of the skull, similar to those I had seen in the Peabody Museum at Yale in skulls from Peruvian excavations. I approached the stranger to question him, but he, having never before seen a white man, fled in fear. He would not even talk to my boys whom I dispatched after him. So the matter of this curious scar and possible skull trephaning among the Kapauku remains a mystery.

Generally, the Kapauku regarded any sickness as the work of an evil spirit. This spirit might act on its own or be sent and manipulated by a sorcerer. Thus, evil spirits that manifested in various diseases and were viewed in visions and dreams belonged to the natural world, whose laws they followed. They were of several well-defined "species" that one could compare with our types of maladies. However, their essence was immaterial. They penetrated their victims in the way two shadows fuse together, or entered the body of a sleeping person when his or her soul temporarily left to engage in the escapades revealed through dreams. To a Kapauku there was little about a spirit that was supernatural. It was manifested in disease and behaved like a living organism. I therefore had little difficulty in explaining to the natives our Western notions about the nature of sickness, as being a consequence of tiny organisms entering the body of a human. As Kaadootajbii, the witch doctor put it: "There is little difference between our and your idea of the nature of disease. We call it *enija*, an evil spirit, because we cannot see it. You have your glasses (*douja*, a word derived from *dou* — to see) through which, as you have told me, you see the little creatures (*jina*). You call it *jina* and we call it *enija*. What is the difference? What we are both interested in is the manifestation, the disease." The Kapauku accepted Western medicine wholeheartedly with its empirically manifested results.

Young natives suffered mainly from bacillary dysentery, which was the main killer of children. When they were older, yaws (frombosia), a tropical type of syphilis, would destroy their faces (palate, nose, and the maxilla especially) and limbs, so that some unfortunate people were horribly disfigured. There was a man in the South Kamu Valley who lost his nose, palate, and maxilla to the disease, so that one could actually see down his throat. Since the man's lower jaw swung freely, unable to articulate with the missing maxilla, his sons had to pre-chew his food for him. This case also signified to me the devotion these people could display toward their loved ones. The main killer of old people was, as far as I could tell, pneumonia and strep throat (with which I was regularly infected). There were also eye diseases that ultimately caused blindness, and skin diseases. However, the malaria, leprosy, tuberculosis, elephantiasis, cholera, and plague found in the New Guinea lowlands had not made their way up into the inland mountains.

As I have described above, the people had several surgeons, most of whom were adept at extracting arrows from warriors' bodies. I witnessed several of these operations. One was an open chest surgery performed on Ijaaj Pigikiiwode. He had been shot with an arrow that penetrated his chest cavity over the sternum, the arrow barely missing his trachea and heart. The surgeon skillfully extracted the arrow, making a deep incision into the patient's chest under his left breast. Into this incision he inserted the stem of a peeled liana, protruding outward by three inches. The wound was dressed with ti plant leaves, and the whole thing was held in position by strips of rattan tied across the man's chest. When I saw the wound I said to myself, "If that man did not die from the arrow, he certainly will from the surgery." To my amazement the man fully recovered. Surgeons at Yale New Haven Hospital later told me that in the absence of antibiotics the measure taken by the Kapauku surgeon was a correct one.

The natives also treated other injuries. For example, Waine Ipouga, brother of one of my adopted daughters, Antonia, came to my place to show me a nasty wound. He had been fighting a wild boar with his bare hands, and his right heel had been completely chewed off and eaten by the beast. The wound, although dressed by Kapauku experts, looked awful to me. Fearing the boy would get gangrene, I urged him to see Dr. Bliek, the Dutch government doctor at Enarotali on Paniai Lake. The boy did not take my advice and instead hobbled to the nearby village of Magidimi. Ijaaj Jokagaibo, my wise best friend, assured me that there was no danger to the boy and that he was in good hands. And indeed, the wound healed and the boy fully recovered except for an awkward gait.

In addition to surgeons, the people had obstetricians, dentists (including specialists in extraction and periodontia), and shamans. Dental surgery was performed with a sharp bamboo sliver with which the abscesses were cut or ligaments of roots were severed prior to extraction. The teeth themselves were extracted by hand.

The most important medical practitioners were, of course, *kamu epi me* — the witch doctors or shamans. They were called in cases of disease or injury, as well as difficult childbirths. Their success lay in creating in their patients a euphoric feeling and a firm belief in their recovery, thus certainly contributing positively to it or at least easing their fears and giving them hope. I do believe that in this respect, Claude Levi-Strauss was right in claiming that shamans have greater success with mental patients than do psychoanalysts. Improvement from psychoanalysis seems to come, at least in part, from the fact that the patient can talk freely about anything and has an attentive and sympathetic audience, and the fact that the patient trusts the skills of the therapist. All this is also true for the work of a shaman. But the shaman has one advantage over the psychoanalyst. He is believed to command supernatural powers, and so his assertions and treatments are blindly accepted, like those of a prophet. Thus his cures seem to be swifter and more successful.

I witnessed a case of such magical treatment of an insane man. The sick individual was Kotouki Mabiipaj from the village of Mogokotu. On 28 February 1955, there was a commotion in front of my house. Several of my boys claimed that a man had stolen from them clothes that I had given them as well as other items. This man, not known to me, suddenly appeared and was confronted by the boys. They berated him, called him a thief, and demanded that the stolen articles all be returned immediately. The man became unreasonably excited and aggressive, threatening to kill me and Ijaaj Pigikiiwode, the son of the headman of the Ijaaj-Enona sub-lineage. I countered "courageously" that if he tried, I certainly knew how to defend myself. Upon this he jumped up and left for the Botukebo village, where he had left his bow and arrows, screaming that he would come back and kill us.

Perplexed by the man's strange behavior, I turned to my boys and exclaimed: "Ogai maagodo dimi beau" (he certainly must be insane). When my boys assured me that indeed this was the case, I exclaimed, "For heaven's sake (actually I used another obscene Kapauku word) why didn't you tell me this before?" What could I do now? I knew immediately — I called for the help of my dear friend Kaadotajbii, the witch doctor, who promptly arrived. Just in case, I took my bow and arrows down from the wall. When Mabiipaj approached, all furious and ready to kill again, it took Kaadotajbii about 20 minutes to calm him down and make him see reason. He returned all the stolen property and left peacefully for his village in the company of Kaadotajbii. A few days afterward Mabiipaj's mother appeared and pleaded with me to have her son removed by the Dutch colonial police. She said the Kapauku were not able to do anything for her son because they believed that a very strong evil spirit possessed him. When he killed his second brother (he has already killed his father and another brother), people shot him several times with arrows. They believed they had mortally wounded him, but he escaped into the forest and miraculously recovered.

Possibly only the white man could help. I wrote a letter outlining the case to the District Officer, Den Haan. He replied that he had no jurisdiction over the valley, that it was officially "uncontrolled and unpacified territory." But because my own life seemed to be in danger he would take care of the insane man. Accordingly, on 20 May seven policemen appeared to take him away to Enarotali, whence he would be flown to Hollandia (the capital of then Dutch New Guinea) and placed in an insane asylum there. The witch doctor Kaadootajbii was dispatched to fetch the man from his native village of Mogokotu. The next day the police tried to persuade Mabiipaj to go with them as far as their first stop, Waghete on Lake Tigi, but he refused. When he became violent, the police overpowered him, then tied him down intending to carry him tied to a pole by his hands and feet. I protested, claiming that the man would not survive such treatment on the four-day trip to Enarotali. "So what should we do then?" the police commander asked me. "Hire the witch doctor." This seemed to the police an impossible solution. Just imagine: the news would travel to Holland and the rest of Europe that the Dutch government was employing and paying a witch doctor for his magical services.

Finally, however, they agreed. It took Kaadotajbii about 20 minutes to calm down the patient. He was untied and then followed Kaadotajbii and the police docilely to Waghete and on to Enarotali. On 25 May I sent a long letter to Dr. Kruijger, the Dutch colonial officer at Waghete, recounting the history of the problem.

On 29 September I was passing a fenced-in area in Hollandia when a man called to me in Kapauku. It was Mabiipaj, the insane man, locked up in the insane asylum. He was the only Kapauku there and could not communicate with anybody. So I got a permit to take him out for a day. He followed me on several of my errands. I gave him a good dinner at a restaurant and returned him to the asylum in the evening. He had improved markedly. When I returned to New Guinea in 1959 I learned that Mabiipaj had been released from the asylum and that a missionary had employed him as his assistant and taken him to a mission in a non-Kapauku area.

Changes Introduced by the Encroaching Western World

When I arrived in the Kamu Valley on 23 November 1954, accompanied by the armed native constabulary and their commander Mr. Lawrence, I received friendly acceptance, land for my future house and an offer of help to build that house. Through an interpreter, Mr. Lawrence explained to the natives the reason for my presence. The police and the local people helped uproot the ground vegetation and expose an area of beautiful yellow sand. After all, the place was called in Kapauku Itoda (properly *iitouda*), "a place of sand." The next day, when I received the gift of a pig from my new landlord Ijaaj Jokagaibo, the headman of the Ijaaj Jamaina sublineage and my future best friend, Mr. Lawrence was satisfied with my friendly contact with the natives and my security. Consequently he and the police left me on 27 November. Just to be sure, he left one Papuan policeman with me as protection.

I was now alone with the Kapauku, whose language I did not yet understand and without the help of an interpreter or any lingua franca. I could barely communicate some basic ideas and felt quite lost. So I was thrilled when, on 12 December, on returning home to my house I saw a white man outside, arguing emotionally with the Kapauku. When I approached to greet him, without even looking at me, he took off on the path to the north. I was, of course, flabbergasted. I tried to communicate with the people to find out who the man was and what his very strange behavior meant. With my incipient Kapauku, gestures, and the help of Damianuuti, the police officer left with me, I gathered that the man was Father Steltenpool, a Catholic missionary priest from Ugapuga to the north of us. Later I found out that he was on a long trip from the southern coast of New Guinea, over the mountains to his parish in the Central Mountains. I found out from the people that, enraged by my presence, he had yelled at them. He castigated them, saying they should not have helped me build my house and should not have allowed me to stay. He said they should throw me out and burn down my house. Indeed, very strange behavior from a priest. Soon after his hurried departure a couple of dozen local people came to my house, armed with bows and arrows in hot pursuit of the priest. It soon became clear that they had decided to kill him. I had to explain to them, as well as I could, that his death would not help matters at all; that, on the contrary, the Dutch police and administration would throw me out. I do not think they understood all I meant to convey but, with my negative attitude to their armed expedition and the refreshments I offered them, the execution-expedition turned into a festive lunch. Awiitigaaj, an excellent politician, made a public show of affection for me, embracing me several times and even managing to produce genuine tears of joy! What a fellow! Had he been born in America, I speculated, he certainly would have been an excellent candidate for president. I promised, of course, to stay, and assured everyone I had not the slightest intention of leaving.

Of course, the affair with Father Steltenpool was not over. Immediately after the party with the natives had ended, I sat down and wrote letters to the priest, the district officer Raphael Den Haan at Enarotali, and my former escort Mr. Lawrence at Tigi Lake. My boys were dispatched to deliver the messages. In the letter to Father Steltenpool I explained who I was, that far from being a Protestant American missionary, which I presumed he had taken me for, I was an anthropologist and — lo and behold! — even a nominal Catholic. The answer from the pastor was quick to come. My boy dispatched to the north brought back a long letter of apology in which the pastor explained that he had taken me for an American Protestant missionary, violating an agreement by which the territory of the Kamu Valley would be missionized by Catholics in the future (Protestants had claimed another region for themselves — if I am not mistaken, the Jawei River catchment). Of course, even if I had been a Protestant missionary it was certainly neither Christian nor decent to incite the natives against me. Who knows? I could have been killed instead of the pastor! He asked for my help because news of the affair had spread to his Edegedide Valley and as a consequence of his precipitous action, many young Papuans and children had left his mission at Ugapuga in protest. I obliged him and later we became good friends. I stayed in his mission overnight on several occasions when I traveled to the north, to Lake Paniai. Later we even reached an agreement that he would not send a Catholic missionary to Southern Kamu Valley prior to my departure in the distant future. Of course, Jokagaibo and the other Kapauku insisted that they would allow only Americans to enter the valley in the future. The pastor proved to be a very learned man who had spent many years in China, spoke and wrote Mandarin, and embarked right away on learning the Kapauku Language. Eventually he perfected his knowledge of Kapauku to the point that he published a comprehensive and accurate Kapauku-Dutch-English-Malay dictionary.

Another visitor to reach my seclusion in the Kamu Valley was Raphael Den Haan, the district officer of the Wissel Lakes region. He came to my place in Itoda to conduct the retrial of an alleged rapist who had committed his crime in the already controlled territory of Tigi Lake. On 24 May, two native policemen came to our confederacy to arrest Pigome Oubii and take him to Ugapuga for questioning about the alleged rape. The police also delivered to me a "treasure chest" filled with 5 kilograms of beautiful cylindrical blue glass beads. I would later purchase these glass beads of German origin from the Dutch to finance my research in the Kamu. My friend, headman Jokagaibo, discussed Oubii's case with me at length, considering all the available evidence, and claimed that the man was innocent. Oubii himself was obviously scared to go with the police because of his general fear of the as yet unfamiliar white man. However, the next day he did leave with them, after I had promised to intervene on his behalf. On 3 June 1955, many Kapauku came to my place enraged because they had heard that Oubii and a man of the Dimi clan had been sentenced in the rape case by government officials at Enarotali. They had to pay a pig each for having committed the rape, and Oubii himself had been thrown into the white man's jail in that distant place. The people refused to pay the fine of two pigs because of what they claimed were trumped-up charges, and prepared for possible armed conflict with the police and the Dutch government to the north of the Kamu Valley. So I sent another letter to the district officer, presenting the available evidence and claiming that the two men were innocent. The whole charge appeared to have been a fraud. Bunajbii, Oubii's brother, took the letter to Enarotali, the seat of the district officer. My arguments and my intervention were successful. Oubii was released from prison pending retrial of his case, and on 7 June he returned to our confederacy to the great rejoicing of our people. They thanked me for my intervention, and my prestige as their defender rose.

On the afternoon of 29 June, Raphael Den Haan, with his judicial and police entourage, arrived at my place in Itoda. A retrial of the case was to be held there. I sent two of my boys to the distant village at Egebutu to bring witnesses for the trial. I spent the next day showing the district officer around, introducing him to local headmen and people, and taking a canoe ride with him on Kugumo Lake in front of my house and on the adjacent Edege River. The retrial was delayed until the witnesses arrived, which they did late at night, and the trial was set for the following day. It started in the morning. The evidence in favor of Oubii was so convincing that Den Haan ruled him innocent of the charges, and also dropped the charge against the Dimi man. No one had to pay Teumiibo any pigs, and the case was closed. The Pigome, Ijaaj, and Dimi Clan members were full of joy and praised the judgment and sense of justice of the district officer. He left my place after the trial, and so ended one of the few breaks I took from my more strictly observational role in the Kamu Valley.

At this time, two visitors descended on my house, although during most of my fieldwork I was alone. Just one day before the arrival of the district officer I had a visit from Father Kamerer, a Franciscan missionary from Okomokebo in the Tigi Lake region. He came on the morning of 28 June 1955, and was a most welcome visitor. He spoke some Kapauku and had published several lengthy treatises on the Kapauku Papuans of his region. So we kept comparing notes and remarked upon the often profound differences between the two regions of the same large language area. The various dialects, while mutually intelligible, often showed etymologically unrelated words that had the same meaning: for example, "fire" in my Kamu-Kapauku dialect was *utu*, while in Paniai dialect it was *bodija*. In Kamu *bodija* meant "large cowry shell," the largest native shell money denomination. Later that day the head of the Christian American Mission Alliance, a Mr. Troutman, arrived. In spite of, or maybe because of the fact that the two clergymen were of competing denominations (Catholic and Protestant) and different nationalities (Dutch and American), we had most interesting discussions the whole day and into the night. Our subjects were not only the Kapauku language and culture, but also the adaptation of the missionary programs to the native society. Both gentlemen fully agreed with me that the Kapauku should be completely free to choose between Catholicism and Protestantism, or any other religion in the future. In the mission schools children should be educated in the basic disciplines but religion should not be forced on them. That night I wrote in my diary that I had spent most of the day "discussing Kapauku language and culture and methodology, but that the day was lost for research." The next day, Mr. Troutman and his entourage departed. Father Kamerer immediately took advantage of his absence by serving a mass at my house. About 25 inquisitive Kapauku attended. Then Father Kamerer also left. No sooner had he disappeared in the direction of the Debei Valley than District Officer Den Haan appeared from the opposite direction, to conduct the investigation and retrial of Pigome Oubii — a rather improbable series of visits from three gentlemen.

Prior to the conclusion of the first period of my fieldwork in the Kamu Valley I was fortunate to offer hospitality to Professor Gressit, a well-known entomologist at Bernice Bishop Museum in Hawaii, and a world expert on the insects of the Pacific. He arrived with his helpers on 12 August 1955 and spent three days with me. Most of these days he spent in the jungle around my house and in the adjacent swamps, hunting insects with his assistants. At night he surrounded my house with several kerosene lanterns to trap insects. Using my house as his base camp, he made two expeditions to the Debei Valley and also climbed the jungle-covered slopes of Kemuge Mountain, which towered over my house. He had some trouble with his assistants due to his ignorance of the native language. Indeed, all my boys who went with him to help catch insects deserted him when he crossed into the territory of their enemy, the Waine clan, as he refused to heed their protests. Luckily he did not encounter any of the Waine people in the forests and returned safely at night. The evenings with him proved to be most profitable. He instructed me on the local insects and advised me how to collect them more effectively. I had been collecting insects for Professor Charles Remington at the Yale Peabody Museum. Professor Gressit idenfitied my insects, making it possible for me to publish my monograph *Kapauku Papuan Economy* (1963b). I was interested in the biology of insects and their scientific identification, while the professor showed a keen interest in the way the Kapauku used the various species for food and manufacture, and in their oral literature and religion. These were three days well spent.

All other visits from the outside world took place during my third fieldwork visit. They were all connected to my attempt to help to establish a mission school in the south Kamu Valley. First to arrive at my place for preliminary talks was Father Van Nuenen, Franciscan missionary and pastor at Tage Lake — who actually had a Ph.D. in Anthropology! Franciscan Father Superior Van Naers accompanied him from the Netherlands New Guinea capital of Hollandia. They arrived on 11 August 1955. As it happened, on that morning I was worn out after a night spent shaking with a high fever from a spell of malaria. Nonetheless, I managed to talk to the two clergymen and we discussed the building of a school somewhere in the vicinity. I suggested a place at the southern border of our confederacy because the people from the southern and hostile confederacies, as well as from our own, would have free access over their own land, meaning that their children would not have to cross hostile foreign territory. They took my advice and, after my departure toward the end of the year and the completion of the building, the school had indeed the highest enrolment in the region, making the project a great success.

Father Van Nuenen himself was a success, not only because of his kindness but also thanks to his anthropology training. By 4 September he had succeeded in purchasing land on our designated spot at the south end of the village of Botukebo, on the bank of the Botu River. The purchase was made from three Kapauku landlords: Ijaaj Awiiti-gaaj; Ijaaj Timajjokainaago; and the rich but timid Ijaaj Timaajjokai-mopaj of Botukebo. Father paid them well, giving them iron axes and beads. They were very satisfied because, in their world, they had made a "killing." After that day, Father Van Nuenen supervised the building of the school until my departure. He received vital support from my by then good friend Father Steltenpool of Ugapuga. He visited us on 14 and 15 September. By that time my people had heard about missionary education, schools, health care, and other benefits from their Kapauku neighbors to the north and east. Members of my Ijaaj-Pigome confederacy came to me on many occasions and urged me to find them a good teacher for their future school, and I was also urged to instruct the future catechist and priest in Kapauku culture, morality, law, and system of justice. My friend Ijaaj Jokagaibo very pointedly made this request to me on the evening when the first missionary assigned to the school paid me a visit: "Teach him our ways, thinking, laws, and sense of justice as I have taught you during all these moons." I promised to, of course. By 17 August 1955, long before the missionary had arrived in South Kamu to start the school project, the people of my region had already cut mugo trees, the best type of building material in our area, in anticipation of the appearance of their future teacher.

The person responsible for the whole school project was Father Van Nuenen, the pastor of the Tage Lake region. The Franciscan mission wanted to build the school right after my departure, so that they could come during my last days and I could acquaint them with the local people and help with the purchase of the necessary land. Father Van Nuenen was a well-educated anthropologist who had done remarkable research among the Moni Papuans to the northeast of the Kapauku territory. He traveled from Ugapuga several times, accompanied by porters carrying the necessary tools and equipment to build the school. When he first came it was a rainy day. He stopped at my house and I had a chance to introduce him to my friends and the Kapauku authorities, and also to the local witch doctor who was to work as his ally rather than as a competitor. Since I realized that the mission would move in after my departure, I tried to make the transition and as smooth as possible. All the mission people assured me that their approach would be rational and nonemotional, and that church attendance would be strictly voluntary, preserving the natives' traditional individualism and emphasizing their right to decide for themselves. The second day of Father Van Nuenen's visit was cloudy but without rain, so he was able to pitch his tent at the village of Botukebo and start dealing with the natives without my help. In the evening he proudly reported to me that a very cooperative and nice man named Bunaibomuuma had asked him to appoint him as his *kapala*, an Indonesian word for "chief." In Kapauku it conveyed the notion of authority, and especially of a facilitator. Van Nuenen was lucky that I was around. Bunaibomuuma, a smooth talker with a servile attitude, was otherwise a notorious crook and embezzler, a man who had already been tried in court and had barely escaped execution by an arrow shooting squad. He offered the priest his own house in exchange for the appointment. This would have allowed him to extort money from the unfortunate local residents, and ultimately might have precipitated an armed rebellion against him as well as against the innocent priest. Of course, after having heard my account of this fellow, the priest dropped his candidacy like a hot potato. In this case I was again reminded of the words of warning of my old professor at the University of Oregon, Professor Homer Barnett: "Avoid people who enthusiastically approach you and offer you their services on your entry into a society to be studied. Very likely they will be misfits in their own community, or even criminals." How true in this case, and also in a similar one at the time of my arrival in the Kamu Valley. Old people may not be as up-to-date or well-educated as younger people, but the young lack a very important thing which old people have: experience.

Another problem Father Van Nuenen faced concerned Papuan school age girls. When he came to the Kamu Valley the priest brought with him carriers and assistants from the Tage Lake area. One of them was a young boy called Simon Mote. One day, Ijaaj Tajwiijokaipouga appeared in my house, quite upset, and asked me to help him with a problem with Father Van Nuenen. He claimed that Simon had started to court his daughter and that the boy had tried to persuade her to leave with him for the Tage Lake region and enter a missionary school there. The unhappy father believed, possibly quite correctly, that the boy wanted to avoid paying an appropriate bride price for the girl, using his position with the pastor to put pressure on Tajwiijokaipouga. So I went to Father Van Nuenen to discuss the problem. The pastor told me he was in favor of taking the girl with him to the school at Tage Lake, and asked what the people could have against such a move. I told him it was quite surprising to me that he failed to see the father's point of view: his daughter would be taken from him without his consent — indeed, without even a proper consultation with him. Furthermore, the girl would be taken to a strange place controlled by a hostile confederacy, where he would not have any access to her. In his place, I told him, getting quite upset myself, I would not only object, but do anything in my power to prevent anyone from taking my child away from me without my consent to a faraway foreign country. Father Van Nuenen saw my point, apologized, and asked me to talk sense to the boy. This I did, and succeeded in talking the boy out of his plan. I suggested that he collect an adequate bride price and marry the girl properly, in which effort I would support him, and to which his future father-in-law would have no objections. Thus was concluded another potentially explosive affair.

During my first research period in 1954–1955 I had to leave the Kamu Valley on several occasions. Invariably my ultimate destination was Enarotali on Paniai Lake, the seat of the Dutch administration of the region and the only government outpost in the central highlands of then Dutch New Guinea. My first trip from Enarotali via the Tigi Lake region, through the Debei Valley and to the Kamu, took me four days. On the advice of my Kapauku friends I rerouted my subsequent trips over the mountain passes of Ogijaajdimi to the Obano village on the western shore of Lake Paniai, or over the Ijaajdimi pass to Tigi Lake, and then after crossing it by boat to Waghete, on foot to the Jawei River, from where I traveled by boat to Enarotali. In Obano on the Western shore of Lake Paniai resided an American missionary who radioed to Enarotali for a boat, which crossed the lake and took me to my destination. Both trips usually took me two to three days only, with overnight stays in the village of Jametadi (the first route over the Ogijaajdimi), or, if I took the second route, the villages of Itugakebo and Waghete.

These trips were always a major undertaking, often including life-threatening dangers. However, even traveling through enemy territory was not as dangerous as flying in a Cessna bush plane to the Kamu Valley on my subsequent visits in 1959, 1962, 1975, and 1979. During my several stays in New Guinea I had three wonderful pilots, all ultimately killed while flying dangerous missions. In 1954-955 the pilot was Mr. Lewis, who also dropped my mail from his plane several times when I was cut off from the outer world by native wars in the north of the Kamu Valley and my boys could not travel through the war-torn territory. Then, one day, I received the sad news that Lewis' plane had been lost while flying near Baliem Valley. Thus I lost my first pilot friend. Flying over New Guinea is more than a hazard. Huge mountains, some as high as 15,000 or 16,000 feet, bad weather, and suddenly developing fog and clouds in the mountain passes pose a deadly danger to the low-flying bush plane trying to make its way through. I myself had several close calls during my flights to and from the central highlands. Once was with my second pilot, Pablo. We were flying from Paniai Lake to Hollandia on the northern coast, past the Carstenz Toppen mountains, the highest peaks of the Pacific islands, covered by glaciers in spite of their location almost on the equator. I was very lucky. The weather was magnificent, and from the plane I was able to film the ice-covered peaks glittering in the tropical sun. My luck, however, did not last. We had on board a missionary boy whom we were to deliver to his parish in a fantastic mountainous area. The airstrip there was cut into the jungle on a mountain ledge overhanging a deep, gigantic gorge. Pablo duly radioed the missionary, asking whether the strip was in order for landing. The answer came: yes, it was all right. We landed, only to find out that it was not "all right" at all. It was covered with mud and several puddles at the end of the runway, where there was a sheer drop into a canyon several thousand feet deep. The parish priest was anxious to get his boy landed, and had misjudged the condition of the runway. Now Pablo confronted me with two possibilities: we could stay at that mission until the area dried out, which could take several weeks, or we could make a daring dash down the runway and if the plane did not have enough speed we could simply drop into the gorge and pick up speed that way. Since childhood, from the age of about five, I had flown with my father in WWI vintage planes and had lived through some very tight moments, so I was accustomed to danger. Because the prospect of sitting idly for possibly several weeks in the New Guinea jungle with the missionary was not attractive, I opted, to the great pleasure of Pablo, for the "muddy dash." So we started, after having properly castigated the missionary. He promised to pray for us, which certainly was a great help. The plane had a hard time taking off. We bounced up and down, reminding me of a takeoff in a biplane from the water's surface. Finally, the windshield partially covered with mud picked up by the propeller, we dropped into the precipice, but with a beautiful ascending curve Pablo cleared the opposite canyon wall — by inches, I reckoned. What a man of courage, and what a pilot! In the excitement I forgot to turn off my movie camera, so I have some shots of the pilot, the cockpit, and me in wild array as a souvenir.

The two other incidents were with my third pilot, Tom, in 1975 and 1979. He was an excellent and seasoned pilot, a wonderful and witty companion who loved the Kapauku and they loved him. Once, when he was bringing me to the Kamu Valley, which by that time had an airstrip, his radio conked out as we entered a mountain pass in a thick fog. He navigated by checking minutes on his clock to figure out when to make an appropriate turn to avoid a mountain wall. I must confess that I felt quite helpless during those moments. It was like swimming in a lake of milk. Although I was not frightened, it was not courage that I felt. As one of my old professors once explained to me, "When you face harm or possible death and you have no fear, that is not courage. You are only brave. Courage is when you are afraid but still perform your dangerous task." So courage requires the presence of fear. I was only brave. However, I was not brave when I peered into the fog and faced a very non-courageous end to my life. A strange thought flew through my mind: if I have to die, why was it not when pilot Pablo dived into a canyon a few years earlier? Would a newspaper bother to report my feat of courage? Hitting a rock face in dense fog was nothing out of the ordinary — it happens to pilots in New Guinea all the time. I looked at Tom, who was smiling at me. I tried to smile back, but most likely I only produced an unconvincing grin. His smile had a purpose — he was trying to give me courage. My grin was nothing but a pathetic grin. I held my breath as the plane finally broke through the clouds, above the beautifully sunlit Kamu Valley. We landed safely.

On the second occasion, Tom was taking me to his airstrip in the jungle area near the coast. Towering monsoon clouds were approaching menacingly and already obscuring the sight of the jungle below. Tom's wife radioed us that there was total cloud cover, and that Tom should ditch the plane in the nearby lagoon. After prodding by her husband, she admitted that there was a tiny hole in the cloud cover, but for Pete's sake we should not try to find it. "Ditch the plane. I'll get a boat for you," was the order. Tom turned to me. "I know you can swim, but do you want to get wet?" "Certainly not," was my answer. And so we searched and found the hole, went through it, and landed safely — just in time. Before we had even reached the hangar all hell broke loose, and walls of monsoon rain descended upon us. Tom's wife embraced him, with tears in her eyes — but also a stern look. She obviously still thought he shouldn't have taken risk. Like my other two pilots, this dear friend of mine was also killed in a crash in the New Guinea jungle. I felt great sorrow over the loss of my friend, and was especially sorry for his wife and children, who had to wait months before the death of their husband and father, lost in the jungle, was officially confirmed.

The overland trips were not always great fun either, although life-threatening conditions were usually absent. I have already described my initial trip from Enarotali to the Kamu Valley in 1954, the deep mud, the slippery jungle "paths," and the treacherous "bridge" crossings over streams and gorges. These native "bridges" often consisted of only one or two poles, made slick by algae and moss. My

Australian army boots with their brass studs proved invaluable in this enterprise. However, when soaked with water and mud in the swamps they became heavy as stones. For that type of terrain I changed into gym shoes — lightweight, nicely drained by holes, and easily dried in the evening over the campfire. I have already mentioned Gais- seau's movie *The Sky Above, the Mud Below* about a journey through the New Guinea jungle, but again that did not always apply to my walking experience. There was mud below my feet all right, but the canopy of the rain forest often obscured the sky. The flooded areas of the swamps were quite treacherous. A "bridge" consisting often of one single pole might then be submerged in the water so that I sometimes preferred to swim through a muddy stream rather than fall into it. Once, while crossing swamps in the northern Kamu Valley in 1959, we made use of a floating grassy island to traverse a stagnant stretch of water. Pushed off from the "shore", it slowly, very slowly floated with us to the other side.

Then there was the quicksand. The natives could distinguish it from safe mud by certain ripples and the quality of the surface. At the be- ginning, ignorant of such dangers, walking for the first time in the swamps and foolishly leading the party (one should never do that in an unfamiliar environment), I dropped into one of these mud holes in the carpet of floating vegetation near Ugapugaa. I sank in up to my shoul- ders, and the natives, making a human chain by joining hands, very slowly pulled me out. The suction of the mud was terrific. The natives laughed and told me that now, covered with mud, I really resembled the Kapauku. The best walking for me was usually in a small brook with its pebbles and sand. Unfortunately this was not the ideal surface for my barefooted companions, so after a while we had to leave the stream, for me a most comfortable "highway" of clear water.

The swamps and streams were dangerous not only to the inexperi- enced. Some Kapauku also drowned in the swamps, I was told.

Simply walking in wet shoes in the jungle may have serious con- sequences. So when on 22 July 1955, after several days' walk, I ar- rived in Enarotali and settled into my room at District Officer Den Haan's house, I noticed a large white area on the instep of my right foot. It was insensitive even to needle pricking, so I was alarmed. I went to see the doctor from the Dutch government, who worked at Enarotali in a small hospital. I feared that I might have contracted leprosy as all the symptoms were there. The doctor looked my foot over and rather cheerfully announced that indeed it looked like leprosy, but if I were lucky I only had the beginnings of gangrene. A nice choice indeed. The prospect of walking among lepers on their island with a disfigured face and no chance of recovery was not appealing. It would have been much nicer to die of the peritonitis I had as a child, or the tuberculosis I inherited from my mother. The thought of gangrene was not much better, with the possibility of my leg being amputated. Although then I would have preferred gangrene to leprosy, nowadays, with the cure for leprosy available, I certainly would change my preference. "We have to wait several days to know the answer," the doctor told me. I might get sensation back if it was the start of gangrene and if it had not progressed too far. I was lucky. After three days my sensation returned, and the discolored area slowly changed to a light brown. The cause of my condition was lack of blood circulation due to my tight boots. During the walk the soaked leather dried out, tightening around my ankle and preventing normal blood flow to my foot.

My first trip outside of the Kamu Valley came in January 1955, when the Dutch colonial officer Fanoy appeared at my house with an escort of armed police. On that day, 20 January, he brought some gifts for the local natives, supposedly to make them friendly towards me. He had come to invite me to go with him to Enarotali to meet Professor Theodor Fischer of Utrecht University, one of the two professors responsible for my research in what was uncontrolled and unpacified territory. Fanoy stayed in my house for a couple of days and then made a short trip to visit our hostile neighbors of the Waine-Tibaakoto confederacy in the south. On his return he reported that those people wanted to wage war on us, the Ijaaj-Pigome people, because three men from one of our villages (Botukebo) had spread the news there that they should not cross the borders of the two confederations and come to my place to trade with me. If they came, they had claimed, there would be a war in which our Ijaaj-Pigome people would be supported by the Dutch police, who would invade their hitherto uncontrolled territory. This lie was obviously spread in order to give Ijaaj-Pigome clan members a monopoly on acquiring beads and other white man's goods from me. So I had to castigate the three men, who then traveled south to admit that their statements were a pack of lies and that the Waine-Tibaakoto were free to come trade with me. Our neighbors declared that they had nothing against me — they were only mad at my hosts.

On 24 January, Mr. Fanoy went with his boys to the western part of the Kamu Valley, to the village of Mauwa to make contact with people living there. On 26 January Mr. Fanoy and his entourage left the Kamu Valley and I decided to accompany them. We stayed overnight in the mission at Ugapuga, where we were the guests of Pastor Steltenpool. After several months, I tasted good European food again. The next day we marched up the forest trail of the upper Edegedide Valley and climbed the steep slopes of the Ogijaajdimi pass. At the top Mr. Fanoy stopped for a rest and a cigarette. I continued on the trail down the mountain and arrived at an American Protestant mission station at Obano, on the western shore of the huge Paniai Lake. Mr. Fanoy arrived a few minutes later. We were welcomed by the missionaries and had a nice supper with them and a pleasant evening. At that time I also tried out the mission's organ, whose keys' plastic covers I eventually acquired as part of a Kapauku necklace, in 1959. Little did I suspect that these good people would be killed in a Kapauku uprising in 1956, or that I would purchase a necklace made from those same white organ keys I played on that night. But that was not all. I later bought a pendant, a grisly trophy of a dried, well-shaped finger, supposedly taken from one of the members of the missionary family. It is now deposited as part of my collection in the Yale Peabody Museum.

On 28 January we crossed the lake on a canoe equipped with an outboard motor, passing several canoe flotillas on our way. Kapauku women, who, with their large oval nets were harvesting delicious crayfish from the lake's bed, manned them. When we arrived at Enarotali I stayed in Fanoy's house because Den Haan had not yet returned from his trip to the coral island of Biak. The next day the district officer arrived with Professor Fischer. I moved to Den Haan's house and had lengthy discussions with him and Professor Fischer concerning my research and my progress in learning the Kapauku language.

On 31 January I had a meeting with Marion Doble, the linguist expert on the Kapauku language, who checked my knowledge of the language and provided me with two more works of hers in the Paniai Kapauku dialect. As I have mentioned already, this lady with her Kapauku texts and vocabulary saved me at least one year of fieldwork. Without her help I would have had to record and analyze the native tongue from scratch. I could offer her little in return. Later on, after my return to the United States, I sent her lists of the Kapauku names of insects, spiders, and plant species which she did not have but which I had accumulated through my animal and plant collections. At that time scientists typically identified them (that is, most of them) by Latin names. Many of these Kapauku species were unknown and had not been described in the scientific literature, to the delight of people like Professor Gressit or Professors Petrunkevitch and Remington of Yale. So we had to be satisfied at that point with the specimens' generic names.

I was scheduled to start my trip back to the Kamu Valley on 2 February. The preceding evening the district officer informed me that he could not accompany me to Obano as we had planned. He had to leave for Kelso village, where his friend, a local headman, had been shot with an arrow and seriously wounded. So I said goodbye to Den Haan and, accompanied by Professor Fischer, left by boat for Obano. There I parted with the professor and continued with my friend Ijaaj Jokagaibo and five porters to my home in Itoda, in the Kamu Valley. We stayed overnight in the village of Jametadi, then took a short cut across the swamps of the northern Kamu Valley. The trip was, as I wrote in my diary, "horrible." We waded through constant knee-deep mud, and three times I fell into "quick mud," waist deep, so that my Papuan companions got a good day's exercise pulling me intermittently from mud holes. In Itoda I was greeted by all my forty-eight sons and five daughters. Etepaanuuti even ran out into the rain to meet me in the swamps, a couple of hours' "walk" from Itoda.

My second trip from the Kamu Valley took place three months later, when I received an invitation from the district officer to the celebration of Queen Juliana's birthday. Den Haan wanted me to bring along a lot of warriors so that guests from the outside world could see real tribesmen, and he promised all my people good food, shelter, and gifts. I explained the nature of the occasion to Ijaaj Awiitigaaj, headman of the Ijaaj-Enona sublineage of the village of Botukebo and a famous connoisseur of female beauty who had collected ten beautiful specimens of womanhood through his multiple-marriage arrangement. He listened attentively and then asked me the most pertinent question for a true Kapauku: "How much did her (the queen's) husband pay for her?" When I answered "Probably nothing," he was no longer impressed and flatly refused to go. It took me quite a long time to persuade him of the lady's importance. Finally he gave in and promised to go. So on 26 April 1955, my 33rd birthday, I was joined by fifteen of my sons, two of my daughters, my best friends Ijaaj Jokagaibo (accompanied by two of his five wives), Ijaaj Awiitigaaj, and additional people from the village of Obajbegaa. Others attached themselves to our caravan during our trip through the Kamu Valley, which we crossed in record time, climbing and descending the Ogijaajdimi pass and arriving at Obano that same night. We made the trip, which usually took two days, in only seven hours, doing the Kapauku version of fast walking, which meant running continuously. I felt so fit that I was not even tired, but my friends seemed weary, and Ijaaj Jokagaibo injured his elbow in a fall in the jungle.

At Obano I again stayed with the American missionaries, and in the afternoon we went down to the shore of the lake. While waiting for the boat to arrive from Enarotali to take us across the lake, we were attacked by the hostile inhabitants of the area, their arrows hitting the soft grassy ground all around us. I forbade my people to shoot back and instead asked them to collect the arrows that missed us — I would send them to the Peabody Museum. When the enemy stopped shooting, I stepped forward from behind our luggage, which served as a defensive wall, and hurled insults up the mountain slopes to receive another volley of arrows, thus enriching my alma mater's collection.

I repeated this several times until the enemy ran out of ammunition or grew tired of our non-reciprocation. At four o'clock in the afternoon we were picked up by the government motorboat and a large flotilla of native canoes and started to cross the huge lake. The crossing proved dangerous due to strong winds, which whipped up high waves that threatened to sink our boats. The Kapauku were scared, shivering from cold and fear as the waves swept steadily onboard. The wife of Ijaaj Jokagaibo, Ijowau Amaadii, performed a *kamu tai* (white magic) ritual to save us. And not without success: our motorboat arrived in Enarotali at sunset. The passengers of the large rowboats had a more difficult time and arrived exhausted from the rain, fighting the waves, and rowing. Four of my boys admitted that they had cried in fear. Only the witch doctor Kaadotajbii appeared undaunted and at ease. No wonder — he was shielded by the departed souls of his ancestors and an assortment of evil spirits under his control.

On the following day, 28 April, the district officer did indeed supply my people lavishly with food. Unfortunately the festive occasion was spoiled by the news that my friend and pilot Mr. Lewis was reported lost over the jungles and precipices near the Baliem Valley. Although we hoped for the best, all of us knew that the news was grave indeed. On 29 April the district officer canceled a reception and party in his house, although my people were well rewarded. In joy and gratitude they and other Papuans spent the whole night dancing and singing around our (that is, Den Haan's) house. The next morning there was a flag parade at the police barracks, followed by a Catholic mass and an official ceremony at Den Haan's office. He gave several speeches in honor of the queen, for guests from abroad in Dutch, English, Malay, and French, and I had to deliver the gist of his talk in Kapauku. Several loyal Kapauku headmen received decorations. Then games and sport events started at which Kapauku could win prizes of tobacco and beads. Arrow shooting, stone carrying, throwing balls through a hole, climbing a pole, and swimming were some of the activities. Mr. and Mrs. Den Haan joined the Papuans' swimming race, to the delight of Papuans and guests alike. In the evening there was a party at the "hotel," with prizes awarded to the winners, dancing, games, gambling, and drinking. "A very nice party," reads my diary. The next day I spent distributing food supplies and gifts to my people, and in discussion with Den Haan and Marion Doble. My two adopted daughters Antonia and Peronika received several pieces of clothing from Mrs. Den Haan. So on 2 May, all well satisfied, we left by boat again for Obano and walked over the mountain pass to the village of Jametadi where, soaked with rainwater and cold, we spent the night in an abandoned catechists' house. The next day, crossing the Kamu Valley, we reached Itoda in a record five hours' time. This we accomplished in spite of the fact that at the time the valley was half-flooded.

My last trip beyond the Kamu Valley during my first research period began on 21 July, 1955. What necessitated the arduous journey to Enarotali was a visit from my old professor from the University of Oregon, Homer Barnett. So I made preparations, which included special instructions to my boys to pull Professor Barnett's leg. For example, I told them that it was polite to give a wolf whistle when meeting a white woman. I also told them that if they were quizzed about their kinship terminology by anybody, they should explain to their interrogator that their terminology was of the Iroquois type. I also gave them other "good advice." So on the designated day I departed with six of my boys and Ijaaj Jokagaibo. Unfortunately, at the village of Jotapuga Ijaaj Jokagaibo and one of my boys fell sick and had to stay behind. I continued to Ugapuga village, in the vicinity of which I fell, as usual, into a quickmud hole, this time almost to my neck, and my boys had to pull me out. In the next brook I took a good bath. After a pleasant visit at Father Steltenpool's in Ugapuga, we departed toward Tigi Lake via Ijaajdimi pass. When we arrived at the American mission station at Itugakebo on the western bank of Tigi Lake we were disappointed to find that Mr. and Mrs. Cato, the American missionaries, were absent. So one of my boys walked around the lake, having received proper remuneration, to fetch a boat for us from the village of Waghete, where Mr. Lawrence, the Dutch administrative officer, had his station. He arrived in his motor boat around seven o'clock in the evening, and we traversed the lake in the darkness under a beautiful starry southern sky.

The next day we continued our walk over the mountains to Udatei-da on the Jawei River. After we had waited there for a couple of hours a police boat took us to Enarotali, where I stayed overnight, as usual, in Den Haan's house. The next day Professor Barnett arrived by amphib-ious plane. We spent the day talking, and the local doctor showed us his slides. In the afternoon Professor Barnett, helped by an interpreter, quizzed the natives and my boys on Kapauku culture. As I had hoped, he started to note down kinship terms. After a fifth term (of a paternal parallel cousin) one of my boys stopped him and told him bluntly: "We need not continue with this. It is obvious that we have an Iroquois kinship and terminology system, which differentiates cousins (cross and parallel) on the basis of their (relative) sex of the first and the last link." After overcoming his shock, Professor Barnett declared that the boys could easily take a Ph.D. examination in anthropology. The next day we went to visit the Catholic pastor Van Nuenen at the neighbor-ing Tage Lake. His mission school accommodated 50 children. We had an enjoyable dinner with three nuns and five Franciscan missionaries. In the evening we returned to Enarotali. As we took an evening stroll down the hill to the pier on the lake, we met three female missionar-ies — two American and one Dutch — one of whom was Marion Doble. As we approached them, the nice quiet evening with a red sunset over the lake was shattered by a salvo of wolf-whistles, nicely arranged in unison. Of course, the ladies blushed, and Professor Barnett started to stutter rather incoherently: "That's impossible!" I assured him that there were many such parallels between the American and Kapauku cultures. To pull one's professor's leg may not be acceptable from an American point of view, but since my old Czech culture and Kapauku customs indulged in practical jokes, and Professor Barnett knew my ways from my student days at Oregon, I felt it was quite excusable. In the end, of course, so did the ladies and Professor Barnett who, after his initial shock, burst into laughter. By the next day every Kapauku in the neighborhood had heard about my jokes and my reputation rose to enviable heights. To compensate Miss Doble for her embarrassment I presented her with my partial Kamu Kapauku dictionary. The next day, Professor Barnet left by plane for Biak Island, having had enough instruction in Kapauku culture. I left Enarotali with my boys by boat to Obano, then crossed the Ogijaajdimi pass and continued through the forest down the slope. This was a very fortunate day for me because on the way down we met a party who were dragging a large dugout canoe up the steep slope on long rattan ropes. It had been cut and hollowed out in the forests, and would now be dragged down the slope and floated on the Edege River. Quite an instructive experience, of which I took several pictures and many notes.

Inside the Kapauku territory and the Kamu Valley I made numerous trips to the various villages, to inspect floods, bridges, drainage systems, and, of course, partake in many *juwo* (pig feasts), *tapa* (money gathering ceremonies), and *deodami* (pig markets). Although all these expeditions were fascinating and exciting, none — not even the two wars I witnessed nor climbing the tabooed Mount Deijaaj was as mysterious as my trip to and exploration of *ditoobii*, a precipice high on a mountain overhanging the source of the Botu River, and located south of the imposing entrance to the Debei Valley. The people told me that the area was haunted by evil spirits and *tene*, the departed shades of the dead. No one had ever dared to descend the almost vertical slopes of the precipice, and thus brave the both the danger of the terrain and the supernatural. What really prompted me to try to descend the abyss was the claim that in days long past, dead people had been thrown down into the deep, possibly with some of their belongings. So on 12 August 1959, I set off up the mountain to *ditoobii* with several of my boys and two men from Pueta, a village of the Waine-Tibaakoto confederacy, formerly hostile to us. The precipice was magnificent, rising from the midst of huge tropical trees, with the forest vegetation partially spilling down the walls of this karst limestone formation. Once it had been a huge grotto, but the ceiling had collapsed a long time ago. Although I had no ropes, and the gradient and walls were forbidding, curiosity and excitement made me attempt the descent. Over the protests of my boys I started to climb down, holding on to the stems, branches, and roots of trees and bushes, using any ledge or crack in the wall as a foot support and often hanging onto lianas and vines. As good Kapauku sons, my boys could not let me climb alone into what they thought was deadly danger, so they followed me over the edge. Down we went, slowly, testing any vegetation or rock for support. Indeed it was quite an adventure. It seemed to me to be more challenging and exotic than any mountain climbing I had done previously.

Finally, after about an hour, we reached the bottom. The sight was magnificent. Above me towered the walls of the precipice, tree cover on the slopes, and at the rim of the opening above, trees partially obscuring the blue sky gently filtering the sun's rays. The bottom of the great depression, covered with boulders and gravel, was mostly devoid of vegetation. When we started to search the area, however, we were disappointed. No skeletons or artifacts were to be found. If dead bodies had ever been thrown down here, they must have been buried under rocks and debris falling from the cliff face. However, we did discover an opening to a large cave, a grotto with stalagmites and stalactites, and climbed down some way into it. Unfortunately, for want of light and a battery torch I had to abandon further underground exploration. Not so my boys. They had spotted several giant fruit bats (flying foxes) suspended from the walls and ceiling of the cave and killed several for their evening meal. The upward climb proved not as difficult as the descent, and, of course, less mysterious. I have to admit that although I intended to return with ropes and a flashlight to explore the depths of the cave, I somehow never did find the time for that excursion and failed to penetrate *ditoobii*'s secrets.

Before any development of a society can be attempted in an area brought under the control of a foreign government, there must be a firmly established, safe and efficient means of communication. As we have seen, to travel any distance in the Kapauku territory had always meant to wade through often knee-deep mud; to cross treacherous swamps; to slide on slick roots in the jungle; and to balance oneself on a pole across a ditch, stream, or crevasse often thirty feet or more deep.

Natives have been known to drown on some of these "roads" through the swamps. So it is obvious that for the Dutch Government building roads was almost mandatory. Everyone can benefit from roads. Consequently the Dutch decided to build roads through valleys under their control by employing the natives and providing them with necessary tools and reasonable pay in Dutch money, for which Kapauku could buy desirable items of food, clothing and tools at the government store in Enarotali. At first the natives showed considerable enthusiasm, but it quickly dwindled. In the end the unfortunate official in charge had trouble getting people to work even for the higher wages offered in 1959.

Exasperated by broken agreements and lack of labor, the official in the Debei Valley sent out the native police to forcibly round up recalcitrant workers from the nearby communities. In the process excess force was sometimes used to induce the people to work. So, for example, Bobii Ipouga of Tadauto was bound and taken by the native police to their barracks in the summer of 1959. This happened, according to my Kapauku informants, in spite of the fact that Bobii's community had already sent twelve people to build the roads. Later three more men, with their hands tied behind their backs, were sent to do the road work. The desperate Debei people, not wanting to start an armed conflict, sent a deputation to me with their grievances. One of their headmen complained to me bitterly: "I was taught Christianity by American people (Protestant missionaries). They claimed that we should love each other, that violence and killing is bad. However the white man is violating his own principles whenever it is profitable to him. It seems that Christianity should be good only for the Kapauku." I knew the Dutch official in charge and I was sure he was a good man who most likely did not know what his zealous native police were doing behind his back. So I wrote him a letter in which I deplored forced labor and stated that during the Second World War in Czechoslovakia we were also forced by the Nazis to work, and received good pay, but that none of us was happy about it. The letter worked like a miracle and the situation was swiftly corrected. Of course there remained the problem of how to induce the Kapauku to work and enjoy their employment. So I made a bet with the Dutch District Officer. If he provided the tools, I would convince the Kamu Valley Kapauku not only to build roads, but to build them for free! The bet, which consisted of a bottle of good champagne, was accepted. We received the tools, and

I delivered several public lectures about the importance of solid and reliable roads. To be more convincing I accompanied my lecture with magazine pictures showing highways, country roads, and bridges. My audience was duly impressed. Eventually they held a meeting, to which I was not invited so as not to influence their judgment, where they decided to construct a road system in the Kamu Valley.

However there was one more problem. They asked how much I would pay a worker. As a good Kapauku orator should do, I exclaimed in surprise, and yelled that I was an American, that New Guinea was not my country, and that the road would be theirs and not mine. It was they who would make use of it and profit from its safety and convenience, while I would have to return to America. Indeed, I told them they should pay me for my advice and the negotiations regarding the tools. My good Kapauku were at first astonished, but then they burst into laughter, pummeling each other with their fists for joy. "You are really quite a guy, you are now like a Kapauku. You know when to give and when to refuse nonsense." And so it was, no pay on either side. So on 9 March 1959 the Botukebo people, helped by some of my boys, started to dig ditches along the straight strip of land that would become the road connecting Itoda and Botukebo villages. They worked, while I criticized, gave advice, and here and there treated the workers to meals and some goodies from the government shop which had to survive a three to four day trip from Lake Paniai. Construction work proceeded well and swiftly, so that by 21 March the people had finished the stretch Itoda—Botukebo. The very next day, augmented by residents from the Jamaina sublineage, the team started work on the connector between Itoda and Kojogeepa, the next village north from Itoda. On 27 March the people of Jagawaugii, a village to the southwest of Botukebo, decided to work on their section of the first public road system in the Kamu Valley, and the Obajbegaa people (to the north of Kojogeepa) started on their road. To help the people of Kojogeepa my boys built a bridge on their road over a small stream on 5 April. The work progressed so splendidly that on 5 May I hosted a feast for the workers and distributed lots of rice, the most appreciated white man's food. On 13 May, Mr. Post, with the Dutch chief of police, and Mr. Veltkamp, assistant to the District Officer of Paniai, came to see the unbelievable construction. They were certainly impressed and gave two blankets, three knives, and two packages of tobacco to the workers. Of course there were many who received nothing, and were sad. Jokagaibo advised me to confiscate the gifts and keep them until I had accumulated more items to make an equitable distribution. Since I could not disappoint the donors, I simply threw into the dissatisfied workers' assembly handfuls of beads. In the ensuing confusion as the scattered beads were retrieved from the ground and in the enjoyment of their finds, they quite forgot the inequitable distribution procedure. On 6 May more gifts came to the workers from the District Officer in the form of 9 chickens. In the end the Kamu Kapauku road connected the villages of Botukebo, Jagawaugii, Itoda, Kojogeepa, and Obajbegaa. A further section was later built to Nottito, another village of our confederacy. The final product traversed several swamps, crossed three streams, and climbed the steep ascent to the village of Obajbegaa.

The reason for success of this project was certainly not my oratory, but the fact that

Kapauku could do it themselves without being ordered around. It was their road, and they employed a very different system of management in its construction. Instead of communal labor and a communally owned facility, the new road, like their main drainage ditches, was owned individually: each segment of it that traversed somebody's property was owned, worked upon, and maintained by the owner of that land. The road was public only in the sense that all people could use it. Naturally, I refrained from lecturing to the people about existence of toll roads in the United States.

In 1962, I returned to the Kamu Valley and, lo and behold, "our" road was still in operation and well maintained, while some of the government roads had suffered from neglect. This example shows that the industrialized nations should help developing states, but never impose a particular development model on newly independent (emerging) nations. Such imposition, no matter how well designed and meant, is doomed to failure if it incorporates ideas basically foreign to and incompatible with the principles of the native culture. Neither the Dutch nor the Indonesian government can transform the individualistic and ideally egalitarian Kapauku into communally minded socialists who would accept projects planned and directed by a foreign and often unwieldy bureaucracy. Advice from an objectively minded anthropologist who has done a long term research among the people, learned the native language, worked as a participant observer, and is not burdened by adherence to any contemporary -isms (e.g. Marxism, capitalism, interpretism, evolutionism, etc.) should be invaluable to a public administrator and national government. In closing this chapter I should mention that I won a bottle of excellent French champagne from Den Haan, which we drank together. At that time the Kapauku hated alcoholic beverages.

Wege Bagee

After my departure from the Kamu Valley the Catholic missionaries and the Dutch Administration moved in, the latter represented by a Dutch officer and hired Kapauku policemen. Whereas the Dutch Administration chose the western part of the valley as their seat of administration, the Catholic catechist settled in my eastern part in the village of Botukebo. The reaction of the Kapauku, as I had the opportunity to observe during my later visits (1959, 1962, 1975, 1979), was certainly not one of dismay or resistance. Western individualism and entrepreneurship appealed to them, and they were enthusiastic about technology, which they did not regard as mystical or supernatural, but as a clever product of the Western mind. Since in their culture the greatest prestige was gained not through warfare, head hunting, or cannibalism but rather through economic success, Christianity, save for its prescribed monogamy, was found to be quite compatible with their philosophical orientation. Given these positive attitudes toward Western capitalism, it is not surprising that when a nativistic movement sprang up in the Kapauku area, as it did in many parts of New Guinea, it did not resemble the irrational cargo cults, with their negative and often destructive aspects, that were so widespread in the eastern part of the island. The members of the Kapauku movement called themselves *Wege bagee*, or even better *dimi beu bagee*, meaning "crazy people" (lit: "people without thought"). Except for a few strange practices stemming from misinterpretation rather than mysticism, their tenets and program were quite progressive, adaptive, and rational, at least in the Kamu Valley.

The founder of the movement was Pakage Amoje, later known as Zacharias Pakage, from the village of Kokabaja in the Tigi Lake region. During World War II he had attached himself to the Dutch District officer Victor de Bruijn (known as "Jungle Pimpernel" for his resistance behind the Japanese lines, see Rhys 1947) and gone with him to Australia. He became a Protestant teacher. Later he turned against the white man, proclaimed himself district officer, burned the houses of his native adversaries, and even planned to kill a missionary. His outbursts of violence were judged criminal by the Dutch Administration, and later as symptoms of insanity. Indeed, after a term in jail he was committed to an institution in Hollandia (now Jayapura). After his release he fell under the influence of the Seventh Day Adventists and became a convinced pacifist. He began to preach the end of the world, love for thy neighbor, tolerance to the enemy, and a general aversion to violence. "Even if somebody comes intending to kill people, one should take it with resignation," was one of the principal commandments of the movement. Pakage preached these beliefs and distributed gifts to his followers. They were expected to be industrious, cultivate their gardens, walk weaponless, and reject temptation to crime, especially the Kapauku's notorious predilection to theft. As a reward for such noble behavior they would be saved at the coming of the end of the world. They were told they would go straight to Ugatame (the Creator), while infidels would carry luggage for all eternity, the same as porters do for the white man.

When I arrived in the Kamu Valley for my second research in 1959, the Wege Bagee was in full swing. Not far from my place in Itoda their members had built two new villages, Obadoba and Idabagata, on the slopes of the southeastern part of the valley. As so often during my research in New Guinea, I was very lucky with respect to this movement. One of my adopted sons, Tibaakoto Tibaipouga of Mogokotu (whom I named Johannes to honor Professor Wilber, one of my old anthropology friends) became the leader of the Kamu Valley chapter of the movement. Consequently I secured good access to the new communities and to available data and insights provided by Tibaakoto and his fellows. He himself took another name and started to call himself Jegedidi (meaning "sick because of crying").

On 31 July 1959, I made my first visit to the two villages with five of my adopted sons. I was amazed at what I encountered there. Although religious beliefs were discussed, and preaching was important, including the observation of Sunday (called *Daa naago* — "tabooed day"), the secular and economic aspects of the movement were especially striking. The two communities were built in large fenced-in areas, which effectively excluded the pigs. These were provided with special stalls on the periphery of the enclosures, and were thus free to roam outside the jungle. The inside areas were subject to intensive complex cultivation using fertilized earth mounds surrounded by drainage ditches. Consequently the two villages and their surroundings were devoid of the notorious New Guinea mud. Furthermore, the Wege Bagee copied my outside privy by building a communal latrine. In order to utilize the building to its full capacity, the villagers planted beans on its walls so that the occupant, while obeying the call of nature, could inspect the crop at his leisure. The houses were spotlessly clean; the paths were dry and mostly covered with sand, running through nicely landscaped beds of flowers and clumps of palms, bananas, and cycads. Cleanliness was much emphasized. The people washed in the morning and in the evening, as I used to do, and shaved or plucked their beards. They wore clothing (if they could afford to buy it from the Dutch stores), which they kept scrupulously clean. Their hair was washed and combed. To my amazement they planted a large area with coffee trees received from the Dutch Administration. Many European vegetables and other cultigens were grown in their garden plots.

They had rejected the old cowry shell money, using only the blue beads that I had brought into the Valley in 1954 and the Dutch paper currency. For enjoyment they constructed a soccer field, where the master himself, Tibaakoto Tibaipouga, functioned as coach in the late afternoons and on Sundays. He had learned to play soccer in 1955 as a member of my soccer team, which had beaten all the teams put up by the other lineages. In those days Kapauku had added their own refreshing innovations such as kicking one's opponent in the buttocks, or eliminating rules that slow down the game like those concerning "out" and "foul". All this gave the game a very dynamic quality. One could see action not only around the ball but also on other parts of the playing field, where members of opposing teams would sneakily stalk each other to score a good kick on the adversary's buttocks —

kicks that were enjoyed as much by the audience as by the kickers. Unfortunately, all these ingenious innovations were now gone thanks to the peaceful bias of the Wege Bagee doctrine. At the end of my inspection of the two villages the people again caught me by surprise. They asked me to give a lecture on the growing of European plants and vegetables and their various modes of cultivation. Having had plenty of experience as a gardener and a former farmer for five years in the Old Czechoslovakia, I was able to oblige them. After the lecture, I was paid for my instruction with four chickens. This was a surprise, as just three years earlier the Kapauku had paid no one for speaking or lecturing. When they saw my surprise they said that among them it was now established practice to pay speakers, as they remembered my claim that in the States I was paid for my lectures to students. My five sons who accompanied me proudly carried the chickens back to our house in Itoda, showing off my professional earnings to passers-by. After that, whenever our household was out of meat, they urged me to go and deliver more lectures to the Wege Bagee.

My Research
and the Dutch Administration

In my research, the cooperation and help I received from the officials of the Dutch colonial government was invaluable. Not only did the governor, Jan Van Baal, allow me to go into an uncontrolled area and provide me with an escort from the administration officer and his police to protect me; his employees helped me purchase equipment at Hollandia, a Catalina plane transported me into the interior to Paniai Lake in the central highlands, and government pilots on several occasions, especially when a local war prevented me from reaching the government outpost at Enarotali on Paniai Lake, dropped my mail and made sure that they saw me well and alive in front of my hut. Although the district officer at Enarotali, Raphael Den Haan, had been asked by the governor to give me support, he went above and beyond this duty and offered me hospitality in his home, periodically sent me letters asking how I was doing, and arranged purchases from the government-run store for me on a fortnightly basis. As time went by we developed a solid friendship. I enjoyed his wit and, when circumstances demanded it, his firm personality, as well as his extraordinary patience with the natives and, as a matter of fact, with me too. I also appreciated his sporting sense of humor, his personal courage, and his generosity. He was a tall, very handsome man — so handsome, in fact, that he could have easily been picked up by some movie agency and made into a film star. He was well liked and respected by his men, by the missionaries, and especially by the Kapauku. He was their "Hapeebee" (HPB), as they used to call him. What a man, and what an administrator! Although I was then only a graduate student, he listened to me and asked for my advice. Amazingly, he even implemented my suggestions, thus inadvertently helping me with my research by raising my prestige among the Kapauku.

There were, however, times when the government relied too much on my material and applied the law of the Ijaaj-Pigome confederacy, as presented in my book (1958a), to other political entities of the Kapauku region, not realizing that different regions and different confederations of lineages within the Kapauku territory had different customs and legal codes that could be accessed only through the memories of old men. They did not fully comprehend the implications and consequences of my concept of the multiplicity of legal systems (now popularly called "legal pluralism"). And so it happened that, on 8 August 1959, I visited the administration at Moanemani village in the western part of the Kamu Valley. This post had been opened after my departure from the valley in 1957, and administered justice and order to the whole Kamu Valley. The officers tried to adjust their decisions as much as possible to the native culture, especially in deciding problem cases brought to their attention and their court by the people.

In Moanemani some of the local residents eyed me with hostility, something I had not experienced during my first research in 1954-1955. I soon found out why. When I entered the courtroom I found my book on Kapauku law, used as a codification of law governing all the Kapauku, on the judge's table. Thus the legal system of the Ijaaj-Pigome confederacy had, *de facto*, been elevated to cover the whole of Kapauku society and applied to parties with often different legal traditions. The local residents were of course told of the source of the law — the "new tribal law"— and were furious not only with me but with all the members of my Ijaaj-Pigome confederacy. My authority prevailed at the court over their protests. Furthermore, my people exploited the situation beautifully, warning those from the various confederacies: "If you do not follow the Itoda Tuani's (meaning me), writings, we shall make him write an even tougher code." No wonder my popularity plummeted among the unfortunate and misunderstood people of the other confederacies. Of course I tried to correct the matter. But the administrators would not hear of it, arguing that without using my book as a guide to the laws of that region they would be facing a plethora of at least sixteen legal systems, each different at least in some respects from all the others. "You send over another sixteen Pospisils and only then can we comply with this legal multiplicity." In the United States I could not find a single student willing to study the

Kapauku confederacy system. They all wanted to study other tribes and be independent of my findings. I had to respect their right to do so, and even praised their insistence on independence and originality. And so it happened that lots of Ijaaj-Pigome legal ideas and principles spread throughout the Kamu Valley.

I will never forget my Christmas of 1954 in the jungles of the central highlands of New Guinea, then a strange land to me, with mysteries and potential dangers abounding. True enough, I had no time for fear, but Raphael Den Haan's letters and his constant concern gave me much-needed psychological security. So, on that Christmas Eve, I sat in my hut after a day of construction on my fireplace, thinking of my wife, my daughter detained in Czechoslovakia by the Communists, my parents, and all the wonderful, bygone past Christmases. Never before had I been alone on that day. There were my Papuans and my boys and girls around, but I had not yet had time to get close to them and develop the deep affection which slowly evolved over several subsequent months. As I sat contemplating the past, a Papuan emissary from Den Haan arrived unexpectedly, bearing six letters (three from my wife), and a bottle of champagne, biscuits, cookies, and other goodies from Den Haan. He made my Christmas that year and dispelled the feeling of loneliness. Indeed, when I opened the champagne by properly blasting off the cork, the natives were all thrilled and watched me take a sip of the bubbling liquid. Naturally they wanted to taste the stuff. I warned them that it was "sharp," but they insisted. So my son Peetideeti (the Kapauku version of Latin Petrus, English Peter) took several courageous gulps and almost dropped the bottle. His eyes just about popped out of their sockets, he turned red and started to gulp for air, emitting howling sounds that reminded me of a hornbill in flight. Then he became more coherent and started to scream that he was burning inside. So we had to name alcoholic beverages "uto uwo," or "fire water" (reminding me of the Native American epithet). I had to distinguish alcoholic beverages from the kerosene for my pressure lamp, which I called uwo-utu "the water fire." After Peetideeti's courageous trial there were no tasting volunteers at all, then or ever after. When I drank a full glass of the champagne with gusto, they regarded me as a superhuman with specially designed entrails to withstand the burning heat. Thus I did after all have a memorable Christmas in New Guinea.

On several occasions Den Haan sent me gifts. Especially appreciated were the live chickens and a rabbit. Additional gifts came from the missionaries (Catholic and Protestant) from the other regions. Thus my flock of chickens started to grow and I did not feel lost, alone, and forgotten in the tropical jungle.

Although the Dutch administration and missions had the best of intentions and their dealings with the natives and the projects they devised for them were most often exemplary, they could not avoid problems and even crises. During my stay these troubles could be divided roughly into two categories. One of these had its origin in the misbehavior of native government employees — Papuans who were hired as policemen, clerks, or catechists. The other type of trouble was serious and was caused by applying Western principles to the native culture and society. During my stay in the region I was mostly exposed to trouble caused by the Kapauku police and catechists. In both instances they were exploiting their advantageous position with the white man, using their power and influence to their own advantage. I earlier described the crime committed by the policeman who was supposed to protect me, but who, by raping the wife of Auwejokaamoje, endangered not only my research but also my personal safety and life. Were the Kapauku not wise, dispassionate, and just, how easily they could have retaliated and killed both of us! In their eyes, and possibly in the eyes of the Westerners, I was after all partly responsible for his mischief since he was my "employee." As in all other cases the Dutch administration punished the culprit rigorously. On 14 June 1955, I received news that a Malay police boy had been extorting money from the Debei people. On 22 June we received a complaint from the village of Degeipige of another case of extortion by a Kapauku policeman from the Paniai region, and on 4 August came more news of extortion by a policeman in Degeipige. On all these occasions I intervened on behalf of the natives and sent a complaint to the Dutch authorities. In the last two cases I was assisted by my friend

Ijaaj Jokagaibo, who went to Degeipige to obtain objective facts and to collect testimonies. In all these cases we were successful and the culprits were punished and forced to return the loot. In all these cases the police had threatened the people with the power of the white man if the victims did not surrender a "gift."

In 1959 another such incident, as well as the misbehavior of a catechist in the Debei Valley, caused all the catechists to flee the valley, claiming that the people there had decided to kill all the white men. We were told that they were coming in full force to "clean out" the Kamu Valley. I decided to stay and face them, especially since my Ijaaj-Pigome confederacy sided with me and decided to fight the invaders if necessary. On that day I noted in my diary: "Should I be killed it will be by the enemy of the people I am studying and not by the latter." Thus I tried to uphold the reputation of anthropology. Fortunately this was not necessary because, as I described earlier, the whole problem was settled peacefully.

In 1959, during my second field trip, some of the Catholic and Protestant gurus who were in charge of the native schools were found to be behaving as teachers often did in the white man's schools: chastising and even physically punishing their misbehaving youngsters. Kapauku boys who behaved in a disorderly fashion were castigated and slapped or caned. This, of course, went against the Kapauku ideas of individual integrity and proper treatment of youngsters, and provoked a negative reaction. Corporal punishment became so common that at a time when the Kamu Valley should have been missionized (after my departure), Ijaaj Awiitigaaj, the headman of the Ijaaj-Enona sublineage, pleaded in my presence with the Catholic priest Father Van Nuenen and complained about the catechists: "We are giving them our children and we love our children — we beat them very, very seldom, therefore the gurus should be kind and refrain from beating."

Sometimes a catechist would even chastise an adult Kapauku, causing serious problems. In February 1955, while traveling through the upper Edegedide Valley (then already missionized), I heard from some Obaajo people about the mistreatment of porters hired by a Catholic catechist traveling to the Mapia Valley. After they had done their work the catechist not only failed to pay them the promised fee, he also refused to give them any food. These boys, being in a strange and politically hostile land, suffered from such hunger, that they ate dirt to fill their stomachs. They had no place to sleep, no fire to warm them night, and were exposed to torrential rain. The guilty guru simply deserted them in Mapia. Although the narrative given to me sounds exaggerated, it was in essence true, as I later corroborated with other sources. In another instance a Catholic guru allegedly killed two pigs belonging to the people, burnt three houses during a dispute with the natives, and extorted food from them. He claimed he had a right to the food because he had taught their children. The people, of course, did not see it that way. They had not asked to be missionized or schooled. These problematic situations were usually consequences of the fact that incompetent, semi-educated individuals, often even non-Kapaukus from Mimika on the south coast of New Guinea, were recruited to fill these posts. Often they did not even speak Kapauku and were placed in the Kapauku region without adequate means of subsistence. This drove them to extortion and even theft of crops and animals,

During my first research and my subsequent visits I tried to help the people adapt to the new colonial order brought to them by government officials and missionaries. One of the ways I tried to reduce the tension between the administration officials and the Kapauku was to attempt to help them solve their disputes by themselves without resorting to the colonial courts. So, for example, several members of the Dimi clan from the Egebutu region came to me with the complaint that the *tonowi* of the village of Ginopigi had extorted cowry shells from them by exploiting his friendly relations with the Dutch colonial administrator at Moanemani. I sent word to him requesting the return of the shells. If he did not comply, I warned, the district officer from Enarotali would most likely interfere and punish him severely with a jail term. Soon, two of my sons returned from Ginopigi with the good news that my scheme had worked very well and the extorted shells had been returned with not much resistance from the headman.

On another occasion in 1955 I had to intervene physically in a fight between two brothers, Ijaaj Amojepa of Kojogeepa, a strongman known for his volatile temper, and his younger brother. The two got into an argument and Amojepa beat his younger brother over the head with a stick, causing deep and bloody wounds. The boy fled and came to my house for help. I cleaned the wounds, dressed them, and tried to calm him down. Before long his older brother appeared with profuse apologies for his violent emotional outburst and offered his wounded brother beads and shell money as compensation for the injury. I thought this gesture would solve the problem, but the wounded and deeply offended youth rejected the rather generous offer and charged at his brother with a knife. I seized him just in time, disarmed him, and after a lengthy argument persuaded him to accept the compensation. "Would a clever and reasonable young Kapauku reject such a profitable deal, and by giving vent to your emotions forfeit the receipt of such a handsome income?" I argued. The young man agreed that this would be inadvisable and said he would rather be regarded as clever and reasonable.

In return for all the assistance I received from the colonial administration with my stay and research, I always tried to be helpful with advice and negotiations with the Kapauku. Although I was able to answer most of the officials' questions and requests promptly, there were some instances which puzzled me and I had to give only tentative answers, or I gave them my opinion at a later date, after I had had a chance to properly analyze the situation. For example, when I returned to the valley in 1959, four years after my initial research, government officials confronted me with a complicated situation for which I had neither a ready explanation nor advice for a remedy. After the administration had pacified the Kamu Valley and put it under its administrative control in 1955 and after my departure that year, the local *tonowi* started to lose power and influence over their former followers, despite the efforts of the government to keep the old political system going. The Dutch administration had taken away from the Kapauku the power to declare war, negotiate peace, or make judicial decisions that might result in a death penalty. The remaining powers of the *tonowi*, however, were left unchanged and their importance was actually enhanced by their new role as intermediaries between their constituencies and government officials. So in 1959 I made my inquiries, studied the new situation, and looked at my new data, but I still had no explanation for the power collapse phenomenon. Only a year later, after my return to Yale, did I make the breakthrough. In 1954-1955 I had collected quantitative data on the people's economy and their socio-political structure. These data enabled me to examine the amount of credit extended by the headmen to their people, and it was this that gave me the solution to the mystery. A comparison of the total credits extended over three years revealed that the natives owed their rich headmen only about one fourth of what they owed in 1955. This explained the loss of power and influence of the local headmen. Most Kapauku followed the decisions of their headmen because they were indebted to them and were afraid of being asked to repay what they owed if they did not comply, and also because they felt grateful for past loans. Also they hoped for future monetary favors. It was now obvious to me that the spectacular decrease in indebtedness of the common people to their leaders was commensurate with the decrease in *tonowi* influence. The young men who formerly had to borrow heavily from headmen in order to buy themselves wives or pigs found, with the advent of the white man, a way to escape indebtedness. They could instead secure lucrative employment with the Dutch administration, which was building an airstrip at Moanemani in the western part of the Kamu. Thus the construction of the airstrip had an unexpected effect on the native culture: by eliminating the necessity to borrow, it caused the natives' political structure to start to disintegrate.

There were, of course, issues over which neither side would yield on its demands and position. One such issue was the Administration's practice of punishing offenders, even murderers, with jail. The Kapauku believed that a man deprived of his personal independence and liberty was doomed. His soul eventually leaves him and he dies. Thus thieves and other minor offenders were, in their eyes, being punished by the Dutch with a slow death resulting from jail sentences of even a few months. I predicted an early uprising should the abolishment of jail be rejected. Accordingly, prior to my departure in 1955 I made several recommendations to the Dutch administration, one of which was to substitute jail sentences with adequate fines. This advice was rejected and one year later, as I had predicted, the Kapauku revolted. After bloody fighting in which over a hundred natives and several policemen died and a Cessna plane was destroyed on the ground, the Kapauku were defeated and "pacified." As I described earlier, in this revolt I suffered a personal loss. My missionary friend in the village of Obano, along with his wife and child, were killed by a band of Kapauku who did not know that the family was very well liked by the local people and were actually their friends, not their enemies.

After 1962, opposition to the new rule of Indonesians was similarly ill-fated, but it assumed much larger proportions. The Kapauku simply wanted to be free and independent. Early after the takeover of Irian Jaya (Indonesian West New Guinea) the animosity of the Kapauku culminated in a second revolt, which ultimately proved to be recurrent, seemingly without a conclusion, and even bloodier than the first. Violence subsided and erupted again periodically. By that time, however, the Kapauku had learned how to use firearms, a supply of which they had secured by theft from the native police, by combat, and by smuggling from outside their territory. Indeed, upon my return in 1975 the Kapauku approached me with a request to get them weapons. I explained that if I did so I would never be able to return, and that it was up to them whether they wanted weapons or my future presence. Fortunately they opted for the latter. All the same, they were apparently still able to shoot down an Indonesian airplane carrying the Indonesian commanding general. With a single rifle shot they hit the pilot, who had the presence of mind and skill to crash-land, saving the general's life but losing his own. Again in this conflict I suffered a personal loss when one of my adopted sons, Ijaaj Wijaagowode, was shot and killed in one of the engagements. Another son of mine became a war hero, fighting off Indonesian paratroopers. He and others told me that my stories from the Second World War and my recounting of my experiences in the underground had come in very handy in their own struggle. Thus it was that old guerilla fighting methods were successfully used in the Kamu Valley. In 1979, during my last stay with the Kapauku, the temporary outcome of hostilities for the Kamu Valley was not a defeat but a reasonable compromise. The Indonesian administration kept the region under control through an Indonesian district officer, a very decent and understanding man, while the police force, composed of uniformed Kapauku, kept peace and order in the valley.

There were two other issues on which I could not agree with the Dutch administration and missionaries: the introduction of the European pig as an improvement to the native stock of pigs (*Sus scrofa papuensis*), and the stocking of formerly fishless rivers, swamps, and lakes. The Kapauku pigs, although much smaller and shaggy-looking creatures compared to their European relatives, had one tremendous advantage: they were virtually disease-free, carrying neither trichinosis nor tapeworm (*Taenia solium*). I warned the Dutch not to bring a new strain of pigs into the territory because I suspected that no matter how carefully the introduced animals might be inspected for disease and parasites, there would inevitably be some individuals that might escape even the most careful scrutiny and bring European parasites into this healthy region. My arguments were not taken seriously. After all, I was only an anthropologist and they were agricultural and biological experts. Unfortunately, my fears and predictions proved to be well-founded. In the seventies, after the introduction of the European pig, the first infestation made its appearance in the pig population. This has become what is now regarded as the worst affliction in the area. The people were not only hosts to this horrible worm, which in European countries lives only in the human colon, but unlike Europeans the Kapauku were also hosts to the parasite's larvae, whose hosts in Europe were exclusively pigs. Today, these enter the digestive system of the natives with contaminated food and especially water, penetrate the bloodstream, and form abscesses not only in the muscles but, most dreadful and lethal, also in the brain, causing severe seizures comparable to epilepsy. During such seizures several Kapauku have fallen into their fires and sustained severe burns. The unexpected difference in the worm's behavior in Europe and in New Guinea is accounted for by the fact that the Kapauku did not wash with soap and that toilets were not available — they defecated freely in the bush and grasslands.

Thus their feces contained the worm eggs, infesting not only their food but also their fresh water system and springs, which became the main source of the dissemination of this plague. In the country where I used to safely drink ice-cold, excellent water from every spring during my trips, and from the small brook, which emerged from the limestone cliffs behind my house, I was suddenly threatened, thanks to our "scientific" experts, with a dreadful parasite infestation which could destroy my brain. There are few more horrible fates. Carleton Gajdusek's photographs of dissected human brains teeming with tapeworm larvae and abscesses testify to the folly of our "experts." To eliminate the parasites in the native situation is virtually impossible under present conditions, short of exterminating the whole pig population and enforcing strict hygiene (washing hands, using toilets, etc.). And even then there are the infected wild boars!

Possibly an even greater catastrophe for the Kamu Valley was the thoughtless introduction of fish. While the lakes and rivers of the region were devoid of fish, which could be a very good source of food and essential proteins for the population, they were the breeding waters for millions of succulent crayfish, a delicacy in Europe. When the idea of introducing fish was presented to me I objected, fearing that the fish would exterminate the crayfish population, a potential source of hard currency for the natives in the future. A future crayfish cannery could bring the natives a true financial boom and long-term prosperity. My arguments, however, were ignored and the lakes and rivers were stocked with several species of fish. As I suspected, the immediate effect was a radical reduction of the crayfish population, a major source of protein for many communities in the old days. Women were soon catching fish in their nets instead of crayfish. "They had to change their method and be much quicker than before," I was told by an informant during my last visit to the valley. Generally the women still used the old crayfish nets, especially in times of flood when beaters drove fish in the flooded shallow waters of the grasslands toward a line of fisherwomen waiting with their nets. Otherwise the fish were now taken with hook and line, both of which were bought from the missions. The hook was now called *keipo*, the Kapauku word for a bone needle. So my dream of a prosperous cannery and Kamu Valley crayfish flooding the European markets was dashed.

Unfortunately, the loss of potentially large revenue for the Kapauku was by no means the worst consequence of the presence of fish in their waters. The profound effect on the ecology was felt in different quarters. In 1954 when I first came to the Kamu Valley the place seemed to me like a paradise. Beautiful scenery, dense virgin forests reaching down the mountain slopes toward the flat, swampy valley floor, an area devoid of the venomous insects (even the honeybees had no stings!), deadly snakes, and crocodiles that made the lowlands of New Guinea a rather inhospitable area for the white man. However, the most important advantage of this highland ecology was the absence of dreadful tropical diseases, especially plague, leprosy, cholera, an assortment of lowland skin diseases, and especially malaria, with all its deadly strains in the lowlands. The fish, together with introduced pigs, devastated this paradise, making it a territory almost as dangerous as the coast.

When I came to the Kamu Valley in 1975 I was greeted in the evening by a swarm of mosquitoes, an insect that I had not seen in the valley during my first three research periods in spite of the fact that my house stood next to Kugumo Lake and a vast adjacent swamp. Even worse, the mosquitoes were of the *anopheles* species, a malaria carrier. This had been a place where I did not have to sleep under mosquito nets or swallow malaria pills. I hated this change and tried to figure out what had actually happened. As it turned out, the fish almost exterminated not only the crayfish, but also the formerly abundant aquatic dragonfly larvae. The millions of dragonflies had eliminated any threat of mosquito infestation, decimating these insects in flight, and their larvae took care of the mosquito progeny in the water. Because of the lack of mosquitoes, the major food of the dragonflies had to be flies and other insects. Having lost their archenemy, the mosquitoes multiplied freely and made living in the Kamu Valley miserable. But the worst is still to come. It is only a question of time before malaria is introduced and decimates the Kapauku population.

As everywhere, these major ecological problems were aggravated by unchecked overpopulation. During my first visit it was officially estimated that there were about 45,000 Kapauku living in territories already brought under Dutch control and in the regions not yet pacified or even explored. So it happened that most of the Kapauku territory remained virgin land and was uninhabited. The Kamu Valley presented a unique feature as a vast, partly dried-out lakebed with exposed rich soil, especially in its eastern and southeastern parts. There the population density was quite high, and many villages were separated from one another by less than two kilometers and counted more than 180 inhabitants. Even with this density there was no lack of land, and the agricultural cycle of fallowing and cultivating could safely allow the land to stay fallow for a period of about fourteen years, the time needed for reforestation and land recuperation. The population increase, although significant compared with other Kapauku regions, was not alarming. It was effectively checked by endemic warfare, disease, and especially high child mortality. A woman who hoped to have four children grow to adulthood had to give birth to ten. With the advent of the white man and later the Indonesians, a profound change took place. The elimination of warfare, which came almost overnight, saved the lives of many adult males. Modern medicine, whose pills and other remedies — which were brought into the Kamu Valley by myself, and then by government officials and missionaries — checked many diseases, especially the most lethal. The killer of children was bacillary dysentery, and the old people's enemy was pneumonia. Once a horribly crippling disease, yaws (*frombosia*), a highly infectious kind of syphilis, was completely wiped out by penicillin. The disappearance of yaws in the Kamu Valley, to which I contributed by inviting a physician to treat the families affected, was a marvel. Witnessing it reminded me of the advantages we enjoy in Western civilization.

True enough, white people have brought some of their diseases to the shores of New Guinea and the tapeworm to the Kamu. Yet despite new diseases and parasites, the Kamu Valley, and especially its western and southern parts, has experienced an almost catastrophic population increase. For example, the community of Botukebo, which I studied closely, had only 180 inhabitants in both 1955 and 1962. In 1975 it boasted 272 residents. Moreover, many Botukebo villagers had moved to other villages or to the coastal towns. This represents a population increase of about 50 percent in residents only. With emigrants added in, it comes to 57 percent, and that in a period of only thirteen years! For me the population pressure created a special problem. Early in my research I had to buy gifts for only 55 of my "sons and daughters"; in 1975 and 1979, however, I faced several hundred of my "grandchildren," all demanding gifts from their "grandpa." My first gifts were beads, knives, machetes, and pots. As time went on, however, my growing family expected gifts of watches, radios, and jewelry.

Ecologically the population increase in the Kamu Valley resulted in a remarkable loss of most of its virgin tropical forest. Of course the large-scale drainage of the southeastern Kamu Valley, completed by the Kapauku on advice from the Catholic mission (and my own advice in 1959), eliminated some of the periodic flooding of the valley floor, even when torrential rains lasted for several days. The increase in the size of the valley floor that was suitable for growing crops resulted in an unprecedented surplus of sweet potatoes and other edibles. However, because of this enlargement of the area of fertile land, the swidden cultivation on the mountain slopes of Kemuge Mountain was virtually abandoned. This area had traditionally provided security for the people in times of flood, when crops on the valley floor were destroyed. The old men in the community responded to this loss by saying: "There may come a huge flood, and when it happens then what? We shall all starve, as old accounts of such disasters tell us." In addition, the increase in population has placed a heavy demand on the forests for construction material and firewood. By 1975, several mountain slopes had become semi-desert, supporting only some grass and scant vegetation, and unable to regenerate any forest cover. Erosion set in. In 1975 and 1979 it was a sad sight for me to see the past beauty of the valley gone, probably forever.

Departure from the Kamu Valley

All things come to an end, and so did my research among the Kapauku. Of my five departures from the Kamu Valley, the first in 1955 was the most dramatic. After my long stay, my adoption into the Ijaaj clan lineage, my economic impact and role as a liaison between the people and the Dutch government, not to mention my attachment to my adopted sons and daughters, best friends, and their primary relatives, departure proved really difficult. The Kapauku knew right from the start of my research that I was not to stay, and toward the end of my first stay the number of "moons" remaining of my residence in Itoda were well known and many times discussed. The Kapauku, being very pragmatic and adaptive, convened a meeting of headmen and other important individuals in the house of Auwejokaamoje, the strongman of the village of Jagawaugii (of Jamaina sub-lineage), to discuss their adaptation to my future departure and their relations with the Dutch administration. They did this in August 1955, far ahead of my leaving the valley. The planned increase in the production of food crops for trade with the white man was an important topic. During my stay we had traded with the Dutch settlement in Enarotali at Paniai Lake, supplying the Dutch primarily with limes, ginger, and several types of bananas, which did not grow at the more elevated region around the lake. Discussions also included plans to hire the white man's planes in order to engage in intensive trade with the coastal people. In those days a great sensation was created by the arrival of a shipment from the United States of some of my developed slides and prints showing the Kapauku at their work, wars and festivities. All the people admired them, identified the individuals in the pictures, and invited their friends to come and see my picture collection. Many people from the Kamu Valley and the adjacent regions came for the viewing, and many expressed a wish to be photographed.

As the time of my departure drew closer the concern about my leaving became quite intense. Over and over again I had to explain that I would return and would stay with them again. In August 1955 a deputation came to my home from the southern part of the Kamu Valley, together with many people of Botukebo, inviting me to the Dogimani pig feast in the western part of the valley. I had to refuse the invitation, explaining that I had little time to complete my planned research. They reluctantly accepted my explanation, promised to intensify their teaching of the Kapauku way, and assured me that all the Kamu people were very sad that I would soon be leaving them. "Who will help us against the injustice of the colonial police? Who will tell the administration officials and present them with the Kapauku point of view? And stand up in the white man's court of justice and defend the Kapauku way of life?" To my surprise they pointed out several things that I had not considered important and that they had never mentioned to me. They praised the fact that I had never hit a boy, even if he misbehaved, that I never got mad (I did, but tried not to show it) and always sought amicable solutions to controversies. Toward the end of September, the anxiety surrounding my departure became acute. Daily, people clustered around my house, I heard many expressions of sorrow, and my adopted sons and daughters wept, embracing me at every opportunity. I had to constantly assure everybody that I was coming back. The most serious problem seemed to be with my "mother," that is, the mother of my best friend Ijaaj Jokagaibo. Not only did she shower me with gifts and heirlooms (beautiful stone axes and a stone machete carved from the green semiprecious stone serpentine, for example), crying and hugging me many times a day, but the evenings and early part of the night she spent wailing on a cliff over my house, performing as if her own son were dying. Finally she wanted to cut off segments of her finger (cleverly, the left hand) as the old mourning custom prescribed. Here I had to intervene, declaring that if she did that, she would look so dreadful that I would certainly think twice about coming back. That worked well and there was no more talk of mutilation.

When my daughters and many other girls decided to follow me to Paniai Lake to see me off, I had no objection. Indeed, I promised to feed them well during the trip, and in Enarotali I distributed lots of bead, axes, knives, machetes, kitchen utensils, mirrors, scarves, and blankets to the people. I surrendered my three chickens, and to my best friend Jokagaibo I gave my beloved pig. As a crowd of Kapauku gathered around my house I threw handfuls of my blue glass beads, since it was the custom to reimburse mourners for their pain and sorrow. I even gave away some spare planks from my house, so that it looked as if I were taking it apart. My best friend Jokagaibo, several lineage headmen, and especially Ijaaj Ekajewaijokaipouga, the headman of the whole Ijaaj-Pigome confederacy, pleaded with me not to dismantle my house since I had promised to return. In return they assured me that they would take good care of it while I was gone. As an expression of utmost grief some men broke their penis sheaths, smeared their faces with ashes, and Kaadootajbii, the witch doctor and a friend of mine, ate dirt. I offered him some freshly roasted pork and cooked crayfish.

When the day of my departure from Itoda arrived I found a large gathering of Kapauku in front of my house. Many of them grabbed my forearm and expressed their sorrow. Finally my entourage and I set out northward. As we passed through the villages of our confederacy (Kojogeepa, Obajbegaa, and Bunauwobado) I was greeted by many of the locals who offered me souvenirs and food. After passing the village of Jotapuga we reached Ugapuga — our goal for the day. I stayed overnight in the Catholic mission and the next day we set out to brave the dangers of the forbidden forest and Mount Deijai, and especially the curse of the evil spirits of Madou and Ukwaniija. Three days later, after we had climbed Deijai and returned to Ugapuga, we continued our journey north via the Ijaajdimi pass to the Tage Lake region, where we stopped at Itugakebo. The local protestant missionary, Mr. Cato, an American, transported us across the lake in his motorboat and we spent the night in the Dutch police outpost of Waghete. There I had a long and pleasant talk with my old friend the police commander of the Tigi area, Mr. Lawrence, who had accompanied me in 1954 to the place of my research in Itoda. Next day we crossed the mountain ridge to the east and entered into the valley of the Jawei River, which emptied the waters of the huge Paniai Lake into the Indian Ocean on the south of the island. There, at a place called Udateida, we waited for the arrival of a boat that would take us to Enarotali. The district officer Mr. Den Haan came himself and took me and my party to his place.

The next day I went with Den Haan and several other Dutch officials to the village of Edegetadi, where ceremonial payment was made to the Papuans who had built a road for the government. At Udateida we met Mr. Veltkamp and members of his expedition to Mount Deijai. After the payment ceremony we returned to Enarotali, where a party was given in my honor at the district officer's house. I was presented with a bottle of exquisite French champagne and I played a borrowed accordion and sang some Czech and Russian folk songs. The party lasted until 4 a.m., though my Kapauku companions retired much earlier. Next day I visited my local friends and acquaintances and bid farewell to them and the local Catholic priest, the visiting Father Kamerer, and the America Protestant missionaries.

A great surprise awaited me that day. I was told that Ijaaj Jokagaibo, my best friend, had been rewarded by the Dutch government for the help he had given me with my research. He was offered a free flight with me to the island of Biak with its international airport, where he could inspect a modern European town. He accepted the invitation, and I was thrilled at the prospect of seeing a tribesman's reaction to air travel, automobiles, modern buildings, the ocean, etc. Next morning, accompanied by my Kapauku friend, Den Haan, Marion Doble, and other Kapauku and Dutch officials, I walked to the pier, where I took leave of my friends. My two boys, Marius and Gubeeni, wept bitterly. My attempt to sooth their grief with a gift of beads had little effect. I thanked Marion Doble again for her help with the Kapauku language and Mrs. Den Haan for her hospitality. Then we boarded a motorboat and, accompanied by District Officer Den Haan, his assistant and Jokagaibo, headed to a Cataline amphibious plane floating nearby. I shook hands with Raphael Den Haan, thanked him again and invited him to visit me in the United States. The plane was already half full of members of the local missions.

The takeoff was smooth. We cleared the water of Paniai Lake and flew north, to a mountain pass at the entrance to the Paniai Lake region, which was covered in cloud. I closely watched Jokagaibo's reactions to the flight. He showed no signs of anxiety over the shaking and tilting of the plane, and was not troubled by motion sickness. On the contrary, he asked me to open the side window of the plane (formerly a machine gun emplacement). Then he reached out into the clouds. Withdrawing his hand, he inspected it carefully and declared: "So I was right. Clouds are nothing but water vapor!" Then he asked me whether it would be possible for him to see how the pilot flew the plane. We crawled between passengers and their baggage, through the narrow entrance into the cockpit, where I asked the pilot if we could observe. Far from being annoyed, he was amused by my friend's interest. He asked the copilot to let the headman sit in his seat and then showed him how, by moving and turning the steering wheel, he could direct the plane to fly up and down and left and right. Then, to my surprise, he asked Jokagaibo to try steering for himself. And so we were making left and right turns and went up and down, to the great enjoyment of the headman and the pilot. Unfortunately this merriment ended when one of the missionaries climbed into the cockpit, his eyes popping, and inquired whether the plane was in trouble. I answered casually, "No trouble. We were just trying to teach the headman how to fly the plane." This rather cool summation of the situation provoked a revolution among the passengers, and Jokagaibo and I had to retreat to the passenger area, where we remained under close supervision for the rest of the flight.

Finally we arrived at Biak. The headman, minus his gourd penis sheath and properly dressed in trousers and a shirt, became the guest of the district officer of Biak. In the afternoon, after scuba diving over the coral reef, I joined him and took him for a ride through the town, showing him the various buildings and explaining their functions. As I mentioned earlier in this book, however, he was much more interested in countring the people in the streets to get an idea of the size of the local population.

The next day Jokagaibo fell sick and asked to be returned to Paniai Lake and his highlands. He claimed that he needed a shaman to make him well again. So the local doctor gave him some pills and he was sent home on the next plane. He soon felt better, attributing his recovery, of course, to the skills of our shaman Kaadotajbii rather than to the pills.

My adventures on the way home did not end with my departure from Kapauku territory, nor even from New Guinea. Since I was a friend of Governor Van Baal, himself an astute anthropologist, I had help with all my logistical and departure problems. I was flown to the then capital of Netherlands New Guinea, Hollandia, hosted at dinners, given lunches at local restaurants, and brought to beaches for swimming and to Sentani Lake for water skiing. I was also invited to attend parties and official ceremonies. And so it happened one day that the governor invited me to a ceremonial reception of the crew of a Dutch warship. As I described earlier, I was there mistaken for the governor.

On my many flights home from New Guinea my problem spot on several occasions proved to be Manila. In 1955, when I hailed a taxi to go to a downtown cinema, I was instead driven to a brothel in Manila's red light district. I insisted that I wanted to go to the movies, but the establishment's female employees did not believe me. Finally I became mad and escaped the swarm of prostitutes, who obviously classified me as an eccentric. On other occasions I was pursued by women, and even men, who tried to sell me "their sisters." "This could happen only to you," claimed Yale Professor Harold Conklin, for whom the Philippines and Manila was a second home. Concerned, I inspected my face to see whether I had the look of a sex-hungry tourist.

By far my most dramatic experience in Manila occurred on my third trip to New Guinea, in 1962. Since it is such a strange account, I will quote directly from my students' "objective" and "unbiased" account, which was published in the 1968 Yale yearbook:

The frustrated would-be seductress grabbed his billfold and fled into the hotel. Alarmed at the possible consequences of losing many valuable personal papers, he quickly followed her; but his antagonists, taking advantage of the element of surprise, were waiting for him, and immediately upon entering the hotel he was jumped by four Filipino toughs. A short scuffle ensued, at the end of which one of his assailants was suffering from four crushed ribs, two others had been knocked out, and the fourth was weakening from loss of blood. While still struggling with the last kidnapper, a fifth man appeared on the scene with a gun. Duly alarmed, he fled into a corridor, waited for the gunman, and then floored him with a searing right uppercut. As it turned out, the gunman had been the first policeman dispatched to restore order in the hotel, and after apologizing profusely to the unamused plain clothesman, he treated him to a free dinner and to a night out at the movies. And thus ended another typically untypical day in the life of Yale University's LEOPOLD POSPISIL, Professor of Anthropology (Yale Banner 1968).

A slightly exaggerated version of what actually happened, perhaps.

Kamu Valley (elevation: 1,500 meters). Photographed from the Debei Valley above (2,000 meters).

The author sits on the edge of Debei Valley; a local chief uses an arrow to identify the different villages below. In the background, behind the clouds, is Mt. Deijai (4,114 m).

Panorama shot of the northern Kamu Valley. (1954)

Kapauku crops. (1954)

A local runs over the hot ashes of a field that has been burned.

A local woman plants sweet potatoes on the slope of a mountain.

Sweet potatoes, at various stages of growth, on the mountainous fields of the Debei Valley.

A local ties a sacred tree-top to what will be the central beam of the dance house in Aigii.

Completed dance house in Aigii.

Construction of the author's house.

Locals train in spear-throwing.

Locals doing gymnastics on the bar set up by the author.

The first headstand by a Kapauku.

The author photographed by his adopted son.

Locals drag a canoe uphill near Ijaajdimi.

The locals built a bridge of poles and rattan across the river.

Native dug-out canoe on Paniai Lake. Panorama of Mt. Deijai.

Kapauku woman with her canoe moored at the bank of the Jawei River in Udateida.

Women fishing with wooden tridents on Kugumo Lake.

Marius holding a fruit bat that had been shot.

Marius wearing a butterfly hairpin.

Ijaaj Ekajewaijokaipouga – the extremely wealthy headman of the Ijaaj-Pigome confederacy – giving a political speech in Waghete. (Note the finery. The author esitmates Ekajewaijokaipouga's personal wealth was equivalent to $250,000.)

Close-up of Chief Ijaaj Ekajewaijokaipouga.

The author and Kaadotajbii, the witch doctor.

The author photographed by his adopted son.

The author and his best friend, headman Jokagaibo Ijaaj, standing on the shore of Paniai.

A group of adolescent girls, including Meekaamude.

Antonia and Perenika.

A group of local boys dressed up and on their way to the pig feast in Bunauwobado.

Local boys on their way to the pig feast, running along the path between Itoda and Obajbegaa.

Locals dancing a dance waitataiat a pig feast. Taken in front of Pospíšil's house in 1954.

Counting out strings of cowrie-shell currency at the pig feast.

A native pig inspects Pospíšil's luggage.

A scene from a Kapauku pig feast in 1954.

Jokagaibo butchering his pig before a group of children and women.

Counting out the bride-price in cowrie shells.

Tree burial with Pegabii climbing to his dead father.

The man Pospíšil performed abdominal surgery on, visiting the author's house healthy. (1954)

Goo, Pospíšil's 'son,' holding an impressive bow and arrows. (1959)

Defendant weeps while the judge passes his decision.

The defendant standing before the court, her hands are tied and skirt is torn.

Native court in session: a native pleads his case while the judge holds his head and contemplates.

Headman urges his followers to war.

War-dance: everybody armed with bows and arrows, dancing clockwise.

Fighting on the battle line, hiding in the tall grass. Panorama of the Kamu Valley in background.

A Kapauku who has just shot his arrow.

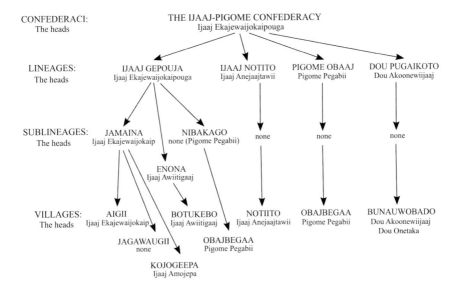

CONFEDERACI: THE IJAAJ-PIGOME CONFEDERACY
The heads   Ijaaj Ekajewaijokaipouga

LINEAGES: IJAAJ GEPOUJA   IJAAJ NOTITO   PIGOME OBAAJ   DOU PUGAIKOTO
The heads   Ijaaj Ekajewaijokaipouga   Ijaaj Anejaajtawii   Pigome Pegabii   Dou Akoonewiijaaj

SUBLINEAGES: JAMAINA   NIBAKAGO   none   none   none
The heads   Ijaaj Ekajewaijokaip none (Pigome Pegabii)

                         ENONA
                      Ijaaj Awiitigaaj

VILLAGES: AIGII   BOTUKEBO   NOTIITO   OBAJBEGAA   BUNAUWOBADO
The heads Ijaaj Ekajewaijokaip Ijaaj Awiitigaaj Ijaaj Anejaajtawii Pigome Pegabii Dou Akoonewiijaaj
                                                      Dou Onetaka
              JAGAWAUGII   OBAJBEGAA
               none   Pigome Pegabii

              KOJOGEEPA
              Ijaaj Amojepa

Afterword:
Leopold Pospíšil, Anthropology and the Kapauku

Leopold Pospíšil is a living legend of cultural anthropology. He was born on 26 April 1923 in the Moravian city of Olomouc, less than four years after his native Czechoslovakia came into being as one of the successor states of the Austro-Hungarian Empire. After a childhood and school-days spent in Olomouc, his subsequent life could provide material for several adventure novels. Having joined the anti-Nazi resistance he was shot in the knee and operated on by his surgeon uncle — without an anesthetic. Later Pospíšil said his uncle had wanted him to realize that precious anesthetic should be kept for those in the resistance in greater need. During the war he narrowly avoided being executed after he and some friends stole a Nazi flag and (to put it politely) relieved them-selves on it and were then interrogated by the police. After the war he studied law at Charles University (the oldest university in Central Europe, founded in 1348), but before he could graduate he emigrated to Germany, along with his wife and father, to escape the Communist dictatorship. And with good reason: his life was once again in danger after his participation in a student march in support of the Czechoslovak president Edvard Beneš. We should add that he left behind his two-year-old daughter and did not see her again till 1968. In Germany he studied philosophy, but in 1949 he decided to move to the USA, where he took a variety of jobs from baker, verger, and gravedigger to cowboy. He enrolled at Willamette University in Oregon where he obtained a BA, following up with a Masters in anthropology at the University of Oregon. Impressed by his success as a student, the farmer he was working for gave him generous financial support, enabling him to continue his studies. Pospíšil applied to Harvard and Yale, was accepted by both, but chose Yale as they offered him a bigger scholarship. Thus the cow-poke became a full-time student of Social Sciences, eventually gaining a doctorate in 1956. During a summer vacation he carried out a short field study of Native Americans, specifically a community of Hopi. Importantly, he also travelled to New Guinea to study the Kapauku, among whom he spent thirteen months conducting basic research. Originally he was given permission to do his research in the eastern part of what was then Papua New Guinea, but on condition he did his doctorate at the Australian National University — a condition he found unacceptable. In the end, thanks to recommendations from his mentor George Peter Murdock and visiting professor Theodore Fischer, he arranged to work in the western part of the island, at that time still a Dutch colony. This research laid the foundation for his successful professional career, in the course of which he published over a hundred research papers and many books, became a member of the National Academy of Sciences, and served as adviser on human rights to President George H. W. Bush. After the fall of the Iron Curtain he started travelling regularly to the land of his birth, where he lectured, met colleagues and visited family. And finally, after over forty years, he was able to accept in person the degree of Doctor of Law.

The authors of this Afterword, Martin Soukup (a cultural anthropologist) and Jaroslav Jiřík (an archaeologist), are former students of Professor Leoplold Jaroslav Pospíšil and thus had the good fortune to attend the fascinating lectures he gave in the 1990s and 2000s at the Institute of Ethnology of Charles University in Prague. In those days, just after the fall of the Iron Curtain, his lectures came as a breath of fresh anthropological air. Before the 'Velvet Revolution,' anthropology in Czechoslovakia had been based on Marxist-Leninist ideology and had few links with its counterpart in the West. Moreover, many excellent anthropologists had emigrated from communist Czechoslovakia, among them Ladislav Holý, Zdeněk Salzmann and Milan Stuchlík. When Pospíšil began regularly returning to Czechoslovakia (then, after the country split, to the Czech Republic), it was he who introduced the ideas and concepts of American anthropology to new generations of students. Credit for a similar reforging of links must also go to Zdeněk Salzmann[1] and Ladislav Holý, the

---

1] An abridged translation of his key work *Language, Culture and Society* (1963) appeared in the supplement of *Český lid* (Salzmann 1996).

latter using his trips home to conduct field research that resulted in the acclaimed study *The Little Czech and the Great Czech Nation* (1996).[2]

A similar situation obtained in archaeology at that time, where the influence of 'post-Marxist' paradigms regarding the development of primitive communal societies was still apparent. Pospíšil's lectures were a direct challenge to such 'traditional' approaches in Czech archaeology and ethnology. The evolution from matriarchy to patriarchy, the absence of personal property, the absence of social hierarchies in the prehistoric and preliterate societies studied by ethnologists and anthropologists, as well as the absence of a monetary economy — all these entrenched notions of the 'savage' and 'barbarian' stages of human evolution were thoroughly and definitively demolished by Pospíšil in his lectures. Interestingly, it was his work among the Kapauku that proved that 'primitive communal societies' (to use the Marxist term) could be based on a capitalist economy. He thus debunked one of the basic tenets of Marxism: that in so-called primitive communal societies there is no such thing as private property and surplus value, but rather an egalitarian tendency with minimal differentiation in social structure and relations. Preliterate non-European societies such as the Kapauku had usually been regarded as just such hypothetical primitive communal societies.

Even long after he graduated, Jaroslav Jiřík continued to attend university lectures, seeing them as a kind of tonic antidote to the otherwise uniformly drab academic (and not only academic) world of Prague, the beating heart of Central Europe. But he also sought opportunities for guest lectures elsewhere. On 20 May 2015, in partnership with the Fulbright Commission and the American Center in Prague, he arranged a lecture by Prof. Pospíšil entitled 'Anthropological Research of Societies and the Ideologically Divided World in the 20th Century', which was attended mainly by Fulbright scholars. Exactly one year later, on 19 May 2016, there followed the lecture 'Adventures in the Stone Age: Western Papua through the Eyes of an Anthropologist', organised by JJ for students at the University of South Bohemia in České

2] A Czech edition of Holý's book came out five years later (Holý 2001).

Budějovice. The event attracted a lot of interest, not least because of a research expedition bound for Papua that same year by students from the university.

After long discussions in which Prof. Pospíšil 'entertained his listeners long into the night', the idea crystallized to publish his 'Adventures in the "Stone Age"' in book form, to be published by Karolinum, the Prague University imprint. So in late September 2018, JJ set out for New Haven to try and secure the manuscript and any available illustrative material. (At the same time he also managed to acquire a number of useful contacts with Yale University, Prof. Pospíšil's alma mater.) However, the task proved less straightforward than he had imagined. First of all, Pospíšil's personal archive contained multiple preliminary or semi-final versions of the manuscript; it appeared that the final text had remained in Prague in 2014, when Pospíšil had left it with Charles University Arts Faculty to be evaluated with a view to possible publication, and sadly it could no longer be found. Importantly, however, Prof. Pospíšil let us scan a selection of color images to accompany the text, which are in themselves a fascinating find. Indeed, the trip could be counted a success on account of the illustrations alone. During the visit, Prof. Pospíšil also gave JJ a private showing of his extraordinary archive of film footage from his field research among the Kapauku.

Subsequently, Martin Soukup also visited Pospíšil in the USA in search of a few missing manuscript pages in the professor's extensive and meticulously kept archive. By that time, however, the professor was no longer consulting his library and archive, so MS was given a free hand to search. 'Switch on the light and go down those steps,' said the assistant. 'Turn right, then right again — there's another light switch — and somewhere there you'll find the Professor's archive and library. What are you looking for? A manuscript?' His successful search was celebrated with a shared lunch of jointly carved chicken washed down with a glass of red wine.

There followed the demanding task of digitalizing the printed manuscript and completing it with inserts provided by the professor to expand and elucidate parts of the original text. The end product of our efforts is thus the reconstructed text of Pospíšil's book as he had originally planned it. We believe we have been true to the author's intentions.

The final stages of preparation of this volume, in particular our communications with the author, were complicated by the coronavirus pandemic. The plan originally was for JJ to travel to New Haven in April 2020 so that Prof. Pospíšil could sign a contract giving Karolinum the right to publish his work. As that was no longer possible, everything had to be done by mail. We waited and waited for the contract, until at an editorial meeting on 15 July we thought we would have to go through the whole rigmarole again. So imagine our pleasure and surprise when at the start of proceedings Petr Valo, the head of Karolinum, produced the signed contract, which had arrived that very morning. By another almost incredible chance, one of the book's graphic designers, Jakub Krč, turned out to be a distant relative of the professor's. Thus it was that for a while we all became a part of the extraordinary world of Leopold Pospíšil.

Pospíšil conducted his basic field research of the Kapauku from September 1954 to November 1955, followed by further spells in 1959, 1962, 1975 and a brief and final two-week stay in 1979. In the 50s and 60s, important studies were carried out in the New Guinea Highlands, the results of which gave significant new impetus to the anthropology of Oceania and led to the formulation of new approaches and the revision of certain anthropological concepts based on new ethnographic insights such as the so-called 'African model' of descendence and descent groups. The Highlands research was so important that a special number of American Anthropologist (1964, issue 4, 2nd part) was devoted to it. So why was it so significant?

The interior of the island had long been largely unexplored and information about its inhabitants was scant. The terrain being mountainous and inaccessible, it took many years to explore and chart. In the east of the island, the colonial authorities only succeeded in penetrating and mapping the country in the late 1930s, just before WWII; and the situation was similar in the west. That is why, even in twentieth century, there existed some communities far from the coastal areas who still had no idea they had been colonized. Large-scale anthropological studies of the New Guinea Highlanders did not commence until the 1950s; before WWII, only a few researchers had visited parts of the island, notably Reo Fortune who worked in Kainantu, Beatrice Blackwood who studied a group of Anga, and Edgar Francis Williams, who did anthropological research for the Australian government in the Southern Highlands. It was not until the 50s and 60s that groundbreaking studies were undertaken of the Gahuku-Gama (Kenneth Read), the Dani (Karl Heider), the Marind-Anim (Jan van Baal), the Chimbu (Paula Brown), and the Tsembaga Maring (Roy Rappaport). Leopold Pospíšil made a significant contribution to this anthropological discovery of the people and cultures of the New Guinea Highlands.

This means, amazingly, that the research and material presented in this book, including the iconic Kodak color photographs, is almost seventy years old! Today, of course, the Kapauku are not the same as they were when Pospíšil lived among them. Given that long intervening period, we may consider the culture described by Pospíšil as defunct — not only the Kapauku, but the Dani, Asmat, Marind-anim and other cultures in the Indonesian part of New Guinea have changed following contact with state officials, missionaries, researchers and tourists. The transformation of the Kapauku way of life can even be seen by comparing former settlement patterns with modern satellite images, thus qualifying the Kapauku culture of the 50s and 60s as a subject of study by a sub-discipline of anthropology — archaeology. For the trend today is for archaeologists to study not only prehistoric or early historic populations; in Europe we now have post-mediaeval and even contemporary archaeology; and 'overseas' one of the many trends is 'colonial' archaeology. In the same way, we may now postulate a new sub-discipline — the archaeology of ethnographic contact. Following the Czech trail alone, we can mention Emil Holub's famous journey to Galulong, the main settlement of the Mashukulumbs (now the Ila people of Zambia) in 1886, or Alberto Vojtěch Frič's sojourn in the Chamacoco villages of Gran Chaco in Paraguay in 1903–05. But the same approach could be adopted with other places around the world that have been visited by professional anthropologists and their predecessors since the days of Captain Cook (e.g. Yuquot, located on Nootka Island, British Columbia, or Hippah Island in Queen Charlotte Sound in New Zealand, both visited by the explorer in 1777-1778).

For European archaeologists, cultural anthropology and ethnology provide more than mere lists of vague analogies with the life and material culture of prehistoric or early historic populations. In this our discussions with Leopold Pospíšil were very fruitful, indicating any number of possible interconnections between the various subdivisions of anthropology in several directions. The thoughts arising from our conversations could, with a little dramatization, be divided into three interlinked 'Acts'.

Act I: As we have said, archaeology studies cultures that are dead. Among the main sources of data for archaeologists are the graves and cemeteries of long-gone populations. So we could hardly avoid asking Prof. Pospíšil about Kapauku burial rites. To his knowledge there was no uniform rite for the whole Kapauku population, but rather a range of practices depending on the status and manner of death of the deceased. Whereas headmen were laid out in their homes, which were then abandoned by other residents, there were also forms of inhumation (or 'semi-inhumation', where only part of the body was buried and the remainder covered with a mound of stones), as well as funerary rites that have left no traces for archaeologists, such as tree 'burials'. Cultural-anthropological considerations thus require us to revise archaeological methods by pointing to changes in the funerary rites of prehistoric populations, and in particular to the absence of burials in certain phases of prehistoric development — not only in Europe. Even well-known burial sites with a documented number of graves may therefore fail to give us an accurate reflection of total prehistoric populations, with obvious consequences for paleodemographic research.

Act II: In the course of our many conversations, Prof. Pospíšil mentioned an old Kapauku legend according to which in former times the local people used to bury their dead in one of the nearby cave. His curiosity aroused, the anthropologist decided to visit the caves in the hope of finding a hoard of cowrie shell jewelry, which at the time of his research still played a central part in living Kapauku culture and was highly prized. Such a find of antique artefacts would have been an exceptional acquisition for any anthropological museum. The expedition was unsuccessful, however, which raises the question whether actual excavations might be needed to unearth any potential artefacts. Either way, there is no doubt this is a field that remains open for future generations of archaeologists.

Act III: Cowrie shell ornaments were important and distinctive artefacts differentiating the wearer in terms of social status and gender. At the same time, we know cowrie shells were a central part of the economic and financial system of the Kapauku, as described by Pospíšil in his studies *The Kapauku Papuans of West New Guinea* and *Kapauku Papuan Economy*, both published in 1963. And just as in East Africa domestic cattle have an important economic function, so for the Kapauku and other tribes of the New Guinea Highlands a key means of sociopolitical exchange was the domestic pig.[3] It was more than simply a source of vital protein; the ownership of a pig was a reflection of the individual's power and prestige. Wealth as expressed in the possession of domestic pigs was an essential precondition for determining bride price and asserting political and legal authority. Along with the cultivation of sweet potatoes and the circulation of cowries, pig ownership formed the basis of the native economy. The more pigs an individual possessed, the higher they automatically rose in the social hierarchy (Pospisil 1963, 10–11).[4]

3] Expressing the price of a commodity in terms of numbers of cattle seems to have been a widespread practice, indicated in some passages of Homer, or in the etymology of the Latin *pecunia* (money) and its cognates *pecus* (cattle) and *peculatus* (embezzlement). An analogous term is the Germanic *Kūgildi* or *Kuhgeld* (Göbl 1978b, 143-144).

4] This applied to many cultures of the New Guinea Highlands, in which pigs were not only a nutritionally rich source of food; owning large numbers of them was a measure of social prestige, influence and success. Marie Reay, who studied the Kuma, paraphrased Herskovits's term when she wrote of the 'pig complex' (Reay 1959: 20-22) to describe how pig breeding and ownership was more than simply a way of providing food — it permeated Kuma and other societies on every level.

Cowrie shells were a means of expressing the price of commodities such as food, domestic animals, land and various artefacts, as well as labor and specialist tasks. As such they fulfilled the primary criterion for a monetary system: they were *precium* (a token of value) rather than *merx* (a commodity). The native economy recognized a fixed exchange rate between *buna bomoje* and *kawane* shells of 1:20. After glass beads were introduced, the price of one *bomoje* was fixed at 30 beads. Specifically, the most valued shells were two types of cowrie, *bomoje* (15 *kawane*) and *buna bomoje* (approx. 20 *kawan*), which were differentiated by color. Also used as currency were necklaces made of *dedege* (nassarius shells) and *pafadau* (glass beads). The necklaces had a standard length — the human arm — and a value of one *bomoje*. (Pospisil 1963: 6–9).

We now come to a question that JJ put to Prof. Pospíšil at our 2017 meeting in Prague. 'Would it be possible to break up a cowrie necklace into its component parts and use them for economic transactions?' He replied: 'In theory, yes. But the value of the intact necklace would be greater than that of its separate parts added together.' This is because the complete necklace also had aesthetic and, in the case of inherited jewelry, sentimental value. This is well illustrated by the exceptional fee Pospíšil was paid for operating on an old man: a treasured necklace (see the chapter *Non-horticultural Food* in this book). As an archaeologist, JJ is already familiar with shell jewelry and its functions. Think of the spondylus shell body ornaments of Neolithic Linear cultures, found predominantly in graves and usually interpreted as markers of social status. For archaeologists investigating the beginnings of agriculture this raises a fundamental question: Is what we see here — as in Papua and other regions of Oceania — a comparable clue to the existence of a (semi-)monetary system in prehistoric Central Europe?

It appears that the Kapauku culture and economy described by Pospíšil is a static model, unchanging in time and place. On the hori-

Roy Rappaport, who focused on pig breeding and slaughter among the Tsembaga Maring, showed in his monograph *Pigs for the Ancestors* the importance of pig ownership in maintaining the social fabric and managing the demands that large-scale pig breeding placed on the human environment (Rappaport 1967).

zontal level we can follow, in great detail and in a variety of situations, interactions between individuals and in society as a whole. What is missing is the dimension of time, which on the vertical axis shapes culture and its long-term development. But here too Pospíšil has an answer. In *Kapauku Papuans and Their Law* (1958: 63-64) he mentions the legendary figure of Me Ibo (the Great Old Man — his real name was Ijaaj Gepouja), who came from the village of Jugeibega in the Mapia region and settled in Kamu Valley. There he married and founded five villages (Botukebo, Aigii, Jagawaugii, Kojogeepa and Obajbegaa), becoming the great-ancestor of every one of their inhabitants. That was in about 1840 — maybe seven generations before the arrival of Leopold Pospíšil. Another legend concerning the origins of the Ijaaj confederacy tells us that the village of Obajbegaa was settled by the Pigome people.

However, in this book (the chapter *Kapauku Mathematics*) Pospíšil proves that some of the numerals in the Kapauku language are of Malayo-Polynesian origin. He therefore assumes that their original home was the coastal lowlands of North New Guinea, somewhere on the shores of Cenderawasih (formerly Geelvink) Bay, where they could have come into contact with Malay fishermen and traders. The ancestors of today's Kapauku did not settle the Highlands until much later, when the Portuguese introduced new species of crops.[5] It was perhaps in that same period that the Kapauku adopted their financial system based on a steady and controlled supply of cowrie shells. It was the thought of this migration that prompted Prof Pospíšil to un-

---

5] In the Professor's view (personal communication), the Kapauku expression *nada*, meaning 'no quantity', might also be of Portuguese origin. Chief among the imported crop types was the yam or sweet potato, which has the virtue of thriving at high altitudes. This led to the so-called Ipmoean Revolution (Bayliss-Smith et al. 2005). Yam grew there so well that the local population increased and people could afford to breed whole herds of pigs. It should be noted, however, that these new plants simply added to the wide variety of cultivars already known in New Guinea. Recent research shows that the first extensive cultivation of taro (*Colocasia esculenta*) at the lowland site Lake Wanum, and pandan (*Pandanus antaresensis* or *P. brosimos*) at Lake Draepi and other places in Central Papua took place at around the same time as in centers of neolithization in other parts of the world (Haberle 1995).

dertake an expedition to the Bouma River area in 1962, in the hope of finding a residue population of lowland Kapauku. Leopold Pospíšil thus paved the way for future research, an important part of which is sure to be archaeological.

Prof. Pospíšil's contribution to world anthropology is undeniable. He is one of the few Czech-born anthropologists to significantly influence theory development in his field. Along with Zdeněk Salzman, Ladislav Holý and Milan Stuchlík, he has without a doubt left the greatest Czech mark on world anthropology. It is worth noting that a certain František Pospíšil, his uncle, made a research trip to the USA, where he studied Native American cultures. The outcome was the first volume of *Etnologické materiálie z jihozápadu U.S.A* (Ethnological Materials from Southwest USA, 1932, Czech only). The second was never written.

His nephew Leopold realized three important research trips, the findings of which he presented in a number of books and scientific papers. His writings on the Kapauku include *The Kapauku Papuans of West New Guinea* (1963), *Kapauku Papuan Economy* (1963), and *Kapauku Papuans and Their Law* (1958). Pospíšil also worked with the Nunamiut people in Alaska and published a number of studies about them. He also conducted research in Europe, specifically a long-term study of a peasant community in Obernberg in Austria that led to the publication of *Obernberg: A Quantitative Analysis of a Tirolean Peasant Economy* (1995). Pospíšil is also a pioneer of legal anthropology, a subject to which he devoted a number of papers and, principally, two authoritative volumes, *Anthropology of Law* (1971) and *Ethnology of Law* (1972; second expanded edition 1978), now established in the canon of that branch of anthropology. His interest in the anthropological aspect of law can be traced to his youth in pre-communist Czechoslovakia, when he studied law at Charles University in Prague.

His achievement as a teacher was also considerable. He influenced generations of students, always urging them to be diligent in their fieldwork while stressing that the key to success in the field is the ability to work in the local language. Many of his students later became leading anthropologists. One especially gratifying example is Patrick Kirch, well known for his archaeological work in the Pacific; but there are many others who have excelled in their field. Drawing on his wide experience teaching general anthropology, he wrote his own textbook, *Sociocultural Anthropology* (2004), which can be seen as a summary of his views on the aims and scope of the subject and its methodological principles. The introductory chapter outlining these views was published in Czech translation under the title *Antropologie a věda* (Anthropology and Science, 1991) with the support of Palacký University, Olomouc. Two further chapters of the planned textbook also came out in Czech, *Culture* and *Belief Systems: Religion and Magic*. Both chapters appeared in the supplement of the 80th annual edition of *The Czech Ethnological Journal* (Czech title: *Český lid*). In the textbook itself he proposes that anthropology be treated as a science — a trend that, at least in American cultural anthropology, is today in the minority, though by no means a diminishing one. An abridged edition of his famous work *Ethnology of Law* also appeared in Czech (*Etnologie práva*, 1997).

One work likely to remain inaccessible to the Anglophone world is Pospíšil's memoir of his schooldays, *Horribile visu* (2016), which he refused to publish under a different, perhaps more reader-friendly title. After all, why should a book not have a Latin title? After the fall of the Iron Curtain he returned to his homeland every year, though it was some time before his achievements were widely recognized here. In 2016 he received an award from the Czech Neuron Foundation for his contribution to world science. MS recalls how Prof Pospíšil enjoyed the after-party and insisted on staying till the very end. MS cannot resist adding one further note. After many hours of conversation with the Professor about his long and colorful life, an edited version of the tapes was to be broadcast on the radio. The producers cut it drastically, however, arguing that so many things could never have happened to one person: being in the anti-Nazi resistance, then on the Communists' death list; doing pioneering research in New Guinea; advising the president of the USA; and founding a whole new branch of research.

Pospíšil's work among the Kapauku is well known to anthropologists and is now regarded as a classic example of anthropological field research in more traditional days, before the advent of self-reflexive and critical postmodern anthropology in the 1980s. Since his findings on the Kapauku have all been published, whether in periodicals or books, it may be asked with some justification whether the present volume has anything new to offer. Indeed it has. Here Leopold Pospíšil gives us a glimpse behind the scenes into his 'anthropologist's kitchen'. He lets us see the day-to-day progress of his research. He shares with us his difficulties and challenges, as well as some amusing anecdotes. We should remember that he was working before such a thing as a manual of field research existed, unless we count the hopelessly antiquated *Notes and Queries on Anthropology*, last revised in 1954. Students learnt the basics in seminars; all the rest they had to figure out on the ground. The three books mentioned above are about the Kapauku; this one is about an anthropologist among the Kapauku.

With this volume, published in the year of the author's 98th birthday, we also wish to express our admiration for Prof Pospíšil and our gratitude for the view of the world he revealed to us in his unforgettable lectures.

Prague, 6 January 2021

Martin Soukup and Jaroslav Jiřík

References
for Afterword:

Bayliss-Smith, T. et al. "Archaeological Evidence for the Ipomoean Revolution at Kuk Swamp, Upper Wahgi Valley, Papua New Guinea," in *The Sweet Potato in Oceania,* eds. Chris Ballard, Paula Brown, Michael Bourke, and Tracy Harwood. Pittsburgh: University of Pittsburgh, 2005. 109—120.

Göbl, Robert *Antike Numismatik. Einführung, Münzkunde, Münzgeschichte, Geldgeschichte, Methodenlehre, Praktischer Teil.* Bd. 1. München: Battenberg, 1978.

Haberle, Simon G. "Identification of Cultivated Pandanus and Colocasia in Pollen Records and the Implications for the Study of Early Agriculture in New Guinea." *Veget. Hist.* Archaeobot. 4, 195-210.

Holý, Ladislav *Malý český člověk a skvělý český národ.* Praha: Sociologické nakladatelství, 2001.

Pospisil, Leopold *Kapauku Papuans and Their Law.* New Haven: Yale University Press, 1958.

Pospisil, L. *Kapauku Papuan Economy.* New Haven: Yale University Press, 1963.

Pospisil, L. *The Kapauku Papuans of West New Guinea.* New York: Holet, Rinehart & Winston, 1963.

Pospisil, L. *Anthropology of Law.* New York: Harper & Row, 1971

Pospisil, L. *Ethnology of Law.* Reading: Addison-Wesley, 1972.

Pospisil, L. *Obernberg: A Quantitative Analysis of a Tirolean Peasant Economy.* New Haven: Connecticut Academy of Arts and Sciences, 1995.

Pospisil, L. *Sociocultural Anthropology.* Boston: Pearson Custom Publishing, 2004.

Pospíšil, L. "Kultura," *Český lid* 80 (1993). Supplement.

Pospíšil, L. *Antropologie a věda.* Olomouc: Univerzita Palackého, 1997.

Pospíšil, L. *Etnologie práva.* Prague: Set Out, 1997.

Pospíšil, L. "Systémy víry: náboženství a magie," *Český lid* 80 (1993). Supplement.

Pospíšil, L. *Horribile visu.* Olomouc: Burian & Tichák, 2016.

Rappaport, Roy *Pigs for the Ancestors.* New Haven: Yale University Press, 1967.

Reay, Mary *The Kuma.* Melbourne: Melbourne University Press, 1959.

Salzmann, Zdeněk "Jazyk, kultura a společnost." Úvod do lingvistické antropologie. *Český lid* 83 (1996). Supplement.

Bibliography

Buettner-Janusch, John, Henry Gershowits, Leopold J. Pospisil and Peter Wilson. "Bloodgroups of Selected Aboriginal and Indigenous Populations." *Nature* 188, no. 5745 (October 1960) 153–155.

Price, Derek de Solla, and Leopold Pospisil. "A Survival of Babylonian Arithmetic in New Guinea?" *Indian Journal of History of Science* 1 (1966) 30–3, 95–6.

Doble, Marion. *Kapauku-Malayan-Dutch-English Dictionary*. The Hague: Martinus Nijhoff, 1960.

Dollard, John and Neal E. Miller. *Personality and Psychotherapy*. New York: McGraw-Hill Book Company, 1950.

Durkheim, Emile. *De la Division de Travil Social*. Paris: Félix Alcan, 1893.

Gaisseau, Pierre Dominique, *The Sky Above, the Mud Below*. Film. 1961.

Gluckman, Max. *The Juditial Process among The Barotse*. Manchester: Manchester University Press, 1967.

Herskovits, Melville J. 1949 *Man and His Works*. New York: Alfred A, Kopf.

Johnson, Allen. "Horticulturalists: Economic Behavior in Tribes," in *Economic Anthropology*, ed. Stuart Plattner, 49–77. Stanford: Stanford University Press, 1989.

Levy-Bruhl, Lucien. *Primitive Mentality*. New York: Praeger, 1923.

Lewellen, Ted C. *Political Anthropology*. Massachusetts: Bergin and Garrey Publishers, 1983.

Llewellyn, Karl N. and E. Adamson Hoebel. *The Cheyenne Way*. Norman: University of Oklahoma Press, 1941.

Lounsbury, Floyd G. "The Structural Analysis of Kinsl Kinship Semantics," in "The Proceedings of the Ninth International Congress of Linguistics*, ed Horace G. Lunt. The Hague; Houton, 1964.

Maine, Henry Sumner. *Ancient Law*. Boston: Beacon Press, 1963.

Malinowski, Bronislaw. *Argonauts of the Western Pacific*. New York: E.P. Dutton and Company, 1961.

Marx, Karl. *Pre-Capitalist Economic Formations*. New York: International Publishers, 1966.

Murdock, George P., Clellan S. Ford, Alfred E. Hudson, Raymond Kennedy, Leo W. Simmons, and W. M. John, Whiting 1961 *Outline of Cultural Materials*. New Haven: Human Relations Area Files.

Ovid. *Metamorphoses*, ed. Daniel Crespin. London: R. Knaplock, 1719.

Pershits, A. T. "The Primitive Norm and Its Evolution." *Current Anthropology* 18, no. 3 (1977) 409–413.

Polanyi, Karl."Our Obsolete Market Mentality," in *Primitive, Archaic, and Modern Economies, Essays of Karl Polanyi*, ed George Dalton. Garden City: Doubleday and Company, 1947. 59–77.

Polanyi, Karl, Conrad, Arensberg and Harry Parsons, eds. *Trade and Market in the Early Empires*. Glencoe: Free Press, 1957.

Pospisil, Leopold. "Kapauku Papuans and Their Law." PhD diss, Yale University, 1958.

Pospisil, Leopold. "Social Change and Primitive Law: Consequences of a Papuan Legal Case." *American Anthropologist* 60, no. 5 (1958) 832–7.

Posipsil, Leopold. "Kapauku Papuans and Their Kinship Organization." *Oceania* 30, no. 3 (March 1960) 188–206.

Pospisil, Leopold. "Papuan Social Structure; "Rejoinder to Leach." *American Anthropologist* 62, no. 4 (August 1960) 690–1.

Pospsil, Leopold. *Kapaku Papuans of West New Guinea*. New York: Holt, Rinehart and Winston, 1963.

Pospisil, Leopold. *Kapauku Papuan Economy*. Yale University Publication in Anthropology, no. 67. New Haven: Yale University, 1963.

Pospisil, Leopold. *Anthropology of Law*. New York: Harper and Row, 1971.

Pospisil, Leopold. "Kapauku Papuan Kinship Terminology: Its Genealogical and Behavioral Components," in *Blood and Semen: Kinship Systems of Highland New Guinea*, eds. Edwin A. Cook and Denise O'Brien. Ann Arbor: The University of Michigan Press, 1980. 2–39.

Pospisil, Leopold. "Traditional Egalitarian Society, Its loose Structure, Emerging Inequality and Other Widely Held Myths," in *Peoples on the Move: Current Themes: Current Themes of Anthropological Research in New Guinea*, eds. Paul Haenen and Ján Power. Nijmegen: Center for Australian and Oceanic Studies, University of Nijmegen, 1989. 18–30.

Pospisil, Leopold. "I Am Very Sorry I Cannot Kill You Any More: War and Peace among the Kapauku," in *Studying War: Anthropological Perspectives, War and Society*, eds. Stephen P. Reyna and R.E. Downs. Philadelphia: Gordon and Breach, 1993. 113–26.

Radcliffe-Brown, A. R. *Structure and Function in Primitive Society*. New York: The Free Press, 1952.

Rhys, Lloyd. *Jungle Pimpernel*. London: Hodder and Stoughton, 1947.

The Royal Anthropological Institut. *Notes and Queries on Anthropology*. London: Routledge and Kegan Paul, 1929.

Sahlins, Marshall. *Stone Age Economies*. Chicago: Aldlne publishing Company, 1972.

Smeds, Matthew. *No Tobacco, No Hallelujah*. London: William Kimber, 1955.

Starr, June and Jane F. Collier. *History and Power in the Study of Law*. Ithaca and London: Cornell University Press, 1989.

Stoltenpool, J. *Ekagi-Dutch-English-Indonesian Dictionary*. The Hague: Martinus Nijhoff, 1969.

Thurnwald, Richard. *Economies in Primitive Communities*. London: Oxford University Press, 1932.

Van Der Leeden, A.C. *Hoofdtrekken der Sociale Struktur in het Westellike Binnenland van Sarmi*. Leiden: Eduard Lido N.V, 1956.

Yale Banner. "Leopold Pospisil," *Yale Banner*. New Haven: Yale University, 1968. 138–139.

(286)

Index

Magidimi (village) 215
Malay
    enclaves in New Guinea 134
    fishermen and traders 133, 136–7,
    252
    language 14, 15, 21, 37, 236
Malaya 133
Malayo Polynesian (language and
    speakers) 133–4, 136
Malenkov, Georgy (Soviet Premier) 140
Malinowski, Bronislaw
    (anthropologist) 11, 37
Mandarin 221
Manila 268
Mapia (people) 68
Mapia Valley (region) 68, 105, 200,
    253–4
Marius (aka Ijaagodooti; adopted son
    of Pospíšil) 64, 75, 211, 266
Marx, Karl 119, 202
Marxism 9, 42, 129, 136, 137, 166,
    168, 244, 10
Masaryk, Tomáš Garrigue (first
    President of Czechoslovakia) 160
Mauwa (village in Kamu Valley) 233
Mead, Margaret (anthropologist) 141
Meekaamude (beautiful young
    Kapauku girl) 87, 88, 89, 90
Mein Kampf 202
Meissen porcelain of Germany 100
Melanesian (inhabitants) 135
Mimika (region on the south coast of
    New Guinea) 254
Moanemani (village in Kamu Valley
    with an airstrip) 250, 256
Mogokotu (village) 179–80, 216–7
Mokmer (town on the Island of Biak)
    140
Moni (Papuans) 225
Moore, Sally (anthropologist, Harvard)
    37

Mount Deijai 203–7, 265–6
Mujikebo (village in Kamu Valley) 55,
    126, 187–8
Murdock, George Peter (anthropologist,
    Yale) 11, 14, 49, 66
Mussolini, Benito 202

Nabire (coastal harbor of New Guinea)
    75, 134–5
Nader, Laura (anthropologist,
    Berkeley) 37
Nakemougi (Kapauku personal name) 51
Nakepajokaipougamaga (Kapauku
    personal name) 51
Napan (New Guinea, coastal
    settlement) 134
Napeetioti (adopted son of Pospíšil) 64
Navajo Indians 11
Nazi concentration camps 9, 53
Nazism 9, 20, 63, 161, 191, 212, 241
Netherlands New Guinea (now Irian
    Jaya, Indonesia) 12, 268
New Guinea
    biosphere 100
    central highlands 17, 98, 105, 134–5,
    140, 219, 227–8, 267
    coast 17, 128, 133, 134
    diet 58–9
    interior 29, 53–4, 134
    island 12, 14, 20, 33, 41, 78, 89, 97,
    107, 140, 168, 174, 183, 203, 218, 228,
    230, 242, 246–7, 252, 260, 261, 268
    lowlands 99, 208, 214
    sculpture 100
New Haven 194, 211
New York 114
Nibakabo sub–lineage 174
Nottio (village in Kamu Valley) 243

Obadoba (village in Kamu Valley, built
    by the Wege Bagee) 33, 246

Ulpian (Roman jurisconsult) 43
United States 10, 53, 56, 62, 81, 87,
   104, 109, 114, 118, 125, 159, 182,
   220, 242–3, 263, 266
University of Oregon 10, 35, 168, 185,
   226, 237–238

Van Baal, Jan (governor of the Dutch
   colony) 14–6, 249, 268
Van den Leeden, Alexander (Dutch
   anthropologist) 14, 50
Veltkamp, Mr. (assistant to the district
   officer of Paniai) 243, 266

Waghete (village on Lake Tigi with
   Dutch police outpost) 21, 217,
   227–8, 237, 265
Waine (enemy) clan (see: Waine–
   Tobaakoto confederacy) 92
Waine Ibo (adopted son of Pospíšil) 64
Waine Ipouga (brother of Antonia)
   215

Waine–Tibaakoto confederacy 84, 146,
   149, 152, 179, 185, 232–233, 239
Walhalla 202
Wege Bagee (Kapauku religious
   movement) 245–248
West New Guinea 159
Western civilization and influence 84,
   168, 220–44
   legal scholars 43
   medical knowledge 214
   thinking 169, 245
Wewak (West Guinea) 210
Wilber, Johannes (Professor,
   anthropologist) 246
Wissel Lakes area 15, 221

Yale New Haven Hospital 210, 215
Yale University 11, 16, 26, 35, 49, 57,
   99, 112, 159, 164, 194, 256, 268–9

Zinoviev, Grigory (Soviet politician)
   203

Adventures in the 'Stone Age' was edited by Jaroslav Jiřík and Martin Soukup.

Jaroslav Jiřík is an associate professor at Charles University and chair of the archaeology department at the Museum of Prácheň in Písek.

Martin Soukup is an associate professor at Charles University, specializing in cultural anthropology and Melanesia.